GROWING OLD IN AMERICA

The major source of statistics on American life is the Bureau of the Census of the U.S. Department of Commerce. Many of their publications were essential for the preparation of this book, including a number of Current Population Reports: Household Wealth and Asset Ownership:1991(WDC, 1990), Money Income of Households, Families, and Persons in the U.S.:1990 (WDC,1991), Marital Status and Living Arrangements:1990 (WDC,1991), Poverty in the United States:1990(WDC, 1991), and The Need for Personal Assistance with Everyday Activities:Recipients and Caregivers (WDC, 1990).

The Social Security Administration, an agency of the U.S. Department of Health Services, is responsible for the financial security of millions of older Americans. Fast Facts and Figures About Social Security (WDC, 1990) answers the most commonly asked questions about Social Security benefits, the SSI program, and Medicare.

The Office of the Inspector General of the U.S. Department of Health and Human Services is responsible for the study, "Resident Abuse in Nursing Homes: Understanding and Preventing Abuse"(WDC, April 1990). Information Plus drew from that study regarding victimization of the elderly in nursing homes.

The problems of aging have become a major political issue in America. Both the U.S. Senate Special Committee on Aging and the U.S. House Select Committee on Aging have held numerous hearings and published innumerable reports on the lives of elderly Americans. Of special importance in the writing of this Information Plus publication wasAgingAmerica:Trends and Projections (WDC,1991), prepared by the U.S. Senate Special Committee on Aging, the American Association of Retired Persons, the Federal Council on the Aging, and the U.S. Administration on Aging. Information Plus gratefully acknowledges use of a number of charts and statistics from that volume.

The Bureau of Labor Statistics of the U.S. Department of Labor publishes information and weel-researched articles on the U.S. workforce in its Monthly Labor Review.

Another helpful report used to prepare this publication was "Americans Over 55 at Work Program," a study conducted by ICF, Inc. for the Commonwealth Fund. The study was released May 21, 1991 at the annual meeting of the National Council on the Aging. Information Plus would like to thank the Older Women's League for permission to use material from 1991 Mothers' Day Report, "Paying for Prejudice: A Report on Midlife and Older Women in America's Labor Force" (WDC, May 1991). Information Plus also thanks American Demographics (May 1991) for permission to reprint material from "Quitting Time" by John P. Robinson.

EDITORS:
CORNELIA B. CESSNA, B.A., M.S.
ALISON LANDES, B.A.
CAROL D. FOSTER, B.A., M.L.S.

124543

CHAPTER I

OLDER AMERICANS -A DIVERSE AND GROWING POPULATION

"Age is a thing of mind over matter --- if you
don't mind, it doesn't matter." Mark Twain

WHO IS OLD?

According to Webster's Dictionary, the word "old" means "having lived or been in existence for a long time." This definition works well for a car or a piece of pottery, but when applied to people, it shows only a small part of a much larger picture - it refers only to the number of years a person has been alive. Even that standard has changed through history. A citizen of ancient Greece was "old" at 18 because the average life expectancy of an ancient Greek was 20 years. An American Indian warrior in the pre-Columbian Southwest could expect to live 33 years. The low life expectancy was based on a high infant mortality rate. Once a child survived through childhood, he or she had a better chance of making it into the fifties or sixties. In 1900, the life expectancy of the average American was 47 years; an American male born in 1990 can expect to live 72.1 years and a female, 79.0 years. (See Table 1.1.)

WHAT IS OLD?

There are many ways to characterize an old person, and everyone has his or her own idea of what old means. Aside from the obvious measure of number of birthdays, people may be labeled old because of their appearance, their physical functioning, their mental capacity, or their lifestyle.

A Working Definition

Old age does not happen overnight; aging is a process that begins before birth and ends only with

TABLE 1.1

PROJECTED LIFE EXPECTANCY AT BIRTH AND AGE 65, BY SEX: 1990-2050
(in years)

Year	At birth			At age 65		
	Men	Women	Difference	Men	Women	Difference
1990	72.1	79.0	6.9	15.0	19.4	4.4
2000	73.5	80.4	6.9	15.7	20.3	4.6
2010	74.4	81.3	6.9	16.2	21.0	4.8
2020	74.9	81.8	6.9	16.6	21.4	4.8
2030	75.4	82.3	6.9	17.0	21.8	4.8
2040	75.9	82.8	6.9	17.3	22.3	5.0
2050	76.4	83.3	6.9	17.7	22.7	5.0

SOURCE: U.S. Bureau of the Census. "Projections of the Population of the United States, by Age, Sex, and Race: 1988 to 2080," by Gregory Spencer. *Current Population Reports* Series P-25, No. 1018 (January 1989).

death. At what point does one become "old"? The problem of defining old age is reflected in the terminology used to describe those who are no longer "young" adults: they are elderly, older, aged, mature, or senior. Some researchers distinguish between various stages of the later years: young-old, middle-old, and oldest-old. For statistical and legislative purposes, however, some definition of "old age" is necessary. The easiest approach has been to designate a chronological age as the dividing point between "not old" and "old."

The U. S. government has assigned a person's 65th birthday as the age when U.S. citizens become eligible for government benefits such as full Social Security, Medicare, and reduced taxes. Age 65 was not selected by any scientific process; it follows a precedent set by German Chancellor Otto von Bismark in 1899. In that year, Germany became the first western government to assume financial support of its older citizens by passing the Old Age and Survivors Pension Act. Chancellor von Bismark arbitrarily decided that eligibility for benefits would begin at age 65 (although he himself was an active and vigorous 74 years old at the time).

TABLE 1.2

Growth of the Older Population, Actual and Projected: 1900–2050

(Numbers in thousands. Data for 1900 to 1990 are April 1 census figures. Data for 2000 to 2050 are July 1 projections.)   revised 8/20/91

YEAR	Total (all ages) Number	65–74 Number	65–74 Percent	75–79 Number	75–79 Percent	80–84 Number	80–84 Percent	80 and over Number	80 and over Percent	85 and over Number	85 and over Percent	65 and over Number	65 and over Percent
1900	75,995	2,187	2.9	520	0.7	252	0.3	374	0.5	122	0.2	3,080	4.1
1910	91,972	2,793	3.0	667	0.7	322	0.4	489	0.5	167	0.2	3,949	4.3
1920	105,711	3,464	3.3	856	0.8	403	0.4	613	0.6	210	0.2	4,933	4.7
1930	122,775	4,721	3.8	1,106	0.9	535	0.4	807	0.7	272	0.2	6,634	5.4
1940	131,669	6,376	4.8	1,504	1.1	774	0.6	1,139	0.9	365	0.3	9,019	6.8
1950	150,697	8,415	5.6	2,128	1.4	1,149	0.8	1,726	1.1	577	0.4	12,269	8.1
1960	179,323	10,997	6.1	3,054	1.7	1,580	0.9	2,509	1.4	929	0.5	16,560	9.2
1970	203,302	12,447	6.1	3,838	1.9	2,286	1.1	3,695	1.8	1,409	0.7	19,980	9.8
1980	226,546	15,581	6.9	4,794	2.1	2,935	1.3	5,175	2.3	2,240	1.0	25,550	11.3
1990	248,710	18,045	7.3	6,103	2.5	3,909	1.6	6,930	2.8	3,021	1.2	31,079	12.5
MIDDLE SERIES (Middle fertility, mortality, and immigration assumptions)													
2000	268,266	18,243	6.8	7,282	2.7	4,735	1.8	9,357	3.5	4,622	1.7	34,882	13.0
2010	282,575	21,039	7.4	6,913	2.4	5,295	1.9	11,410	4.0	6,115	2.2	39,362	13.9
2020	294,364	30,973	10.5	8,981	3.1	5,462	1.9	12,113	4.1	6,651	2.3	52,067	17.7
2030	300,629	35,988	12.0	13,023	4.3	8,464	2.8	16,593	5.5	8,129	2.7	65,604	21.8
2040	301,807	30,808	10.2	14,260	4.7	10,790	3.6	23,041	7.6	12,251	4.1	68,109	22.6
2050	299,849	31,590	10.5	12,042	4.0	9,613	3.2	24,900	8.3	15,287	5.1	68,532	22.9

Source: U.S. Bureau of the Census. Data for 1900 to 1940, 1960, and 1980 shown in 1980 Census of Population, PC80–B1, General Population Characteristics, Tables 42 and 45; Data for 1990 from 1990 Census Population, (CPH-L-74, modified age and race counts). 2000 to 2050 shown in "Projections of the Population of the United States by Age, Sex and Race: 1988 to 2080," Current Population Reports, P-25, No. 1018, Washington D.C.; U.S. Government Printing Office, 1989. Data for 1950 shown in "Estimates of the Population of the United States and Components of Change, by Age, Color, and Sex: 1950 to 1980," Current Population Reports, Series P-25, No 519, U.S. Government Printing Office, Washington, D.C., 1985. Data for 1970 from unpublished table consistent with "United States Population Estimates by Age, Sex, and Hispanic Origin: 1988," Series P-25, No. 1045, U.S. Government Printing Office, Washington, D.C. 1990.

The national median age (half of all Americans are below and half are above this age) exceeded 32 years for the first time in 1987. The median age was 16.7 in 1820, then reached 30 years in 1950.

Why is America getting older? One of the main reasons is that in the 20 years after World War II (1939-1945), as soldiers returned home eager to start families, as the world's political climate stabilized and the U.S. economy prospered, there was an explosion of births (Figure 1.2). Children born during these years make up what is called the "baby-boom generation." The baby boomers will begin to turn 65 around 2010. The 65+ population will increase dramatically between 2010 and 2030 as the baby-boomers complete their transition from "not-old" to "old." So while the baby boom generation initially reduced the median age, as it grows older, it is moving the median age upward.

As shown in Figure 1.2, there was a dramatic decline in births beginning in the mid-1960s (the "baby-bust generation"), followed by only a modest increase in the 1980s. Declining birth rates mean that the number of young people decreases relative to the number of older people in the population.

In this book, the terms "old," "older," and "elderly" are used interchangeably to describe people aged 65 and older. The term "oldest old" refers to people 85 and older.

AMERICA GROWS OLDER

In 1900, one American out of every 25 (4 percent of the total population) was over 65 years old. The 65+ age group made up 12.5 percent of the total population in 1990. By 2050, 22.9 percent of the U.S. population (more than one person out of every five) will be 65 or older (Table 1.2 and Figure 1.1).

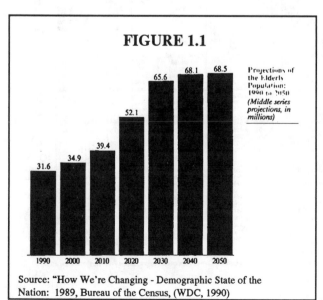

FIGURE 1.1

Projections of the Elderly Population: 1990 to 2050 (Middle series projections, in millions)

1990	2000	2010	2020	2030	2040	2050
31.6	34.9	39.4	52.1	65.6	68.1	68.5

Source: "How We're Changing - Demographic State of the Nation: 1989, Bureau of the Census, (WDC, 1990)

The Oldest Old

Even more dramatic than the growth of the 65+ population will be the increase in the number of Americans over the age of 85. While the 65 to 84 age group will decline slightly after 2030, the number of people over 85 will continue to grow through 2050. By 2050, the 85+ age group will make up 5 percent of the total U.S. population and

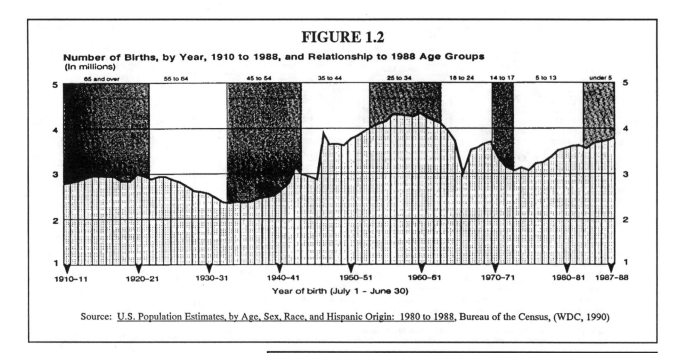

FIGURE 1.2

Number of Births, by Year, 1910 to 1988, and Relationship to 1988 Age Groups
(In millions)

Year of birth (July 1 - June 30)

Source: <u>U.S. Population Estimates, by Age, Sex, Race, and Hispanic Origin: 1980 to 1988</u>, Bureau of the Census, (WDC, 1990)

22 percent of the 65+ age group (Table 1.2). Women made up 72 percent of the oldest old in 1989. Because women will continue to have longer life expectancies into the middle of the next century, it is likely that they will make up an even larger proportion in the future (Table 1.3).

Living to be 100

America will likely experience a "centenarian boom" within the next 60 years. The chances of living to age 100 have increased 40 times since 1900. The U. S. had 61,000 centenarians in 1989 (Table 1.3). Dr. Gregory Spencer, a demographer with the U.S. Census Bureau, predicts that America will have 108,000 centenarians by 2000, 441,000 by 2025, and 1.3 million by 2050 - a phenomenal growth when compared to the 4,000 centenarians living in the United States in 1960. Most centenarians live past the age of 100 by only a few years, the majority (90 percent) being less than 105 years.

TABLE 1.3

Total Population, by Sex, Race, and Age: 1989
[In thousands, except as indicated. As of July 1. Includes Armed Forces abroad. See headnote, table 1]

AGE	Total [1]	Male	Female	White	Black
Total	248,762	121,445	127,317	209,326	30,788
Under 5 yrs. old.	18,752	9,598	9,155	15,050	2,890
Under 1 yr. old	3,945	2,020	1,925	3,163	619
1 yr. old	3,717	1,904	1,813	2,983	577
2 yrs. old .	3,660	1,872	1,788	2,931	567
3 yrs. old .	3,710	1,898	1,812	2,983	561
4 yrs. old .	3,721	1,904	1,816	2,989	565
5-9 yrs. old .	18,212	9,321	8,891	14,628	2,802
5 yrs. old .	3,605	1,844	1,761	2,895	550
6 yrs. old .	3,678	1,883	1,795	2,959	558
7 yrs. old .	3,733	1,910	1,822	3,000	573
8 yrs. old .	3,573	1,831	1,742	2,874	549
9 yrs. old .	3,624	1,853	1,770	2,900	573
10-14 yrs. old.	16,950	8,689	8,260	13,574	2,879
10 yrs. old .	3,563	1,826	1,737	2,846	571
11 yrs. old .	3,418	1,751	1,667	2,740	540
12 yrs. old .	3,384	1,735	1,649	2,712	534
13 yrs. old .	3,257	1,668	1,589	2,608	513
14 yrs. old .	3,327	1,708	1,619	2,668	522
15-19 yrs. old .	17,847	9,123	8,725	14,367	2,767
15 yrs. old .	3,278	1,681	1,596	2,619	520
16 yrs. old .	3,355	1,718	1,637	2,672	542
17 yrs. old .	3,536	1,815	1,720	2,832	561
18 yrs. old .	3,794	1,936	1,858	3,068	583
19 yrs. old .	3,884	1,973	1,911	3,177	561
20-24 yrs. old.	18,886	9,529	9,356	15,490	2,695
20 yrs. old .	3,772	1,913	1,859	3,078	549
21 yrs. old .	3,625	1,835	1,790	2,964	523
22 yrs. old .	3,671	1,851	1,820	3,014	521
23 yrs. old .	3,777	1,899	1,879	3,101	538
24 yrs. old .	4,040	2,031	2,008	3,332	563
25-29 yrs. old .	21,830	10,979	10,851	18,192	2,861
25 yrs. old .	4,242	2,136	2,106	3,519	571
26 yrs. old .	4,282	2,153	2,128	3,564	566
27 yrs. old .	4,400	2,210	2,191	3,666	578
28 yrs. old .	4,326	2,173	2,153	3,618	555
29 yrs. old .	4,580	2,307	2,273	3,825	591
30-34 yrs. old.	22,218	11,151	11,068	18,622	2,767
30 yrs. old .	4,575	2,299	2,276	3,812	590
31 yrs. old .	4,483	2,251	2,233	3,764	552
32 yrs. old .	4,507	2,263	2,244	3,778	561
33 yrs. old .	4,297	2,149	2,147	3,602	527
34 yrs. old .	4,357	2,168	2,168	3,666	536
35-39 yrs. old.	19,676	9,782	9,894	16,664	2,273
35 yrs. old .	4,204	2,101	2,103	3,545	504
36 yrs. old .	4,033	2,008	2,025	3,417	462
37 yrs. old .	3,934	1,954	1,980	3,332	456
38 yrs. old .	3,744	1,853	1,891	3,183	419
39 yrs. old .	3,762	1,866	1,896	3,187	431
40-44 yrs. old.	16,908	8,319	8,589	14,571	1,731
40 yrs. old .	3,761	1,856	1,905	3,200	419
41 yrs. old .	3,583	1,768	1,815	3,091	364
42 yrs. old .	3,855	1,903	1,952	3,376	357
43 yrs. old .	2,825	1,381	1,444	2,430	287
44 yrs. old .	2,885	1,411	1,473	2,474	303
45-49 yrs. old.	13,528	6,608	6,921	11,678	1,396
45 yrs. old .	2,846	1,391	1,455	2,447	299
46 yrs. old .	3,068	1,499	1,569	2,676	296
47 yrs. old .	2,748	1,339	1,409	2,359	296
48 yrs. old .	2,440	1,193	1,247	2,112	246
49 yrs. old .	2,427	1,185	1,241	2,083	260

AGE	Total [1]	Male	Female	White	Black
50-54 yrs. old.	11,377	5,511	5,866	9,790	1,223
50 yrs. old .	2,411	1,165	1,247	2,063	267
51 yrs. old .	2,312	1,123	1,189	1,991	245
52 yrs. old .	2,209	1,070	1,139	1,896	240
53 yrs. old .	2,210	1,073	1,137	1,908	234
54 yrs. old .	2,235	1,079	1,155	1,931	237
55-59 yrs. old.	10,725	5,121	5,605	9,310	1,116
55 yrs. old .	2,102	1,010	1,092	1,809	228
56 yrs. old .	2,076	995	1,081	1,796	219
57 yrs. old .	2,176	1,039	1,137	1,886	230
58 yrs. old .	2,163	1,027	1,135	1,886	219
59 yrs. old .	2,209	1,049	1,160	1,933	219
60-64 yrs. old.	10,867	5,079	5,788	9,569	1,035
60 yrs. old .	2,229	1,053	1,176	1,937	234
61 yrs. old .	2,235	1,053	1,182	1,970	212
62 yrs. old .	2,114	984	1,129	1,858	203
63 yrs. old .	2,103	978	1,125	1,859	194
64 yrs. old .	2,187	1,010	1,176	1,945	192
65-69 yrs. old.	10,170	4,631	5,538	9,029	916
65 yrs. old .	2,175	1,001	1,174	1,921	204
66 yrs. old .	2,045	935	1,111	1,812	187
67 yrs. old .	2,089	954	1,135	1,857	186
68 yrs. old .	1,987	905	1,082	1,781	164
69 yrs. old .	1,874	837	1,037	1,657	176
70-74 yrs. old.	8,012	3,464	4,549	7,193	661
70 yrs. old .	1,741	772	969	1,552	154
71 yrs. old .	1,708	751	956	1,541	134
72 yrs. old .	1,619	700	918	1,457	131
73 yrs. old .	1,487	632	855	1,338	120
74 yrs. old .	1,458	608	850	1,306	123
75-79 yrs. old.	6,033	2,385	3,648	5,430	486
75 yrs. old .	1,376	566	811	1,237	113
76 yrs. old .	1,297	521	776	1,165	106
77 yrs. old .	1,212	476	735	1,089	98
78 yrs. old .	1,120	432	688	1,009	89
79 yrs. old .	1,028	391	637	930	79
80-84 yrs. old.	3,728	1,306	2,422	3,409	256
80 yrs. old .	921	338	583	832	72
81 yrs. old .	815	290	526	750	51
82 yrs. old .	720	253	467	661	47
83 yrs. old .	669	228	441	614	44
84 yrs. old .	603	198	405	552	42
85-89 yrs. old.	1,962	588	1,374	1,791	142
85 yrs. old .	515	164	351	470	37
86 yrs. old .	448	137	311	406	32
87 yrs. old .	387	114	272	353	28
88 yrs. old .	332	95	237	303	24
89 yrs. old .	281	78	203	257	20
90-94 yrs. old.	790	195	594	719	61
90 yrs. old .	234	62	171	213	17
91 yrs. old .	190	48	142	174	14
92 yrs. old .	151	36	115	138	12
93 yrs. old .	117	26	91	107	9
94 yrs. old .	97	23	74	87	9
95-99 yrs. old.	229	53	176	200	25
95 yrs. old .	77	19	59	69	8
96 yrs. old .	58	14	44	51	6
97 yrs. old .	42	10	32	37	5
98 yrs. old .	30	7	23	25	4
99 yrs. old .	22	5	17	19	3
100 yrs. old and over	61	13	48	50	9
Median age (yr.)	32.6	31.5	33.8	33.6	27.7

[1] Includes other races, not shown separately.

Source : U.S. Bureau of the Census, *Current Population Reports*, series P-25, Nos. 1045 and 1057.

RACIAL CHARACTERISTICS

The non-white and Hispanic populations have a smaller proportion of elderly than the white population (Table 1.4). In 1989, 13 percent of whites were age 65 and over, compared to only 8 percent of blacks and 5 percent of Hispanics. These differences in racial proportions are expected to continue until the next century, when the minority elderly are predicted to increase more rapidly than the white population. This growth will be due to greater fertility among minority populations resulting in a larger proportion of younger people among non-whites.

Table 1.3 demonstrates a result of the larger proportion of younger persons in the black community. The median age among whites in 1989 was 33.6 years, for blacks, 27.7 years.

ADDITIONAL REASONS FOR THE AGING OF AMERICA

In addition to the large number of births after World War II, there are several other reasons for the aging of the American population. Foremost are medical advances that have greatly reduced infant mortality and death from childhood diseases; people have a greater chance of surviving the first years of life. (An extremely high infant and child mortality rate was the main reason that average life expectancy was so low in early civilizations.) Medical advances, life-sustaining technologies, and a greater awareness of and desire for a healthy lifestyle have helped lengthen the lives of Americans.

WHERE IS OLDER AMERICA - AND WHERE IS IT GOING?

In 1989, over half (16.2 million) of the country's elderly lived in just nine states: California, New York, Florida, Pennsylvania, Texas, Illinois, Ohio, Michigan, and New York (Table 1.5). Although California had the largest number of elderly residents (over 3 million), Florida had the highest percentage (18 percent) relative to its total population. Alaska had the fewest elderly residents, both in absolute numbers (22,000) and in percentage of population (4.1 percent).

The number of 65+ residents will increase in all regions of the U. S. into the next century, with the South gaining the greatest number and the Midwest the fewest. 1980 marked the first time in American history that a greater number of elder people lived in the suburbs than in central cities. They were older neighborhoods known to have lower resident income levels, more rental housing, lower home values, and higher population densities.

Most older Americans still live in, or have returned to, their native states. They tend to remain where they spent their adult lives. Although migration is less common among the elderly, when older citizens do move, it is to the Sunbelt states, that is to the Southern and Western regions (Table 1.6).

MARRIED MEN -UNMARRIED WOMEN

The ratio of women to men varies dramatically by age, with the disparity becoming most marked among the oldest. Figure 1.3 demonstrates the moving of the baby boom cohort (group) through the population. The diagrams illustrate the swell-

TABLE 1.5

RANK ORDER OF STATES, BY SELECTED CHARACTERISTICS OF THE 65+ POPULATION: 1989

		Number of people 65+		People 65+ as percent of state's population			Percent change in number of people 65+, 1980-1989	
Rank*	State	Number (000s)	Rank	State	Per-cent	Rank	State	Per-cent
1 (1)	California	3,071	(x)	U.S., total	12.5	(x)	U.S., total	21.3
(x)	U.S., total	30,984	1	Florida	18.0	1	Alaska	88.3
2 (2)	New York	2,341	2	Pennsylvania	15.1	2	Nevada	84.5
3 (4)	Florida	2,277	3	Iowa	15.1	3	Hawaii	56.6
4 (5)	Pennsylvania	1,819	4	Rhode Island	14.8	4	Arizona	51.1
5 (3)	Texas	1,714	5	Arkansas	14.8	5	New Mexico	38.5
6 (6)	Illinois	1,437	6	West Virginia	14.6	6	South Carolina	35.9
7 (7)	Ohio	1,399	7	South Dakota	14.4	7	Florida	34.9
8 (8)	Michigan	1,100	8	Missouri	13.9	8	Delaware	34.3
9 (9)	New Jersey	1,021	9	Nebraska	13.9	9	Utah	34.1
10 (13)	Massachusetts	813	10	Oregon	13.9	10	North Carolina	32.4
11 (10)	North Carolina	798	11	North Dakota	13.9	11	Washington	31.5
12 (15)	Missouri	719	12	Massachusetts	13.8	12	Colorado	31.1
13 (14)	Indiana	694	13	Kansas	13.7	13	Virginia	30.0
14 (12)	Virginia	657	14	Connecticut	13.6	14	Oregon	29.3
15 (11)	Georgia	653	15	Maine	13.4	15	Idaho	29.3
16 (17)	Wisconsin	652	16	Wisconsin	13.4	16	Maryland	28.6
17 (16)	Tennessee	625	17	Oklahoma	13.3	17	California	27.2
18 (18)	Washington	567	18	New Jersey	13.2	18	Georgia	26.3
19 (21)	Minnesota	549	19	Montana	13.2	19	Montana	25.4
20 (22)	Alabama	523	20	Arizona	13.1	20	Texas	25.0
21 (19)	Maryland	509	21	New York	13.0	21	Wyoming	24.9
22 (20)	Louisiana	487	22	Ohio	12.8	22	New Hampshire	22.5
23 (23)	Kentucky	472	23	Alabama	12.7	23	Connecticut	20.8
24 (24)	Arizona	464	24	Kentucky	12.7	24	Tennessee	20.7
25 (27)	Connecticut	441	25	Tennessee	12.6	25	Michigan	20.6
26 (29)	Iowa	428	26	Minnesota	12.6	26	Louisiana	20.5
27 (28)	Oklahoma	428	27	Dist. of Col.	12.5	27	Ohio	19.6
28 (30)	Oregon	392	28	Mississippi	12.4	28	Pennsylvania	18.8
29 (25)	South Carolina	390	29	Indiana	12.4	29	Alabama	18.8
30 (33)	Arkansas	356	30	Illinois	12.3	30	New Jersey	18.8
31 (32)	Kansas	343	31	North Carolina	12.1	31	Indiana	18.5
32 (31)	Mississippi	326	32	Idaho	11.9	32	Rhode Island	16.5
33 (26)	Colorado	324	33	Washington	11.9	33	Maine	16.2
34 (34)	West Virginia	272	34	Vermont	11.9	34	Vermont	16.1
35 (36)	Nebraska	224	35	Michigan	11.9	35	Wisconsin	15.5
36 (38)	Maine	164	36	Delaware	11.8	36	Kentucky	15.1
37 (37)	New Mexico	161	37	New Hampshire	11.4	37	Minnesota	14.5
38 (43)	Rhode Island	148	38	South Carolina	11.1	38	West Virginia	14.2
39 (35)	Utah	146	39	Louisiana	11.1	39	North Dakota	14.0
40 (42)	New Hampshire	126	40	Nevada	10.9	40	Illinois	13.9
41 (40)	Nevada	121	41	Maryland	10.8	41	Oklahoma	13.9
42 (41)	Idaho	121	42	Virginia	10.8	42	Arkansas	13.8
43 (39)	Hawaii	119	43	Hawaii	10.7	43	South Dakota	12.9
44 (44)	Montana	106	44	California	10.6	44	Mississippi	12.7
45 (45)	South Dakota	103	45	New Mexico	10.5	45	Kansas	12.0
46 (47)	North Dakota	92	46	Georgia	10.1	46	Massachusetts	11.9
47 (46)	Delaware	79	47	Texas	10.1	47	Missouri	10.9
48 (48)	Dist. of Col.	76	48	Wyoming	9.8	48	Iowa	10.5
49 (49)	Vermont	68	49	Colorado	9.8	49	Nebraska	9.1
50 (51)	Wyoming	46	50	Utah	8.6	50	New York	8.3
51 (50)	Alaska	22	51	Alaska	4.1	51	Dist. of Col.	1.8

SOURCE: U.S. Bureau of the Census. "State Population and Household Estimates: July 1, 1989," by Edwin Byerly. *Current Population Reports* Series P-25, No. 1058 (March 1990), and unpublished data.

NOTE: All rankings in this table are derived from unrounded numbers and percentages.

*Numbers in parentheses represent rank order of states based on population of all ages in 1989.

(x) Not applicable

TABLE 1.6

PERCENT CHANGE IN POPULATION, BY AGE GROUP, FOR REGIONS AND DIVISIONS: 1980-1989
(number in thousands)

Region and Division	All ages			Under 65			65+		
	1980	1989	Percent Change	1980	1989	Percent Change	1980	1989	Percent Change
U.S., total	226,546	248,239	9.6	200,997	217,255	8.1	25,549	30,984	21.3
Northeast	49,135	50,772	3.3	43,063	43,831	1.8	6,072	6,941	14.3
New England	12,348	13,047	5.7	10,828	11,288	4.2	1,520	1,759	15.7
Middle Atlantic	36,787	37,726	2.6	32,236	32,544	1.0	4,551	5,182	13.9
Midwest	58,866	60,148	2.2	52,174	52,408	0.4	6,692	7,740	15.7
East North Central	41,682	42,298	1.5	37,189	37,017	-0.5	4,493	5,281	17.5
West North Central	17,183	17,851	3.9	14,984	15,392	2.7	2,199	2,459	11.8
South	75,372	85,523	13.5	66,884	74,883	12.0	8,488	10,640	25.4
South Atlantic	36,959	43,115	16.7	32,592	37,404	14.8	4,367	5,711	30.8
East South Central	14,666	15,406	5.0	13,009	13,461	3.5	1,657	1,945	17.4
West South Central	23,747	27,002	13.7	21,283	24,017	12.8	2,464	2,985	21.1
West	43,172	51,796	20.0	38,874	46,133	18.7	4,298	5,663	31.8
Mountain	11,373	13,513	18.8	10,312	12,022	16.6	1,061	1,491	40.5
Pacific	31,800	38,283	20.4	28,563	34,111	19.4	3,237	4,172	28.9

SOURCE: U.S. Bureau of the Census. "State Population and Household Estimates: July 1, 1989," by Edwin Byerly. *Current Population Reports* Series P-25, No. 1058 (March 1990).

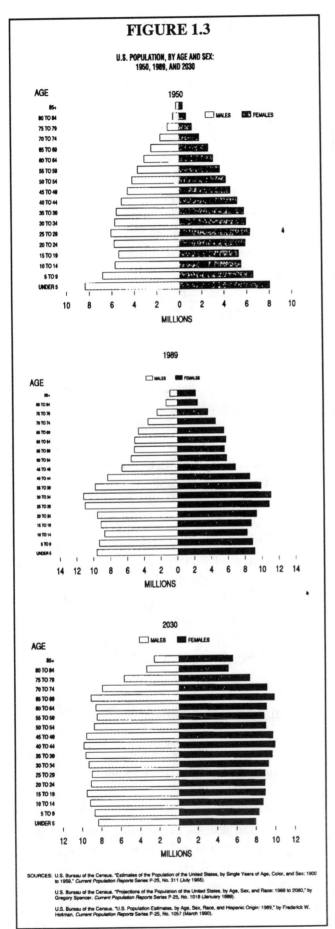

FIGURE 1.3

U.S. POPULATION, BY AGE AND SEX:
1950, 1989, AND 2030

1950

AGE

85+
80 TO 84
75 TO 79
70 TO 74
65 TO 69
60 TO 64
55 TO 59
50 TO 54
45 TO 49
40 TO 44
35 TO 39
30 TO 34
25 TO 29
20 TO 24
15 TO 19
10 TO 14
5 TO 9
UNDER 5

☐ MALES ■ FEMALES

10 8 6 4 2 0 2 4 6 8 10
MILLIONS

1989

AGE

85+
80 TO 84
75 TO 79
70 TO 74
65 TO 69
60 TO 64
55 TO 59
50 TO 54
45 TO 49
40 TO 44
35 TO 39
30 TO 34
25 TO 29
20 TO 24
15 TO 19
10 TO 14
5 TO 9
UNDER 5

☐ MALES ■ FEMALES

14 12 10 8 6 4 2 0 2 4 6 8 10 12 14
MILLIONS

2030

AGE

85+
80 TO 84
75 TO 79
70 TO 74
65 TO 69
60 TO 64
55 TO 59
50 TO 54
45 TO 49
40 TO 44
35 TO 39
30 TO 34
25 TO 29
20 TO 24
15 TO 19
10 TO 14
5 TO 9
UNDER 5

☐ MALES ■ FEMALES

12 10 8 6 4 2 0 2 4 6 8 10 12
MILLIONS

SOURCES: U.S. Bureau of the Census. "Estimates of the Population of the United States, by Single Years of Age, Color, and Sex: 1900 to 1959." *Current Population Reports* Series P-25, No. 311 (July 1965).

U.S. Bureau of the Census. "Projections of the Population of the United States, by Age, Sex, and Race: 1988 to 2080," by Gregory Spencer. *Current Population Reports* Series P-25, No. 1018 (January 1989).

U.S. Bureau of the Census. "U.S. Population Estimates, by Age, Sex, Race, and Hispanic Origin: 1989," by Frederick W. Hollman. *Current Population Reports* Series P-25, No. 1057 (March 1990).

ing of the population at the oldest range and the especially noticeable increase in the female elderly.

In 1989, over three-quarters of men aged 65 and over were married, but only 42 percent of women in this age group had spouses (Figure 1.4). Almost half of all women 65 and over were widowed, but only 14 percent of men were widowed. There is a large discrepancy between the percentage of elderly men who are married and elderly women who are not because women live longer than men; men tend to marry women younger than themselves and, therefore, are more likely to die first; and men who are widowed or divorced remarry more often than do women in the same situation. The gap widens even further for those 75 and over - in 1989, 70 percent of men in this age group were married compared to only 25 percent of women (Table 1.7).

ATTITUDES ABOUT AGING

In non-industrialized countries, old people are often held in great respect and esteem. Not only have they weathered years of what may have been harsh living conditions, but they have accumulated wisdom and knowledge that younger generations need to survive and carry on the traditions of their culture. In many industrialized societies such as the United States, a person's worth is measured largely by the type of work he or she does and the amount of wealth accumulated. When people retire from full-time employment, often on a modest company or government pension, they lose status because they are no longer working, earning money, or "contributing" to society. Their lifetime of experience may not seem relevant in an ever-changing world. Their identity is often bound to their former jobs, and without them, they feel worthless.

While the stereotypes of the elderly were probably never an accurate representation of most older people, they are even less true today than ever before. As technology and better living conditions work to increase the number of years a human being can survive, and people actively strive

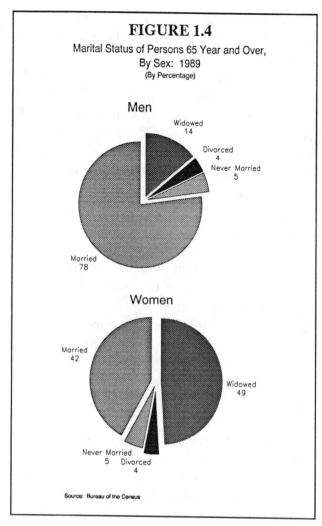

FIGURE 1.4

Marital Status of Persons 65 Year and Over,
By Sex: 1989
(By Percentage)

Men

Widowed
14

Divorced
4

Never Married
5

Married
78

Women

Married
42

Widowed
49

Never Married
5

Divorced
4

Source: Bureau of the Census

four times a week, while another is crippled with arthritis; one 80-year-old couple may volunteer to be foster grandparents, while another spends most of their days in front of the TV set.

Challenging the Myth

During the past few years, a revolution has been taking place. Older people want to be recognized as individuals rather than as stereotypes. Most of them are healthier, and many are wealthier, than at any time in our history. They are demanding the respect and recognition they feel they have earned. Older activists are involved in causes ranging from job retraining to long-term care to changing the public's perception of old age.

RESHAPING OUR SOCIETY

The aging of America means much more than just having more old people around. Attitudes about older people change as the elderly become more numerous and vocal, and the focus of daily life will shift from a youth culture to a mature one. This is unfamiliar territory. America has never been old before.

It is little wonder that the United States has been a youth-oriented society for so many years. The 65+ age group made up less than 5 percent of the population in 1900. But the projection for the year 2030 suggests that the elderly and the under-17 group will then equal one another in number. The complexion of the nation will certainly have changed.

Changing the Marketplace

Because spending power has traditionally been in the hands of young adults and their children, manufacturers and retailers have targeted these age groups almost exclusively. Now a whole new market is surfacing. Those adults worked in the prosperous post-war years, earned good wages and were conscientious about saving, and have completed child rearing responsibilities. Many have discretionary money.

to improve and preserve their health, "old age" becomes harder to define.

One Definition Does Not Fit All

Individuals age very differently. In fact, the differences between individuals in the latter years of their lives are much greater than in their early years. Although they may have diverse personalities and intellects, most babies and young children behave and develop within fairly predictable patterns. Even our educational system, whether right or wrong, presupposes a uniformity among children that allows them to be taught and to learn specific materials at specific ages.

On the other hand, one 65-year-old man may go to work every day as he has for the past 40 years, while another's dependance requires constant care; one 70-year-old woman may play 18 holes of golf

TABLE 1.7

Marital Status of the Population, by Sex and Age: 1989

[As of March. Persons 18 years old and over. Excludes members of Armed Forces except those living off post or with their families on post. Based on Current Population Survey; see text, section 1, and Appendix III. See *Historical Statistics, Colonial Times to 1970*, series A 160-171, for decennial census data]

SEX AND AGE	NUMBER OF PERSONS (1,000)					PERCENT DISTRIBUTION				
	Total	Single	Mar-ried	Wid-owed	Di-vorced	Total	Single	Mar-ried	Wid-owed	Di-vorced
Male.................	**85,799**	**22,195**	**55,279**	**2,272**	**6,044**	**100.0**	**25.9**	**64.4**	**2.7**	**7.0**
18-19 years old............	3,635	3,533	95	2	5	100.0	97.2	2.6	0.1	0.1
20-24 years old............	8,939	6,915	1,912	6	105	100.0	77.4	21.4	0.1	1.2
25-29 years old............	10,650	4,890	5,243	-	518	100.0	45.9	49.2	-	4.9
30-34 years old............	10,811	2,789	7,157	23	842	100.0	25.8	66.2	0.2	7.8
35-39 years old............	9,595	1,461	7,091	33	1,009	100.0	15.2	73.9	0.3	10.5
40-44 years old............	8,086	673	6,432	38	943	100.0	8.3	79.5	0.5	11.7
45-54 years old............	11,917	801	9,661	164	1,291	100.0	6.7	81.1	1.4	10.8
55-64 years old............	10,088	563	8,385	328	812	100.0	5.6	83.1	3.3	8.0
65-74 years old............	7,880	386	6,387	704	402	100.0	4.9	81.1	8.9	5.1
75 years old and over.........	4,199	184	2,915	982	118	100.0	4.4	69.4	23.4	2.8
Female...............	**93,984**	**17,775**	**56,195**	**11,492**	**8,522**	**100.0**	**18.9**	**59.8**	**12.2**	**9.1**
18-19 years old............	3,719	3,366	333	8	11	100.0	90.5	9.0	0.2	0.3
20-24 years old............	9,336	5,838	3,231	11	256	100.0	62.5	34.6	0.1	2.7
25-29 years old............	10,827	3,184	6,755	31	858	100.0	29.4	62.4	0.3	7.9
30-34 years old............	10,950	1,854	7,868	67	1,161	100.0	16.9	71.9	0.6	10.6
35-39 years old............	9,775	969	7,391	133	1,281	100.0	9.9	75.6	1.4	13.1
40-44 years old............	8,418	530	6,311	250	1,327	100.0	6.3	75.0	3.0	15.8
45-54 years old............	12,705	692	9,518	697	1,798	100.0	5.4	74.9	5.5	14.2
55-64 years old............	11,311	492	7,716	2,035	1,067	100.0	4.4	68.2	18.0	9.4
65-74 years old............	9,867	441	5,251	3,614	560	100.0	4.5	53.2	36.6	5.7
75 years old and over.........	7,077	410	1,819	4,646	203	100.0	5.8	25.7	65.6	2.9

- Represents or rounds to zero.

Source: U.S. Bureau of the Census, *Current Population Reports*, series P-20, No. 445.

Ironically, many manufacturers have no idea how to tap this potential market. Their marketing programs fail because they promote an item designed specifically for an "old" person, only to find that older people reject products that remind them of their age. It is often harder to develop a product that universally appeals to the old just because they are old than one that appeals to the young simply because they are young. Older consumers, especially those between 50 and 65, are a very diverse group with wide-ranging interests and needs.

The Need for New Marketing Approaches

Television commercials may look very different in the years ahead. The emphasis on youthfulness may find less acceptance in a generally aging community. Modelling and advertizing agencies increasingly demand the over-50 model. Magazines aimed at the mature audience, such as Modern Maturity, almost exclusively use advertisements with older models. However, the image of older people in advertising will almost certainly retain the healthy, vital qualities of younger models, while emphasizing the wisdom and experience gained with age.

The increasing number of elderly, the hours they spend watching television and otherwise attuned to the media (See Chapter XI), and the discretionary income available to many of them make the elderly a prime target for marketing.

The Need for New and Different Housing

In the future, the privately-owned, one-family residence with lawn may be only one of the housing options preferred by the elderly. Houses that accommodate the physical limitations of the elderly will become more necessary, as will apartment complexes for those who are no longer able or interested in maintaining a single-unit home for physical, financial, or security reasons. Entire developments devoted to elderly retirees have already sprung up in several states, although, as noted in Chapter III, with varying degrees of success. Chapter III explores more fully the possibilities for housing for the elderly.

CHAPTER II

THE ECONOMIC STATUS OF OLDER AMERICANS

The economic status of older Americans is more varied than that of any other age group. The elderly were once popularly stereotyped as poor, ill, and in need of all the public and private economic support they could get. Some observers now suggest that most older people are well off and do not need assistance, especially from the government. Elderly-rights advocates, on the other hand, point out that many older Americans have high, out-of-pocket medical expenses, are sharply affected by inflation and the overall economic climate, and have few opportunities to increase, or even maintain, their income.

The elderly are well represented in every economic bracket - affluence, middle class, and poverty. The major questions are how many elderly are in each segment, how wealth and poverty are defined, and how severe is poverty among the poor.

NET WORTH

A person's net worth is the sum of all his or her financial resources, including assets (items of value) and income, minus all debts and liabilities. When estimating the net worth of Americans, the U.S. Bureau of the Census uses the household*, rather than the individual, as the basic unit of calculation.

Are the Elderly Worth More?

The median net worth of households headed by a person 65 years or older in 1988 (the latest year for which figures are available), including home

---

TABLE 2.1
Median Net Worth, by Age of Householder and Monthly Household Income Quintile: 1988

Monthly household income	Total	Less than 35 years	35 to 44 years	45 to 54 years	55 to 64 years	65 years and over			
						Total	65 to 69 years	70 to 74 years	75 years and over
All households (thousands)	91,554	25,379	19,916	13,613	13,090	19,556	6,331	5,184	8,041
Median income................	$1,983	$2,000	$2,500	$2,604	$2,071	$1,211	$1,497	$1,330	$977
Median net worth.............	35,752	6,078	33,183	57,466	80,032	73,471	83,478	82,111	61,491
Excluding home equity	9,840	3,258	8,993	15,542	26,396	23,856	27,482	28,172	18,819

Source: Household Wealth and Asset Ownership: 1988, Bureau of the Census, (WDC, December 1990)

---

* A household consists of all persons occupying one housing unit (that is, a house, an apartment, a condominium, etc.) and includes related and nonrelated persons. Household income includes the income of every person in the household. One person (usually the person with the largest individual income) is designated as the "householder." The Bureau of the Census assumes that everyone living in one household shares the income and assets, as well as the debts and liabilities.

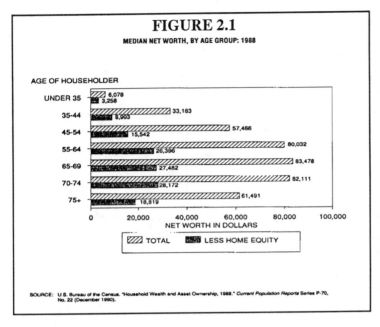

FIGURE 2.1

MEDIAN NET WORTH, BY AGE GROUP: 1988

AGE OF HOUSEHOLDER

UNDER 35   6,078 / 3,258
35-44   33,183 / 8,993
45-54   57,466 / 15,542
55-64   80,032 / 26,396
65-69   83,478 / 27,482
70-74   82,111 / 28,172
75+   61,491 / 18,819

NET WORTH IN DOLLARS

TOTAL   LESS HOME EQUITY

SOURCE: U.S. Bureau of the Census. "Household Wealth and Asset Ownership, 1988." *Current Population Reports* Series P-70, No. 22 (December 1990).

the elderly, net worth is low for unmarried persons and minorities, with unmarried householders' net worth being 40 percent of that of married couples (Table 2.2).

Income

As shown in Table 2.1, net worth in 1988 increased for each successive age group through the 55 to 64 year group and then began to decline. This is largely due to the fact that at some time during their lives most people work, and a working person generally earns more money and accumulates more assets as he or she gets older.

equity (the market value of the home less the amount remaining on the mortgage), was $73,471, the highest of any age group except the 55 to 64 year group (Table 2.1 and Figure 2.1). These figures seem to support the argument that the elderly are more wealthy than the non-elderly. However, many elderly people have fixed incomes and what they own cannot always be easily converted into cash if needed. Older people often have higher per person living costs. In addition, among

By age 65, most people are retired from the work force. They must then rely on fixed resources such as Social Security or pension benefits or compensate by tapping other, perhaps non-replaceable resources such as savings accounts or investments. According to the figures in Table 2.3, median income in 1990 actually began to decline at age 55. The median income of a household with a 75-year-old householder ($13,150) was less than for any other age group.

Assets

The elderly hold more assets than the non-elderly because of people's tendency to accumulate savings, home equity, and property in their lifetimes. Older Americans will usually have a greater percentage of their assets in bank accounts (30 percent) than the non-elderly (13 percent) (Figure 2.2).

In all age groups, home equity accounts for most of the household's net worth. In 1988, it represented 40 percent of net worth of households headed by an elderly householder. Even if a home is very valuable, however, it cannot be used for daily expenses. The only time a house provides any monetary value to the owner is when it is sold. Even then, new accommodations

TABLE 2.2

MEDIAN NET WORTH FOR ELDERLY (65+) HOUSEHOLDS, BY TYPE OF HOUSEHOLD AND RACE AND HISPANIC ORIGIN OF HOUSEHOLDER: 1988 AND 1984
(1984 median net worth is expressed in 1988 dollars)

Characteristic	Median net worth	
	1988	1984
All households	$73,471	$68,600
Type of household:		
Married couple	$124,419	$102,830
Male householder	$48,883	$46,919
Female householder	$47,233	$48,829
Race and Hispanic origin of householder:		
White	$81,648	$74,773
Black	$22,210	$15,972
Hispanic origin*	$40,371	$21,837

SOURCE: U.S. Bureau of the Census. "Household Wealth and Asset Ownership: 1988." *Current Population Reports* Series P-70, No. 22 (December 1990). Also "Household Wealth and Asset Ownership: 1984." *Current Population Reports* Series P-70, No. 7 (July 1986).

*Hispanic people may be of any race.

TABLE 2.3

Age of Householder—Households, by Total Money Income in 1990

[Numbers in thousands. Households as of March 1991.

Total money income	Total	Under 65 years Total	15 to 24 years	25 to 34 years Total	25 to 29 years	30 to 34 years	35 to 44 years Total	35 to 39 years	40 to 44 years
ALL RACES									
All Households									
Total	94 312	73 785	4 882	20 323	9 246	11 077	21 304	10 947	10 357
Less than $5,000	4 901	3 548	648	1 017	537	481	701	369	332
$5,000 to $9,999	9 184	4 795	694	1 397	687	710	968	575	393
$10,000 to $14,999	8 925	5 444	715	1 659	868	791	1 235	678	557
$15,000 to $19,999	8 296	5 704	589	1 912	964	948	1 410	738	672
$20,000 to $24,999	8 427	6 389	595	2 105	1 073	1 032	1 589	842	727
$25,000 to $29,999	7 501	6 039	445	1 914	941	973	1 670	904	766
$30,000 to $34,999	7 363	6 188	365	2 010	879	1 131	1 848	1 002	846
$35,000 to $39,999	6 395	5 545	284	1 669	771	898	1 682	875	807
$40,000 to $44,999	5 372	4 781	147	1 417	549	868	1 510	797	713
$45,000 to $49,999	4 702	4 194	118	1 160	510	650	1 434	713	721
$50,000 to $54,999	4 068	3 741	72	956	381	575	1 372	690	682
$55,000 to $59,999	3 227	2 951	72	680	284	395	1 005	519	487
$60,000 to $64,999	2 767	2 557	35	586	201	385	902	464	438
$65,000 to $69,999	2 170	1 955	30	367	120	247	688	318	370
$70,000 to $74,999	1 809	1 679	15	304	99	204	592	262	331
$75,000 to $79,999	1 555	1 438	6	230	89	141	544	247	297
$80,000 to $84,999	1 204	1 074	15	191	64	127	331	160	172
$85,000 to $89,999	982	901	2	166	60	106	293	118	175
$90,000 to $94,999	769	685	10	95	37	58	221	118	103
$95,000 to $99,999	590	530	4	88	19	69	157	58	99
$100,000 and over	4 085	3 646	19	400	111	289	1 172	501	671
Median income .... dollars	29 943	33 920	18 002	30 359	27 242	32 429	38 561	36 928	40 472
Standard error .... dollars	153	173	488	234	325	329	349	396	439
Mean income .... dollars	37 403	40 969	21 484	34 484	31 394	37 064	45 076	42 838	47 441
Standard error .... dollars	158	184	377	267	361	384	353	460	538
Income per household member .... dollars	14 197	14 226	9 041	12 101	11 896	12 250	13 744	13 119	14 399
Standard error .... dollars	74	78	216	126	190	174	141	189	217
Gini ratio	.426	.402	.411	.369	.366	.367	.373	.371	.373
Standard error	.0037	.0041	.0154	.0075	.0109	.0102	.0078	.0105	.0109

[Numbers in thousands. Households as of March 1991.

Total money income	Under 65 years—continued 45 to 54 years Total	45 to 49 years	50 to 54 years	55 to 64 years Total	55 to 59 years	60 to 64 years	65 years and over Total	65 to 74 years Total	65 to 69 years	70 to 74 years	75 years and over	Mean age
ALL RACES												
All Households												
Total	14 751	8 134	6 617	12 524	6 164	6 360	20 527	12 001	6 365	5 636	8 526	48.2
Less than $5,000	493	242	252	687	336	352	1 353	613	285	328	740	49.0
$5,000 to $9,999	743	371	373	992	337	655	4 388	1 961	876	1 085	2 427	57.1
$10,000 to $14,999	782	409	373	1 054	453	601	3 481	1 870	887	983	1 610	53.2
$15,000 to $19,999	783	406	377	1 010	428	582	2 592	1 472	768	704	1 120	50.2
$20,000 to $24,999	1 041	568	473	1 079	513	567	2 037	1 334	712	622	703	47.6
$25,000 to $29,999	1 042	570	472	967	416	551	1 463	975	583	392	487	46.4
$30,000 to $34,999	1 042	548	494	922	474	448	1 175	812	436	375	364	45.1
$35,000 to $39,999	1 043	580	463	867	421	446	850	606	400	206	244	44.7
$40,000 to $44,999	952	550	402	755	419	336	591	442	251	191	148	44.5
$45,000 to $49,999	882	525	357	601	331	270	508	383	234	191	125	44.4
$50,000 to $54,999	778	427	351	562	291	271	347	247	165	82	100	44.3
$55,000 to $59,999	738	422	316	456	257	199	276	188	102	86	88	44.8
$60,000 to $64,999	644	371	274	390	221	169	210	147	88	60	63	44.8
$65,000 to $69,999	546	318	228	324	194	130	215	172	104	67	43	46.2
$70,000 to $74,999	483	276	207	286	183	103	130	95	49	46	35	45.9
$75,000 to $79,999	417	249	169	241	146	95	117	90	58	31	28	46.1
$80,000 to $84,999	359	224	135	177	87	91	130	90	58	32	41	47.1
$85,000 to $89,999	306	178	128	135	84	51	81	66	39	27	15	46.3
$90,000 to $94,999	260	133	127	100	58	42	84	69	44	25	15	47.3
$95,000 to $99,999	176	92	84	105	68	37	60	53	33	20	7	47.8
$100,000 and over	1 240	676	564	813	447	366	440	317	194	123	123	49.0
Median income .... dollars	41 922	43 169	40 370	32 365	36 338	28 773	16 855	20 292	22 314	17 875	13 150	(X)
Standard error .... dollars	412	671	669	426	602	551	183	272	383	403	238	(X)
Mean income .... dollars	50 003	50 964	48 821	41 459	44 967	38 061	24 586	27 942	30 254	25 331	19 862	(X)
Standard error .... dollars	488	628	702	493	718	671	263	363	525	490	364	(X)
Income per household member .... dollars	16 886	16 407	17 543	17 653	18 246	17 019	14 026	14 757	15 181	14 223	12 773	(X)
Standard error .... dollars	212	276	341	272	389	387	191	251	349	366	299	(B)
Gini ratio	.389	.380	.400	.435	.418	.447	.463	.447	.438	.452	.466	(X)
Standard error	.0090	.0121	.0134	.0103	.0144	.0147	.0088	.0111	.0150	.0165	.0149	(B)

Source: Money Income of Households, Families, and Persons in the United States: 1990, Bureau of the Census, (WDC, 1991)

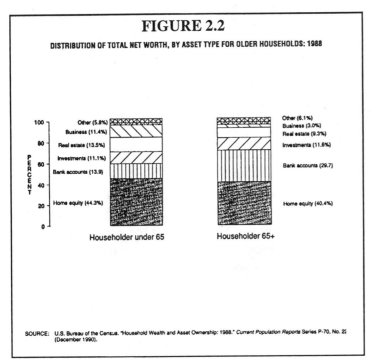

FIGURE 2.2

DISTRIBUTION OF TOTAL NET WORTH, BY ASSET TYPE FOR OLDER HOUSEHOLDS: 1988

Householder under 65

Other (5.8%)
Business (11.4%)
Real estate (13.5%)
Investments (11.1%)
Bank accounts (13.9)
Home equity (44.3%)

Householder 65+

Other (6.1%)
Business (3.0%)
Real estate (9.3%)
Investments (11.6%)
Bank accounts (29.7)
Home equity (40.4%)

SOURCE: U.S. Bureau of the Census. "Household Wealth and Asset Ownership: 1988." *Current Population Reports* Series P-70, No. 22 (December 1990).

must be found and paid for. Many older people have lived in their homes for a long time and do not want to move. In many states, money can be borrowed against the value of a home, but elderly people may be reluctant to take on any new debt, especially if they are on a fixed income.

Assets in the form of bank accounts, including savings accounts and certificates of deposit (CDs), made up almost 30 percent of elderly households' net worth in 1988. Most bank accounts are not "fixed" in the strict sense because they do represent available cash, but many older people are reluctant to "touch their savings" except in an extreme emergency. They know that one major or prolonged illness can use up a lifetime of savings.

Smaller Households are More Expensive to Run

Almost all elderly households are made up of fewer persons than younger households. Generally, the larger the household, the greater the expenses, but not on a one-to-one scale. The Bureau of the Census reports that the basic cost of living for two people is less than twice as much as the cost for one person living alone; the living cost of four people is significantly less than four times that of someone living alone.

Larger and younger households often have multiple incomes. Repairing a leaky roof or buying a new refrigerator costs the same for both households, but the larger the household, the less the cost <u>per person</u> and as a percentage of total income. Buying small quantities of food for one or two persons may be almost as expensive as buying in bulk for three or four. Because the elderly often have limited mobility, they may be forced to buy food and other necessities at small neighborhood stores that charge more than supermarkets.

More Rich Than Poor

Numbers such as net worth do not always accurately describe the condition of most elderly people. Some older people in the United States are, indeed, very rich. When their wealth is averaged into income and asset statistics, it masks the fact that a large number of old people live below, and often far below, the poverty level (see THE ELDERLY POOR, below).

A person's assets change with age. The value of vehicles declines from 16 percent of the household assets among those under age 35 to 3 percent for those 65 and older. Meanwhile, the value of financial assets such as interest-bearing accounts doubles from 11 percent among the non-elderly to 22 percent for the elderly. Unfortunately for most elderly retirees who live off these investments, the recent trend in the U. S. economy toward lower interest rates has led to significant cuts in their monthly incomes, sometimes by several hundred, and even thousands of dollars.

SOURCES OF INCOME

Unlike younger people who may get almost all their income from a regular paycheck, the elderly rely on a variety of sources to meet the expenses of daily living. Unable to improve their incomes through work, they often are vulnerable to circumstances beyond their control, such as the death of a spouse, health problems, Social Security and Medi-

13

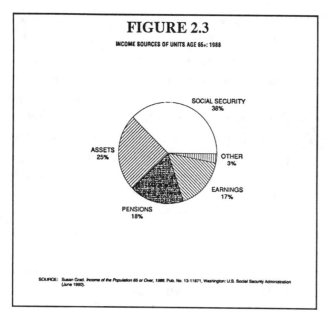

FIGURE 2.3

INCOME SOURCES OF UNITS AGE 65+: 1988

SOCIAL SECURITY
38%

ASSETS
25%

OTHER
3%

EARNINGS
17%

PENSIONS
18%

SOURCE: Susan Grad. *Income of the Population 65 or Over, 1988.* Pub. No. 13-11871, Washington: U.S. Social Security Administration (June 1990).

care shifts, and inflation. As a group, in 1988 the elderly derived 38 percent of their income from Social Security benefits, 25 percent from assets (returns on stock investments, interest from savings accounts, etc.), 17 percent from earnings, 18 percent from government and private employee pensions, and 3 percent from "other" sources (Figure 2.3). Very few elderly people receive income from all these sources at any one time. In addition, the elderly receive favorable treatment in taxes and government in-kind transfers. In-kind benefits include Medicare, Medicaid, food stamps, and housing assistance.

Rising health care costs, rather than funding for retirement, account for most of the increasing public spending on the elderly. In 1991, programs benefitting the elderly accounted for more than 30 percent of the federal budget, a doubling of the 15 percent spent on the elderly in 1960. Over the same period, spending on health programs for the elderly as a proportion of all federal spending on the elderly increased five-fold from 6 percent in 1960 to 32 percent in 1991.

Social Security

The elderly depend on Social Security for their incomes more than on any other source. The Social Security program pays benefits to more than 90 percent of those over 65. For 60 percent of the elderly, Social Security provides more than 50 percent of their income. For one-quarter of the elderly, it provides at least 90 percent of their income, and for 14 percent of the elderly, Social Security supplies all their income.

Assets and Earnings

The trend toward earlier retirement has caused a decline in the role of earnings in supporting the aged. As earnings account for less income, assets and pensions have become more important. Assets are the second most important source of income for the aged, representing one-quarter of their income source. It must be emphasized that this is an average figure; while some elderly have large assets, one-third of the elderly have <u>no</u> income from assets (Figure 2.3).

Pension (Retirement) Funds

Many large companies, along with most local and state governments and the federal government, offer pension plans. (The first employer-provided retirement plan in the U.S. was started in 1875.) Employees are eligible for pension benefits when they retire or leave a company if they have worked for the company for a designated number of years and/or have reached a specified age. A pension benefit is usually money in the form of a monthly check beginning at retirement and ending at death. A few companies pay for 100 percent of pension benefits, but more commonly, companies provide a portion of the benefits, and employees contribute a percentage of their salaries to the pension fund during their working years.

The 1989 Employee Benefits Survey of medium and large establishments showed that 63 percent of full-time employees were covered by pension plans (1991, <u>Monthly Labor Review</u>). Employees in larger firms were more likely to be covered than those in smaller firms. Highly paid workers were more likely to have coverage, as were workers in industries covered by union contracts.

14

TABLE 2.4
Age of Householder—Households, by Total Money Income In 1990

Numbers in thousands. Households as of March 1991.

Total money income	Under 65 years						65 years and over					Mean age
	45 to 54 years			55 to 64 years				65 to 74 years				
	Total	45 to 49 years	50 to 54 years	Total	55 to 59 years	60 to 64 years	Total	Total	65 to 69 years	70 to 74 years	75 years and over	
ALL RACES—Con.												
Nonfamily Households—Con.												
Female householder, total	1 556	774	782	1 973	817	1 156	7 509	3 460	1 548	1 912	4 049	57.9
Less than $5,000	161	78	83	336	163	174	961	396	181	215	565	62.3
$5,000 to $9,999	199	88	111	421	110	310	2 984	1 235	505	729	1 749	68.9
$10,000 to $14,999	180	73	107	277	113	164	1 530	767	351	416	763	62.7
$15,000 to $19,999	148	67	81	238	100	138	761	393	186	208	368	56.3
$20,000 to $24,999	198	110	88	189	87	102	489	252	112	139	237	51.0
$25,000 to $29,999	157	86	71	161	70	91	260	135	64	70	125	48.2
$30,000 to $34,999	126	54	72	102	52	49	166	77	50	27	89	45.7
$35,000 to $39,999	107	56	51	79	45	34	96	62	34	28	34	44.6
$40,000 to $44,999	82	47	35	45	19	26	82	48	25	22	34	45.8
$45,000 to $49,999	43	24	18	23	11	13	32	14	5	10	18	42.5
$50,000 to $54,999	31	21	10	24	16	9	29	18	12	6	11	43.2
$55,000 to $59,999	23	13	9	23	3	20	25	11	1	10	14	45.9
$60,000 to $64,999	24	7	17	13	7	6	9	1	-	1	7	44.2
$65,000 to $69,999	12	12	-	11	5	6	14	12	3	9	2	44.9
$70,000 to $74,999	19	12	7	5	1	3	12	4	3	2	8	(B)
$75,000 to $79,999	3	1	2	11	5	6	7	3	-	3	3	(B)
$80,000 to $84,999	8	4	3	4	2	2	14	10	5	5	4	(B)
$85,000 to $89,999	4	1	3	-	-	-	3	3	-	3	-	(B)
$90,000 to $94,999	6	2	4	1	1	-	5	3	1	2	1	(B)
$95,000 to $99,999	1	1	-	3	3		7	6	6		1	(B)
$100,000 and over	24	17	8	10	5	4	24	9	4	5	15	49.2
Median income .... dollars	21 980	23 364	20 434	14 056	16 166	12 525	9 620	10 552	11 236	10 106	9 039	(X)
Standard error .... dollars	640	1 109	1 198	643	1 030	761	124	235	398	279	151	(X)
Mean income .... dollars	26 248	27 862	24 651	18 554	20 078	17 478	13 477	14 321	14 890	13 861	12 755	(X)
Standard error .... dollars	905	1 249	1 304	568	966	684	241	327	501	429	349	(X)
Income per household member ...... dollars	22 149	23 313	20 978	17 100	17 823	16 554	13 124	13 943	14 429	13 545	12 424	(X)
Standard error .... dollars	1 173	1 688	1 632	827	1 331	1 048	348	515	794	678	476	(X)
Gini ratio	.426	.417	.432	.453	.454	.447	.415	.410	.412	.406	.415	(X)
Standard error	.0295	.0407	.0434	.0260	.0403	.0339	.0159	.0215	.0321	.0291	.0234	(X)

(Continued)

In 1988, pensions accounted for 18 percent of the income of the elderly. The spouse of a person who actually participated in a pension plan is also considered a recipient. Overall, 42 percent of the aged received income from public and/or private pensions other than Social Security. There are fewer government pension plans than private plans, but average benefits are substantially larger.

Individual Retirement Accounts (IRA's) were first established in 1974 as a means of retirement savings for those not covered by pensions. Another thrift plan, which is employer-provided, is the 401(k). Both IRA's and 401(k)'s provide a retirement savings opportunity for those not covered by pensions.

Federal Pension Laws

A company that has a pension plan will often invest the money received into the plan in an investment fund (for example, stocks or bonds), much as a bank does with its depositors' money. If the investment choice is a good one, the company makes a profit on the money in the fund; a bad investment results in a loss. During the early 1970s, several major plans collapsed, leaving retirees without benefits even though they had contributed to the plan for many years. These collapses led to the passage in 1974 of the Employment Retirement Income Security Act (ERISA) (PL 93-406). ERISA established participation and vesting (eligibility for benefits) guidelines and standards to ensure that funds are managed in the best interest of plan participants. It also created the Pension Benefit Guaranty Corporation, a federal agency, to take over benefit payments when underfunded plans are terminated. As of November, 1991, that fund had a two billion dollar deficit.

Women are somewhat less likely to be covered by a pension (64 percent as opposed to 69 percent for men). Before 1983, some plans paid lower monthly benefits to women because, statistically, women had longer lifespans than men and, on average, collected pension benefits for a longer

TABLE 2.4 Continued

Age of Householder—Households, by Total Money Income In 1990

Numbers in thousands. Households as of March 1991.

Total money income	Under 65 years						65 years and over					Mean age
	45 to 54 years			55 to 64 years			Total	65 to 74 years			75 years and over	
	Total	45 to 49 years	50 to 54 years	Total	55 to 59 years	60 to 64 years		Total	65 to 69 years	70 to 74 years		
ALL RACES—Con.												
Nonfamily Households—Con.												
Male householder, total	1 493	868	625	1 225	655	569	2 118	1 169	572	597	949	44.1
Less than $5,000	114	61	53	136	68	67	179	99	48	53	81	47.1
$5,000 to $9,999	138	62	77	200	73	127	578	273	130	143	305	54.0
$10,000 to $14,999	145	85	60	172	82	90	458	245	113	132	212	47.9
$15,000 to $19,999	137	77	60	133	70	63	298	166	75	91	132	44.7
$20,000 to $24,999	134	83	51	106	59	47	189	126	67	59	63	41.3
$25,000 to $29,999	158	97	61	79	43	36	112	73	39	34	39	40.3
$30,000 to $34,999	130	78	52	81	50	31	84	51	25	26	33	40.2
$35,000 to $39,999	89	37	52	82	43	39	36	23	14	9	14	39.4
$40,000 to $44,999	87	61	26	50	36	13	33	21	14	7	12	40.5
$45,000 to $49,999	63	46	17	36	28	9	36	24	13	11	13	39.6
$50,000 to $54,999	58	25	33	30	20	11	20	10	7	2	10	39.7
$55,000 to $59,999	38	25	13	15	11	4	24	15	10	5	9	40.0
$60,000 to $64,999	43	27	17	17	7	10	12	4	3	2	7	40.7
$65,000 to $69,999	17	13	4	8	6	2	9	7	4	2	2	39.4
$70,000 to $74,999	18	12	7	23	20	3	7	7	4	2	4	42.4
$75,000 to $79,999	22	14	7	8	4	4	5	5	3	2	-	42.0
$80,000 to $84,999	20	15	5	4	2	1	-	-	-	-	-	(B)
$85,000 to $89,999	15	9	6	7	2	4	7	-	-	-	7	43.6
$90,000 to $94,999	4	1	3	-	-	-	10	6	1	5	3	(B)
$95,000 to $99,999	3	-	3	4	4	-	-	-	-	-	-	(B)
$100,000 and over	58	42	17	33	26	7	19	14	6	8	5	42.8
Median income _____ dollars_	27 445	28 327	26 007	18 680	22 354	14 996	13 184	14 345	14 891	13 780	11 829	(X)
Standard error _____ dollars_	877	1 155	1 627	1 181	1 615	985	384	495	998	720	455	(X)
Mean income _____ dollars_	34 237	36 626	30 921	26 821	31 643	21 268	18 389	19 602	20 247	18 985	16 895	(X)
Standard error _____ dollars_	1 198	1 726	1 542	1 288	2 112	1 247	576	806	1 109	1 165	813	(X)
Income per household member __ dollars_	27 176	28 766	24 912	22 836	26 631	18 354	17 223	18 161	18 946	17 423	16 040	(X)
Standard error _____ dollars_	1 438	2 016	1 982	1 512	2 426	1 641	828	1 160	1 890	1 598	1 173	(X)
Gini ratio _____	.435	.435	.431	.481	.479	.459	.434	.431	.425	.435	.432	(X)
Standard error _____	.0303	.0407	.0444	.0354	.0490	.0480	.0279	.0364	.0494	.0535	.0441	(X)

Source: Money Income of Households, Families, and Persons in the United States: 1990, Bureau of the Census, (WDC, 1991)

period of time. In 1983, the Supreme Court ruled that pension plans must make payments based on gender-neutral actuarial tables (statistical calculations for insurance purposes) (*Arizona Governing Committee for Tax Deferred Annuity and Deferred Compensation Plan v. Natalie Norris, 463 US 1073*).

The Retirement Equity Act of 1984 (PL 98-397) requires pension plans to pay a survivor's benefit to the spouse of a deceased vested plan participant. Prior to 1984, some spouses received no benefits unless the employee was near retirement age at the time of death. Under the 1984 law, pension vesting begins at age 21 or after 5 years on the job, and employees who have a break in employment for reasons such as maternity leave will not lose any time already accrued.

Family Support

While the contribution by the family, both in financial support and the value of the care and time they give to an elderly parent or relative, has not been statistically determined, numerous studies suggest that it is substantial. According to these studies, income from federal sources (the next largest source of income for the aged), plays a minor role compared to the amount of support contributed by family members. When elderly persons outlive their family members, they are often faced with serious problems concerning financial security and personal care.

MEDIAN INCOME

Table 2.3 shows 1990 median income comparisons between the elderly and those younger than 65. In 1990, the median income for a household headed by someone 65 years and older was $16,855 (i.e., half of all men aged 65 years or older made under $16,855 and half made over $16,855), just under half the income of those 55 to 64 years of age ($32,365). Income continues to decline with age after age 65, with those over 75 receiving approximately three-quarters of the income of the 65 to 74 age group.

16

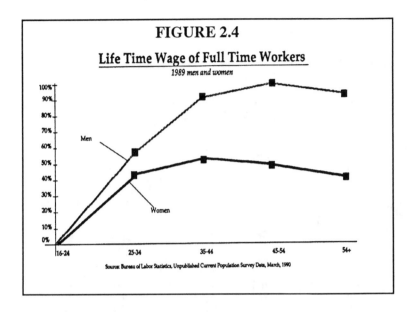

FIGURE 2.4

Life Time Wage of Full Time Workers

1989 men and women

Source: Bureau of Labor Statistics, Unpublished Current Population Survey Data, March, 1990

Only men and women in the 15 to 24 year old group had lower median incomes than the elderly (Table 2.3). However, a great many younger people are students and/or live at home and receive substantial financial support from their parents in addition to their own incomes.

Black and Hispanic elderly have lower incomes than their white counterparts. The 1990 median income for whites 65 and older was $18,689; for blacks, it was $11,264, for Hispanics, $15,641 (Table 2.5).

As with every other age group, women 65 years and older living alone had a lower median income ($9,513) in 1990 than older men living alone ($12,868) (Table 2.4). The U.S. Department of Agriculture, in its Family Economic Review, 1991, Vol. 4, No. 3, reported that husband-wife families fared best when income was adjusted for household size. The women had low median incomes but benefitted from the income of the spouse. The lower income of older women was largely associated with their greater likelihood of lifelong economic dependence on men. Women living alone fared less well than all others.

The earnings gap between American men and women accelerates as people grow older. The already lower women's income increases until age 45, the peak of a woman's earnings, while men's income peaks a decade later (Figure 2.4). This results in substantial differences in male and female earnings among the elderly. Many factors contribute to this wage gap, among them differences in education and experience and union affiliation. A report by the Older Women's League in 1989 concluded that the primary reason was job segregation. Older women are confined more narrowly in traditionally "women's occupations," which are lower paying. Unflattering stereotypes of older women as weak, incapable, and inflexible also encourage discrimination against women in mid-life and older.

EXPENSES

The elderly generally spend their money differently from younger people. Table 2.6 shows the 1989 average expenditure comparisons between elderly and younger people. Expenditures were highest in the under-65 group and decreased through the 75-years-and-older group, with the oldest persons spending the least of any age group. Older households spend less because they have less money to spend, fewer people to support, and different needs and values. The distribution of their expenditures is shown in Figure 2.5.

Not surprisingly, the elderly spend more money on health care than any other age group, both in actual dollars and in percentage of expenditures. Almost 15 percent of all expenditures of persons 75 years and older were for health care ($2,351), compared to 9.4 percent for those 65 to 74 ($1,981), and 4 percent for the under-65 group ($1211). Figure 2.6 illustrates the proportionate use of health-care dollars of those both under and over 65.

One measure of the economic differences among the elderly is shown in those who have discretionary income, that is money left over after the person has paid everything needed to maintain their standard of living. Table 2.7 shows that those over the age of 65 have a smaller percentage of discretionary income than all groups except per-

TABLE 2.5

Presence of Elderly—Households, by Total Money Income in 1990, Race, and Hispanic Origin of Householder

Numbers in thousands. Households as of March 1991.

Total money income	Total	No persons 65 years and over	With persons 65 years and over					
					Some, but not all elderly			
			Total	All members elderly	Total	Elderly householder or spouse only	Elderly other relative only	Elderly nonrelative only
ALL RACES								
Total	94 312	71 822	22 489	15 473	7 017	5 401	1 310	113
Less than $5,000	4 901	3 520	1 380	1 242	139	123	15	-
$5,000 to $9,999	9 184	4 704	4 480	3 980	499	429	50	13
$10,000 to $14,999	8 925	5 298	3 627	2 961	666	571	67	13
$15,000 to $19,999	8 296	5 551	2 745	2 011	734	605	92	6
$20,000 to $24,999	8 427	6 224	2 202	1 466	737	622	91	8
$25,000 to $29,999	7 501	5 926	1 575	967	608	533	63	5
$30,000 to $34,999	7 363	6 019	1 344	735	610	471	105	12
$35,000 to $39,999	6 395	5 363	1 032	503	529	382	123	9
$40,000 to $44,999	5 372	4 654	718	338	380	281	83	7
$45,000 to $49,999	4 702	4 063	639	237	403	288	96	7
$50,000 to $54,999	4 088	3 648	440	176	264	174	74	6
$55,000 to $59,999	3 227	2 863	363	146	217	141	67	3
$60,000 to $64,999	2 767	2 490	277	103	174	116	54	1
$65,000 to $69,999	2 170	1 899	270	102	168	117	41	3
$70,000 to $74,999	1 809	1 613	197	50	146	76	62	-
$75,000 to $79,999	1 555	1 402	154	65	88	54	29	2
$80,000 to $84,999	1 204	1 034	170	78	92	56	33	3
$85,000 to $89,999	982	872	110	35	75	44	24	3
$90,000 to $94,999	769	664	105	37	68	50	16	2
$95,000 to $99,999	590	501	90	19	70	36	27	2
$100,000 and over	4 085	3 515	570	220	350	231	97	7
Median income ... dollars	29 943	33 774	18 062	14 143	30 965	28 041	43 304	34 667
Standard error ... dollars	153	177	211	171	459	563	1 408	3 249
Mean income ... dollars	37 403	40 847	26 403	20 549	39 313	36 438	49 557	44 108
Standard error ... dollars	158	187	263	254	573	630	1 294	5 822
Income per household member ... dollars	14 197	14 277	13 814	14 628	12 982	13 272	12 392	11 600
Standard error ... dollars	74	79	174	244	248	301	473	1 894
Gini ratio	.426	.403	.465	.454	.402	.406	.348	.419
Standard error	.0037	.0042	.0082	.0105	.0136	.0160	.0291	.1089
WHITE								
Total	80 968	60 970	19 998	14 155	5 844	4 606	1 002	89
Less than $5,000	3 256	2 247	1 009	928	82	78	4	-
$5,000 to $9,999	7 161	3 356	3 805	3 465	340	297	31	9
$10,000 to $14,999	7 460	4 153	3 307	2 768	539	464	56	8
$15,000 to $19,999	7 034	4 546	2 488	1 900	589	511	59	6
$20,000 to $24,999	7 262	5 241	2 021	1 398	622	535	66	8
$25,000 to $29,999	6 558	5 109	1 448	915	533	479	50	2
$30,000 to $34,999	6 494	5 250	1 244	718	526	415	83	11
$35,000 to $39,999	5 576	4 629	947	489	458	332	108	6
$40,000 to $44,999	4 809	4 139	670	330	340	261	68	5
$45,000 to $49,999	4 187	3 617	570	225	345	257	72	7
$50,000 to $54,999	3 679	3 279	400	175	225	159	55	4
$55,000 to $59,999	2 953	2 625	328	143	184	119	58	3
$60,000 to $64,999	2 540	2 281	258	103	155	107	45	1
$65,000 to $69,999	1 962	1 722	240	101	140	99	31	3
$70,000 to $74,999	1 626	1 454	173	50	122	65	49	-
$75,000 to $79,999	1 404	1 272	132	65	67	50	12	2
$80,000 to $84,999	1 079	922	157	75	82	52	26	3
$85,000 to $89,999	899	799	100	35	65	41	17	3
$90,000 to $94,999	689	590	99	37	62	47	14	1
$95,000 to $99,999	549	470	80	19	60	31	22	2
$100,000 and over	3 791	3 269	522	216	306	209	76	5
Median income ... dollars	31 231	35 563	18 689	14 831	31 959	29 292	43 699	37 671
Standard error ... dollars	143	171	218	175	497	578	1 329	5 026
Mean income ... dollars	38 912	42 826	26 978	21 402	40 485	37 770	50 416	46 580
Standard error ... dollars	174	207	282	272	639	697	1 462	6 992
Income per household member ... dollars	15 070	15 155	14 671	15 117	14 137	14 368	13 401	13 242
Standard error ... dollars	80	90	197	261	297	352	581	2 461
Gini ratio	.417	.390	.458	.448	.393	.397	.337	.416
Standard error	.0040	.0045	.0087	.0109	.0150	.0173	.0334	.1241

(Continued)

sons under 24. Nonetheless, almost one-quarter of the elderly report having discretionary income.

THE ELDERLY POOR

Poverty standards are based on the "Economy Food Plan," developed by the U.S. Department of Agriculture (USDA) in the 1960s. The plan calculates the cost of a minimally adequate household food budget for different types of households by age of householder. Since USDA surveys showed that the average family spends one-third of its income on food, it was decided that a household with an income three times the amount needed for food was living fairly comfortably. The poverty level, then, is calculated by multiplying the cost of a minimally adequate food budget by three.

In 1966, one in every three elderly Americans lived in poverty (Table 2.8). During the 1960s and

TABLE 2.5 Continued

Presence of Elderly—Households, by Total Money Income in 1990, Race, and Hispanic Origin of Householder—Con.

Numbers in thousands. Households as of March 1991.

Total money income	Total	No persons 65 years and over	With persons 65 years and over		Some, but not all elderly			
			Total	All members elderly	Total	Elderly householder or spouse only	Elderly other relative only	Elderly nonrelative only
BLACK								
Total	10 671	8 628	2 044	1 130	914	672	180	18
Less than $5,000	1 500	1 148	352	298	53	43	10	-
$5,000 to $9,999	1 786	1 195	591	448	143	116	19	4
$10,000 to $14,999	1 240	971	269	154	115	96	9	5
$15,000 to $19,999	1 050	832	218	95	123	82	24	-
$20,000 to $24,999	988	831	157	63	94	70	22	-
$25,000 to $29,999	741	645	96	39	57	41	10	4
$30,000 to $34,999	695	619	75	12	63	47	13	-
$35,000 to $39,999	613	549	64	7	57	45	8	2
$40,000 to $44,999	412	382	30	1	29	15	9	2
$45,000 to $49,999	378	329	49	8	41	27	11	-
$50,000 to $54,999	293	266	28	1	26	13	11	-
$55,000 to $59,999	197	170	26	1	26	19	5	-
$60,000 to $64,999	128	120	8	-	8	6	2	-
$65,000 to $69,999	132	113	19	-	19	13	6	-
$70,000 to $74,999	113	100	12	-	12	11	1	-
$75,000 to $79,999	96	81	16	-	16	4	11	-
$80,000 to $84,999	69	64	6	-	6	4	1	-
$85,000 to $89,999	51	47	4	-	4	2	2	-
$90,000 to $94,999	44	42	2	-	2	-	2	-
$95,000 to $99,999	23	21	2	-	2	-	2	-
$100,000 and over	122	102	20	3	17	15	-	2
Median income ... dollars	18 676	20 862	11 264	7 100	21 190	19 763	27 688	(B)
Standard error ... dollars	426	357	542	198	1 219	1 398	4 001	(B)
Mean income ... dollars	24 814	26 347	18 343	10 327	28 254	26 824	34 195	(B)
Standard error ... dollars	335	382	641	442	1 149	1 339	2 630	(B)
Income per household member ... dollars	8 635	8 785	7 829	8 102	7 712	7 629	8 610	(B)
Standard error ... dollars	157	173	374	616	436	522	993	(B)
Gini ratio	.463	.449	.493	.417	.423	.433	.386	(B)
Standard error	.0110	.0120	.0281	.0413	.0375	.0454	.0737	(B)
HISPANIC ORIGIN[1]								
Total	6 220	5 384	836	362	474	314	144	8
Less than $5,000	466	389	77	64	13	13	-	-
$5,000 to $9,999	849	648	201	149	52	45	7	-
$10,000 to $14,999	804	679	125	52	73	53	14	3
$15,000 to $19,999	679	573	106	46	60	44	15	1
$20,000 to $24,999	633	561	72	21	51	42	9	-
$25,000 to $29,999	531	483	48	7	41	27	13	-
$30,000 to $34,999	498	435	63	11	52	29	20	1
$35,000 to $39,999	404	369	35	2	33	15	15	2
$40,000 to $44,999	286	269	18	3	15	8	5	1
$45,000 to $49,999	233	209	24	1	23	13	10	-
$50,000 to $54,999	182	170	13	1	12	4	8	-
$55,000 to $59,999	121	118	3	-	3	1	2	-
$60,000 to $64,999	99	91	8	1	7	6	2	-
$65,000 to $69,999	95	85	10	-	10	4	6	-
$70,000 to $74,999	71	63	7	-	7	2	6	-
$75,000 to $79,999	53	43	10	1	8	2	7	-
$80,000 to $84,999	40	36	4	1	4	3	1	-
$85,000 to $89,999	24	24	-	-	-	-	-	-
$90,000 to $94,999	30	28	2	1	2	1	1	-
$95,000 to $99,999	9	8	1	1	1	1	-	-
$100,000 and over	111	102	9	1	8	3	3	1
Median income ... dollars	22 330	23 516	15 641	8 599	23 727	20 182	33 364	(B)
Standard error ... dollars	458	515	943	611	1 687	1 805	2 362	(B)
Mean income ... dollars	27 972	28 842	22 370	12 478	29 913	24 705	38 806	(B)
Standard error ... dollars	461	493	1 244	1 083	1 872	1 609	3 259	(B)
Income per household member ... dollars	8 134	8 116	8 288	9 163	8 044	7 866	7 974	(B)
Standard error ... dollars	181	190	607	1 262	667	765	977	(B)
Gini ratio	.422	.414	.461	.429	.395	.381	.338	(B)
Standard error	.0147	.0156	.0448	.0815	.0561	.0654	.0923	(B)

[1]Persons of Hispanic origin may be of any race.

Source: Money Income of Households, Families, and Persons in the United States: 1990, Bureau of the Census, (WDC, 1991)

early 1970s, the average income of the elderly increased. This was largely due to increases in Social Security and pension benefits. As a result, by 1989 the poverty rate of those 65 and older had dropped to 11 percent and then rose slightly to 12.2 percent in 1990 (Table 2.9). The gap is closing between the poverty rates of the elderly and the non-elderly.

The Old-Poor versus the Young-Poor Debate

As shown in Table 2.9, the poverty rate among the elderly in 1990 (12.2 percent) was below that of the general population (13.5 percent). The percentage of people living below the poverty level was greater among those under 24 years of age than among the elderly. In fact, the poverty rate of the

TABLE 2.6

AVERAGE ANNUAL EXPENDITURES OF CONSUMER UNITS BY TYPE OF EXPENDITURE AND AGE OF REFERENCE PERSON: 1989

Type of expenditure	Amount expended				Percent distribution			
		65+				65+		
	Under 65	Total	65 to 74	75+	Under 65	Total	65 to 74	75+
Total	$30,191	$18,967	$21,152	$15,919	100.0	100.0	100.0	100.0
Housing, exc. utilities	7,394	4,475	4,960	3,795	24.5	23.6	23.4	23.8
Shelter	5,332	2,988	3,283	2,574	17.7	15.8	15.5	16.2
Operations, supplies, and furnishings	2,062	1,487	1,677	1,221	6.8	7.8	7.9	7.7
Transportation	5,751	3,092	3,695	2,248	19.0	16.3	17.5	14.1
Food	4,486	2,912	3,205	2,505	14.9	15.4	15.2	15.7
At home	2,520	1,907	2,048	1,713	8.3	10.1	9.7	10.8
Away from home	1,966	1,004	1,157	792	6.5	5.3	5.5	5.0
Health care	1,211	2,135	1,981	2,351	4.0	11.3	9.4	14.8
Utilities, fuels, public services	1,873	1,694	1,813	1,528	6.2	8.9	8.6	9.6
Cash contributions	849	1,091	1,022	1,187	2.8	5.8	4.8	7.5
Clothing	1,765	902	1,138	576	5.8	4.8	5.4	3.6
Personal insurance and pensions	2,938	740	1,059	295	9.7	3.9	5.0	1.9
Entertainment	1,614	719	843	546	5.3	3.8	4.0	3.4
Other*	2,312	1,207	1,436	888	7.7	6.4	6.8	5.6

SOURCE: U.S. Department of Labor, Bureau of Labor Statistics. "Consumer Expenditures in 1989." Press Release USDL: 90-616 (November 30, 1990).

*Includes tobacco products, alcoholic beverages, personal care products and services, reading, education, and miscellaneous expenditures.

dation (formerly the Villers Foundation), vigorously challenge this claim, noting that many elderly people have incomes that barely cover their needs (if it covers them at all), and that the oldest old are among the poorest poor.

A Different Standard for the Old

The Economy Food Plan used in determining poverty levels assumes that a healthy elderly person has lower nutritional requirements than a younger person and, therefore, an elderly person needs less money for food. This assumption has resulted in different poverty standards for the old and for the young. For example, in 1990, the Census Bureau's statistical poverty level for a single adult under 65 years of age was $6,800; for a single adult 65 or older it was $6,268 - 7.8 percent lower. A 64-year-old woman, then, with a yearly income of $6,500 is poor, but on her 65th birthday, she becomes "not poor"! The poverty level for elderly couples in 1990 was $7,905, 10 percent lower than for non-elderly couples ($8,794).

youngest poor was almost twice the elderly poverty rate. The poverty level among blacks and Hispanics is two to three times that of whites.

Many people use these statistics to support the argument that the elderly do not need as much support, especially from the government, as they currently receive. Some people assert that the elderly get benefits at the expense of the young. Other organizations, such as Families U.S.A. Foun-

This method of defining poverty does not recognize specialized problems of the elderly. For example, no household costs other than food are counted, even though the elderly spend a much greater percentage of their incomes on health care than do younger people. In addition, the Economy Food Plan considers only the nutritional needs of a healthy person; many of the elderly are in poor health and may need special diets or nutritional supplements.

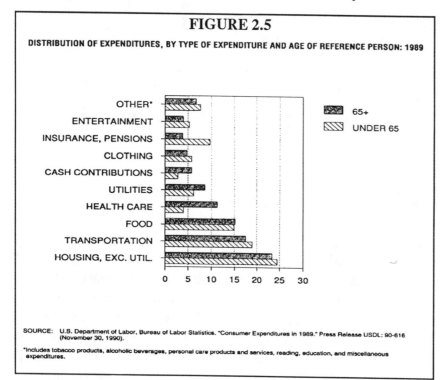

FIGURE 2.5

DISTRIBUTION OF EXPENDITURES, BY TYPE OF EXPENDITURE AND AGE OF REFERENCE PERSON: 1989

SOURCE: U.S. Department of Labor, Bureau of Labor Statistics. "Consumer Expenditures in 1989." Press Release USDL: 90-616 (November 30, 1990).

*Includes tobacco products, alcoholic beverages, personal care products and services, reading, education, and miscellaneous expenditures.

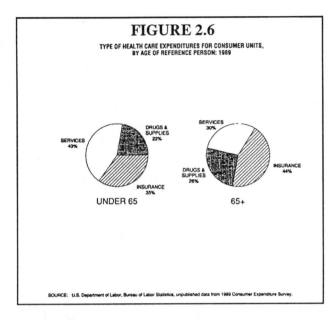

FIGURE 2.6

TYPE OF HEALTH CARE EXPENDITURES FOR CONSUMER UNITS,
BY AGE OF REFERENCE PERSON: 1989

UNDER 65

SERVICES 43%

DRUGS & SUPPLIES 22%

INSURANCE 35%

65+

SERVICES 30%

INSURANCE 44%

DRUGS & SUPPLIES 26%

SOURCE: U.S. Department of Labor, Bureau of Labor Statistics, unpublished data from 1989 Consumer Expenditure Survey.

When comparing the percentage of old and very young people who live in poverty, it is important to note that the same poverty standard is not applied to both groups. If it were, the percentage of elderly poor would increase relative to the younger poor. In addition, most young people are poor for a limited period of time; as they become old enough to enter the work force they often have the opportunity to increase their income. Poor older people, on the other hand, have almost no option but to remain poor, and they may be poor for the rest of their lives.

Differences Among the Poor Old

Twelve percent of all elderly people lived below the poverty level in 1990, but there are significant differences in poverty levels among the eld-

erly. Table 2.10 shows poverty levels among the elderly poor by various characteristics. As a group, women over 65 were almost twice as likely to live below the poverty level (15.4 percent) as men (7.6 percent). Only 10.1 percent of elderly white were poor, compared to 22.5 percent of those of Hispanic origin and 33.8 percent of black elderly. Those who lived alone were much more likely to be poor.

Those over 75 are more likely to be poor. Typically, poverty rates are high among the oldest old, women living alone, and minorities. In 1990, the poverty rate for all persons aged 75 and older was 16 percent, and for women in this age group it was 19.5 percent.

THE AFFLUENT ELDERLY

Certainly, more older Americans live comfortably today than at any other time in history. People now in their 60s and 70s were children of the Great Depression that began in 1929 and lasted through most of the 1930s. Many of them learned to economize and save. In their twenties and thirties, the men returned from World War II to inexpensive housing and G.I. bills that provided a free or economical college education. During their forties and fifties, their peak earning years, they participated in an unprecedented economic expansion. Many of them have raised their children, paid off their mortgages, and are in relatively good health. In addition, Social Security payments are larger than ever.

TABLE 2.7

Households with Discretionary Income—Selected Income Measures: 1986

[Households as of March 1987 and income figures are for the preceding year, expressed in 1986 dollars. Discretionary income is the amount of money which would permit a household to maintain a living standard comfortably higher (30 percent or more) than the average for similar households. For methodology, see source]

CHARACTERISTIC	ALL HOUSEHOLDS		HOUSEHOLDS WITH DISCRETIONARY INCOME						
			Households		Average income		Spendable discretionary income	
	Number (1,000)	Aggregate income after taxes (bil. dol.)	Number (1,000)	Percent of all households	Before taxes (dol.)	After taxes (dol.)	Aggregate income (bil. dol.)	Average income (dol.)
Total	89,479	2,165.1	25,869	28.9	56,605	41,940	319.0	12,332
Age of householder:								
15-24 years old	5,197	78.0	972	18.7	38,241	30,124	7.6	7,790
25-29 years old	9,652	205.9	2,646	27.4	48,547	36,618	24.2	9,130
30-34 years old	10,850	264.3	3,419	31.5	54,243	40,067	37.3	10,919
35-39 years old	10,155	280.2	3,349	33.0	60,049	43,585	41.5	12,405
40-44 years old	8,549	259.1	2,605	30.5	66,133	47,891	36.5	13,999
45-49 years old	6,888	218.3	2,299	33.4	69,412	49,968	33.2	14,448
50-54 years old	6,323	193.0	2,008	31.8	68,181	49,079	27.2	13,550
55-59 years old	6,443	178.5	2,252	35.0	61,480	44,906	32.8	14,584
60-64 years old	6,424	157.8	1,848	28.8	61,001	44,262	26.5	14,356
65-69 years old	6,086	125.3	1,523	25.0	50,447	38,968	19.7	12,921
70-years old and over	12,912	204.6	2,946	22.8	39,117	32,344	32.5	11,015

Source: Bureau of the Census and the Conference, *A Marketer's Guide to Discretionary Income*, 1989

The Center for Social Research in Aging at the University of Miami (Coral Gables, FL) defines the "comfortably retired" as those who live in households with incomes more than double the poverty level. It estimates that 59 percent of 55-to-64-year-olds are comfortably retired, as are 51 percent of 65-to-74-year-olds, and 37.5 percent of those 75 years and older. Hawaii has the highest percentage of comfortably retired per-

TABLE 2.8

POVERTY RATES FOR ELDERLY AND NONELDERLY ADULTS: 1966 TO 1989

Year	Poverty rate		Year	Poverty rate	
	18 to 64	65+		18 to 64	65+
1966	10.5	28.5	1978	8.7	14.0
1967	10.0	29.5	1979	8.9	15.2
1968	9.0	25.0	1980	10.1	15.7
1969	8.7	25.3	1981	11.1	15.3
1970	9.0	24.6	1982	12.0	14.6
1971	9.3	21.6	1983	12.4	13.8
1972	8.8	18.6	1984	11.7	12.4
1973	8.3	16.3	1985	11.3	12.6
1974	8.3	14.6	1986	10.8	12.4
1975	9.2	15.3	1987	10.6	12.5
1976	9.0	15.0	1988	10.5	12.0
1977	8.8	14.1	1989	10.2	11.4

SOURCE: U.S. Bureau of the Census. "Money Income and Poverty Status in the United States: 1989." *Current Population Reports,* Series P-60, No. 168 (September 1990).

Benefits and Beneficiaries

More than 40 million persons received Social Security benefits in December 1991. Seventy-three percent of all beneficiaries were 65 or older; 62 percent of all beneficiaries were retired workers, 19 percent were survivors of deceased workers, 7 percent were disabled workers, and 12 percent were "others."

sons in all three age groups, while Mississippi and South Dakota have the lowest percentage of comfortably retired elderly.

THE SOCIAL SECURITY PROGRAM

Congress passed the Social Security Act in 1935 to provide economic assistance to retirees, the blind, and mothers and dependent children. It has since been amended many times and is currently composed of many sections including Medicare (see Chapter VIII) and Supplemental Security Income (see below). The section entitled the Old-Age, Survivors, and Disability Insurance (OASDI) program provides monthly benefits to retired and disabled workers and their dependents, and to survivors of insured workers.

The Social Security program is funded with a mandatory tax that is withheld from workers' earnings and is matched by the employer. When a covered worker retires (or is disabled), he or she draws benefits based on the amount he or she has contributed to the fund. The longer the time of employment and the higher the earnings, the larger the benefit. In 1989, worker and employer each contributed 7.51 percent of the worker's salary to the fund; the OASDI program took in $240.8 billion (almost twice the amount of all the other Social Security programs combined) and paid out $200 billion in benefits. The contribution was raised to 7.65 percent beginning in 1990.

Beginning January 1992, the average Social Security check for retired workers is $629. For an elderly couple, both receiving benefits, the average monthly Social Security check is currently $1,067. Elderly widows or widowers receive $527.

Although Social Security was not initially intended to be a full pension enabling a recipient to maintain his or her pre-retirement standard of living, many elderly people are almost solely dependent on this income. Before Social Security was created, the poverty rate for those 65 and over was over 47 percent. The Census Bureau has concluded that the program enables 15 million Americans to stay above the poverty level, and that it is the country's most effective anti-poverty program.

Ever since 1940, when Americans first received Social Security benefits, average monthly retirement benefits have steadily increased, but in the early 1970s, they soared. In 1972, the average benefit was indexed to keep up with inflation as reflected by the Consumer Price Index (CPI). This meant that recipients receive periodic "raises" or COLA's (cost of living adjustments) that are based on the economic situation at that particular time. Within a few years, the whole system was facing serious long-range financial troubles which many observers linked to the 1972 amendments. Many legislators felt that indexing vastly overcompen-

TABLE 2.9

Number, Poverty Rate, and Standard Errors of Persons, Families, and Unrelated Individuals Below the Poverty Level in 1990 and 1989

(Numbers in thousands. Persons, families, and unrelated individuals as of March of the following year. An asterisk (*) preceding number and poverty rate difference indicates statistically significant change at the 90-percent confidence level.)

Characteristic	1990					1989					1990-89 difference		
		Below poverty level		Poverty rate			Below poverty level		Poverty rate		Below poverty level		
	Total	Number	Standard error	Percent	Standard error	Total	Number	Standard error	Percent	Standard error	Number	Standard error	Poverty rate
PERSONS													
All persons	248 644	33 585	523	13.5	.2	245 992	31 528	510	12.8	.2	* 2 057	542	* .7
Race and Hispanic Origin													
White	208 611	22 326	438	10.7	.2	206 853	20 785	425	10.0	.2	* 1 540	492	* .7
Related children under 18	51 028	7 696	223	15.1	.5	50 705	7 165	216	14.1	.4	* 531	250	* 1.0
Black	30 806	9 837	250	31.9	.8	30 332	9 302	246	30.7	.8	* 535	260	1.3
Related children under 18	9 980	4 412	138	44.2	1.7	9 847	4 257	137	43.2	1.7	155	144	1.0
Hispanic origin[1]	21 405	6 006	200	28.1	.9	20 746	5 430	194	26.2	.9	* 576	165	* 1.9
Related children under 18	7 300	2 750	114	37.7	1.8	7 041	2 498	111	35.5	1.8	* 253	94	2.2
Family Status													
In families	210 967	25 232	463	12.0	.2	209 515	24 066	453	11.5	.2	* 1 166	481	* .5
Householder	66 322	7 098	144	10.7	.2	66 090	6 784	140	10.3	.2	* 315	149	* .4
Related children under 18	63 908	12 715	274	19.9	.5	63 225	12 001	268	19.0	.5	* 714	284	* .9
Related children under 6 years	22 629	5 198	185	23.0	.9	22 220	4 868	180	21.9	.9	* 330	191	1.1
Other family members	80 737	5 419	224	6.7	.3	80 199	5 281	222	6.6	.3	138	234	.1
In unrelated subfamilies	1 621	907	93	56.0	6.5	1 292	702	82	54.4	7.1	* 204	92	1.6
Reference person	639	337	28	52.8	5.2	534	275	25	51.4	5.8	* 63	28	1.3
Children under 18	888	536	62	60.4	8.3	690	416	55	60.2	9.4	* 120	62	.1
Unrelated individual	36 056	7 446	148	20.7	.4	35 185	6 760	139	19.2	.4	* 686	151	* 1.4
Male	16 912	2 857	85	16.9	.5	16 209	2 539	79	15.7	.5	* 318	86	* 1.2
Female	19 144	4 589	111	24.0	.6	18 976	4 221	105	22.2	.6	* 368	113	* 1.7
Age													
Under 15 years	55 124	11 802	261	21.4	.5	54 200	11 060	255	20.4	.5	* 741	271	* 1.0
15 to 24 years	34 825	5 594	131	16.1	.4	35 255	5 370	129	15.2	.4	224	136	* .8
25 to 44 years	81 570	8 469	166	10.4	.2	80 435	7 808	160	9.7	.2	* 661	171	* .7
45 to 54 years	25 688	2 002	83	7.8	.3	25 304	1 883	81	7.4	.3	119	86	.4
55 to 59 years	10 692	963	58	9.0	.5	10 549	1 027	60	9.7	.6	-64	62	-.7
60 to 64 years	10 854	1 098	62	10.3	.6	10 683	1 017	60	9.5	.6	81	64	.8
65 years and over	30 093	3 658	106	12.2	.4	29 566	3 363	104	11.4	.4	* 294	111	* .8
Residence													
Nonfarm	243 865	33 051	520	13.6	.2	241 374	31 014	506	12.8	.2	* 2 036	538	* .7
Farm	4 779	534	98	11.2	2.1	4 618	514	96	11.1	2.2	20	102	.1
In metropolitan areas	193 052	24 510	457	12.7	.2	191 169	22 917	444	12.0	.2	* 1 592	472	* .7
In central cities	74 936	14 254	357	19.0	.5	75 123	13 592	349	18.1	.5	* 663	370	* .9
Outside central cities	118 116	10 255	305	8.7	.3	116 045	9 326	292	8.0	.3	* 930	313	* .6
Outside metropolitan areas	55 592	9 075	353	16.3	.7	54 824	8 611	344	15.7	.7	464	365	.6
Region													
Northeast	50 799	5 794	199	11.4	.4	50 520	5 061	187	10.0	.4	* 733	203	* 1.4
Midwest	59 914	7 458	259	12.4	.4	59 428	7 043	252	11.9	.4	414	268	.6
South	85 097	13 456	354	15.8	.4	84 044	12 943	348	15.4	.4	514	368	.4
West	52 835	6 877	259	13.0	.5	52 000	6 481	252	12.5	.5	396	268	.6
FAMILIES													
Race and Hispanic Origin[1] of Householder													
All families	66 322	7 098	144	10.7	.2	66 090	6 784	140	10.3	.2	* 315	161	* .4
Married-couple families	52 147	2 981	87	5.7	.2	52 317	2 931	86	5.6	.2	50	98	.1
Male householder, no wife present	2 907	349	28	12.0	1.0	2 884	348	28	12.1	1.0	1	32	-
Female householder, no husband present	11 268	3 768	99	33.4	1.0	10 890	3 504	95	32.2	1.0	* 264	110	1.3
White families	56 803	4 622	111	8.1	.2	56 590	4 409	108	7.8	.2	213	130	.3
Married-couple families	47 014	2 386	77	5.1	.2	46 961	2 329	76	5.0	.2	57	90	.1
Male householder, no wife present	2 276	226	23	9.9	1.0	2 303	223	22	9.7	1.0	4	27	.3
Female householder, no husband present	7 512	2 010	70	26.8	1.0	7 306	1 858	67	25.4	1.0	* 152	81	1.3
Black families	7 471	2 193	73	29.3	1.0	7 470	2 077	71	27.8	1.0	115	82	1.5
Married-couple families	3 569	448	32	12.6	.9	3 750	443	32	11.8	.9	5	36	.8
Male householder, no wife present	472	96	15	20.4	3.3	448	110	16	24.7	3.8	-14	17	-4.4
Female householder, no husband present	3 430	1 648	63	48.1	2.1	3 275	1 524	60	46.5	2.1	* 124	70	1.5
Hispanic origin families[1]	4 981	1 244	54	25.0	1.1	4 840	1 133	52	23.4	1.1	* 110	50	1.6
Married-couple families	3 454	605	37	17.5	1.1	3 395	549	35	16.2	1.1	55	35	1.3
Male householder, no wife present	342	66	12	19.4	3.8	329	54	11	16.3	3.5	12	11	3.0
Female householder, no husband present	1 186	573	36	48.3	3.5	1 116	530	35	47.5	3.6	43	34	.8

[1] Persons of Hispanic origin may be of any race.

Source: Poverty in the United States: 1990, Bureau of the Census, (WDC, 1991)

TABLE 2.10

Age, Sex, Household Relationship, and Hispanic Origin, by Poverty Status of Persons in 1990

[Numbers in thousands. Persons, families and unrelated individuals as of March of the following year]

Characteristic	All races Total	All races Below poverty level Number	All races Below poverty level Percent of total	White Total	White Below poverty level Number	White Below poverty level Percent of total	Black Total	Black Below poverty level Number	Black Below poverty level Percent of total	Hispanic Origin[1] Total	Hispanic Origin[1] Below poverty level Number	Hispanic Origin[1] Below poverty level Percent of total
ALL PERSONS												
Both Sexes												
Total	248 644	33 585	13.5	208 611	22 326	10.7	30 806	9 837	31.9	21 405	6 006	28.1
Under 18 years	65 049	13 431	20.6	51 929	8 232	15.9	10 162	4 550	44.8	7 457	2 865	38.4
18 to 24 years	24 901	3 964	15.9	20 383	2 753	13.5	3 549	1 051	29.6	2 741	752	27.5
25 to 34 years	42 905	5 201	12.1	35 902	3 578	10.0	5 435	1 434	26.4	4 219	1 004	23.8
35 to 44 years	38 665	3 268	8.5	32 905	2 250	6.8	4 272	839	19.7	2 920	603	20.6
45 to 54 years	25 686	2 002	7.8	22 030	1 358	6.2	2 694	569	21.1	1 737	311	17.9
55 to 59 years	10 692	963	9.0	9 248	681	7.4	1 115	246	22.0	658	122	18.5
60 to 64 years	10 654	1 098	10.3	9 316	768	8.2	1 033	288	27.9	582	105	18.1
65 years and over	30 093	3 658	12.2	26 898	2 707	10.1	2 547	860	33.8	1 091	245	22.5
65 to 74 years	18 238	1 765	9.7	16 209	1 234	7.6	1 581	468	29.6	737	152	20.6
75 years and over	11 855	1 893	16.0	10 689	1 472	13.8	966	392	40.6	354	93	26.2
Male												
Total	121 073	14 211	11.7	102 159	9 543	9.3	14 439	4 030	27.9	10 745	2 814	26.2
Under 18 years	33 311	6 841	20.5	26 643	4 240	15.9	5 145	2 263	44.0	3 812	1 508	39.5
18 to 24 years	12 275	1 499	12.2	10 121	1 067	10.5	1 669	370	22.2	1 424	323	22.7
25 to 34 years	21 319	1 923	9.0	18 054	1 404	7.8	2 496	442	17.7	2 190	416	19.0
35 to 44 years	19 032	1 342	7.1	16 434	1 020	6.2	1 931	259	13.4	1 475	260	17.6
45 to 54 years	12 428	821	6.6	10 748	585	5.4	1 198	203	17.0	811	134	16.5
55 to 59 years	5 179	384	7.4	4 525	274	6.0	505	97	19.3	318	50	15.6
60 to 64 years	4 982	443	8.9	4 398	320	7.3	465	109	23.5	255	38	14.7
65 years and over	12 547	959	7.6	11 235	634	5.6	1 031	286	27.8	461	86	18.6
65 to 74 years	8 156	524	6.4	7 267	325	4.5	694	170	24.6	323	58	18.0
75 years and over	4 391	434	9.9	3 968	309	7.8	337	116	34.4	137	28	20.1
Female												
Total	127 571	19 373	15.2	106 453	12 783	12.0	16 367	5 807	35.5	10 660	3 193	29.9
Under 18 years	31 738	6 591	20.8	25 286	3 992	15.8	5 016	2 287	45.6	3 645	1 357	37.2
18 to 24 years	12 627	2 465	19.5	10 262	1 686	16.4	1 881	681	36.2	1 317	430	32.6
25 to 34 years	21 586	3 278	15.2	17 848	2 174	12.2	2 938	992	33.8	2 029	587	28.9
35 to 44 years	19 633	1 926	9.8	16 471	1 230	7.5	2 341	580	24.8	1 445	343	23.7
45 to 54 years	13 258	1 181	8.9	11 282	773	6.9	1 496	365	24.4	926	177	19.1
55 to 59 years	5 512	579	10.5	4 723	407	8.6	610	148	24.4	340	72	21.1
60 to 64 years	5 671	656	11.6	4 918	448	9.1	569	179	31.4	327	68	20.7
65 years and over	17 546	2 699	15.4	15 663	2 073	13.2	1 516	574	37.9	631	159	25.3
65 to 74 years	10 081	1 240	12.3	8 942	909	10.2	887	298	33.6	414	94	22.7
75 years and over	7 464	1 459	19.5	6 721	1 164	17.3	629	276	43.9	217	65	30.1
PERSONS IN FAMILIES												
Both Sexes												
Total	210 967	25 232	12.0	176 504	15 916	9.0	26 296	8 160	31.0	18 912	5 091	26.9
Under 18 years	63 989	12 750	19.9	51 096	7 723	15.1	9 987	4 418	44.2	7 308	2 757	37.7
18 to 24 years	20 490	2 574	12.6	16 563	1 568	9.5	3 140	903	28.8	2 279	549	24.1
25 to 34 years	33 888	3 854	11.4	28 281	2 593	9.2	4 373	1 129	25.8	3 480	805	23.1
35 to 44 years	32 903	2 452	7.5	28 065	1 631	5.8	3 505	667	19.0	2 493	478	19.2
45 to 54 years	21 957	1 339	6.1	18 944	860	4.5	2 143	419	19.6	1 493	243	16.3
55 to 59 years	8 976	540	6.0	7 889	380	4.8	799	129	16.2	549	73	13.3
60 to 64 years	8 727	552	6.3	7 748	397	5.1	722	138	19.2	492	67	13.5
65 years and over	20 038	1 172	5.8	17 918	764	4.3	1 627	357	21.9	819	119	14.6
65 to 74 years	13 413	675	5.0	12 019	425	3.5	1 035	209	20.2	574	83	14.6
75 years and over	6 625	497	7.5	5 899	339	5.7	592	147	24.8	246	36	14.6
Male												
Total	103 591	11 048	10.7	87 579	7 217	8.2	12 056	3 301	27.4	9 279	2 361	25.4
Under 18 years	32 805	6 521	19.9	26 255	4 006	15.3	5 056	2 196	43.4	3 744	1 461	39.0
18 to 24 years	9 992	866	8.7	8 146	525	6.4	1 464	307	21.0	1 145	213	18.6
25 to 34 years	15 841	1 247	7.9	13 432	920	6.9	1 826	275	15.0	1 695	305	18.0
35 to 44 years	15 548	890	5.7	13 521	682	5.0	1 447	154	10.6	1 173	178	15.2
45 to 54 years	10 529	499	4.7	9 199	348	3.8	895	124	13.9	668	98	14.7
55 to 59 years	4 350	207	4.8	3 899	155	4.0	319	42	13.1	252	24	9.4
60 to 64 years	4 287	260	6.1	3 866	210	5.4	317	47	14.8	221	26	11.9
65 years and over	10 239	558	5.4	9 262	373	4.0	733	156	21.2	382	56	14.7
65 to 74 years	6 890	315	4.6	6 225	205	3.3	489	87	17.8	273	39	14.4
75 years and over	3 348	242	7.2	3 037	167	5.5	243	69	28.3	109	17	15.5
Female												
Total	107 377	14 184	13.2	88 925	8 699	9.8	14 240	4 859	34.1	9 633	2 730	28.3
Under 18 years	31 183	6 229	20.0	24 842	3 718	15.0	4 931	2 222	45.1	3 564	1 296	36.4
18 to 24 years	10 498	1 708	16.3	8 417	1 043	12.4	1 676	596	35.6	1 134	336	29.6
25 to 34 years	18 047	2 607	14.4	14 848	1 673	11.3	2 547	854	33.5	1 785	500	28.0
35 to 44 years	17 354	1 562	9.0	14 544	949	6.5	2 058	514	25.0	1 320	300	22.7
45 to 54 years	11 429	840	7.4	9 745	512	5.3	1 248	295	23.6	826	145	17.6
55 to 59 years	4 626	333	7.2	3 990	226	5.7	480	87	18.2	297	50	16.7
60 to 64 years	4 440	291	6.6	3 882	187	4.8	405	92	22.6	271	40	14.8
65 years and over	9 799	614	6.3	8 656	391	4.5	895	201	22.4	437	63	14.4
65 to 74 years	6 523	360	5.5	5 794	219	3.8	546	122	22.4	301	44	14.7
75 years and over	3 276	255	7.8	2 862	172	6.0	349	78	22.5	137	19	13.9
Householder												
Total	66 322	7 098	10.7	56 803	4 622	8.1	7 471	2 193	29.3	4 981	1 244	25.0
Under 18 years	35	27	(B)	28	20	(B)	7	7	(B)	8	7	(B)
18 to 24 years	2 691	928	34.5	2 135	598	28.0	469	304	64.8	415	175	42.1
25 to 34 years	14 590	2 377	16.3	12 189	1 568	12.9	1 943	734	37.8	1 495	441	29.5
35 to 44 years	17 078	1 648	9.6	14 431	1 063	7.4	2 023	482	23.8	1 323	322	24.4
45 to 54 years	11 701	806	6.9	9 990	508	5.1	1 249	263	21.0	808	161	20.0
55 to 59 years	4 691	296	6.3	4 158	198	4.8	404	78	19.3	294	40	13.7
60 to 64 years	4 635	331	7.1	4 074	224	5.5	453	102	22.6	234	27	11.7
65 years and over	10 900	686	6.3	9 797	443	4.5	923	224	24.2	405	69	17.0
65 to 74 years	7 373	387	5.3	6 619	240	3.6	612	134	21.9	287	46	15.9
75 years and over	3 527	298	8.5	3 179	203	6.4	311	90	28.8	118	23	19.9

Source: Poverty in the United States: 1990, Bureau of the Census, (WDC, 1991)

sated for inflation, causing relative benefit levels to rise higher than at any time in the history of the program. Some reports indicated that if the formula had remained in effect, benefit levels for some future retirees would be higher than their earnings before retirement! In an attempt to prevent future Social Security benefits from rising to excessive levels, Congress passed the Social Security Amendments of 1977 (PL 95-216).

The Future of the Social Security Program

Some observers believe that the Social Security benefit program faces a shaky future, that its solvency is threatened in the next 75 years. In November 1982, the OASDI trust fund almost went bankrupt. Then-President Ronald Reagan and Congress instituted higher Social Security taxes, along with a one-time delay in the cost of living adjustment and increased contributions.

The program is currently solvent, the result of a larger number of employees contributing funds to the system and fewer retirees than expected. It pays out $700 billion annually in pension benefits. The earliest wave of "baby boomers," those individuals who were born between the mid-1940s and the 1950s, are still in the work force and reaching their peak earning years. At the same time, people who are now retiring were born during the low birth rate cycle of the Great Depression, so there are now fewer retirees depleting funds than there are workers contributing to it.

At the present time, a retiree who paid approximately $25,000 into the system will have that amount returned in about three years. That will not be the case for a retired worker of the future. He or she will have paid considerably more money into the system and get back much less. Furthermore, since there will be a much larger percentage of retirees as the baby boomers reach 65 (starting in 2010), the younger generation of workers will face greater financial responsibility for the support and care of an increasing population of older Americans.

Supplemental Security Income (SSI)

Supplemental Security Income (SSI) is a joint federal/state welfare program designed to supply monthly cash payments to needy, aged, blind, or disabled Americans. Instituted in 1974, it replaced many local public assistance programs. SSI benefits are financed from general revenues, not from the Social Security Trust fund, and are issued in addition to Social Security benefits. Individual payments vary from state to state, depending on whether the federal or state government administers the program.

SSI payments totaled $14.6 billion in 1989, of which 20 percent went to the elderly. The average payment to an aged individual in December 1989 was $198 and for an aged couple, $412. More than 75 percent of all SSI payments made to the elderly go to women.

The percentage of SSI recipients under 65 years of age increased between 1974 and 1989, while the percentage of recipients over 65 decreased. Many observers believe that the SSI program could do more to help the elderly. For one thing, it provides only enough income to bring an individual to 70 percent, and a couple to 90 percent, of the poverty level. Its strict assets test excludes many elderly people from receiving benefits, and many low-income people are unaware of the program.

CHAPTER III

WHERE THE ELDERLY LIVE

ELDERLY HOUSEHOLDS

The Census Bureau reports that of the slightly more than 93 million households in the United States in 1990, 18.1 million (21 percent) were headed by people 65 years or older. The preference among the majority of the elderly is to live independently as long as possible. Today, most elderly Americans are adequately housed, but the range of conditions is broad, from the affluent "younger-old" homeowner to the very elderly and very poor nursing home resident.

THE "MODIFIED EXTENDED" FAMILY

The "modified extended" family is the dominant form of family organization found in industrialized societies today. It is also the arrangement that most older people say they prefer. In this setting, older and younger generations live in separate households but are in touch with each other on a fairly regular and frequent basis.

LIVING WITH A SPOUSE

The number of elderly people living with a spouse varies greatly between men and women. In 1990, 74 percent of all noninstitutionalized men aged 65 or over lived with their spouse, compared to only 40 percent of women (Table 3.1). The difference is even more dramatic in the 75 to 84 age

TABLE 3.1

Living Arrangements of the Elderly: 1990

(Numbers in thousands)

| Living arrangement and age | 1990 | | | | | |
| | | | | Percent distribution | | |
	Total	Men	Women	Total	Men	Women
65 years and over..... Living—	29,566	12,334	17,232	100.0	100.0	100.0
Alone...................	9,176	1,942	7,233	31.0	15.7	42.0
With spouse.............	16,003	9,158	6,845	54.1	74.3	39.7
With other relatives.......	3,734	953	2,782	12.6	7.7	16.1
With nonrelatives only[1] ...	653	281	372	2.2	2.3	2.2
65 to 74 years .... Living—	17,979	8,013	9,966	100.0	100.0	100.0
Alone...................	4,350	1,042	3,309	24.2	13.0	33.2
With spouse.............	11,353	6,265	5,089	63.1	78.2	51.1
With other relatives.......	1,931	528	1,401	10.7	6.6	14.1
With nonrelatives only[1] ...	345	178	167	1.9	2.2	1.7
75 to 84 years .... Living—	9,354	3,562	5,792	100.0	100.0	100.0
Alone...................	3,774	688	3,086	40.3	19.3	53.3
With spouse.............	4,145	2,537	1,607	44.3	71.2	27.7
With other relatives.......	1,237	264	974	13.2	7.4	16.8
With nonrelatives only[1] ...	198	73	125	2.1	2.0	2.2
85 years and over....... Living—	2,233	758	1,475	100.0	100.0	100.0
Alone...................	1,051	213	838	47.1	28.1	56.8
With spouse.............	505	356	150	22.6	47.0	10.2
With other relatives.......	567	160	406	25.4	21.1	27.5
With nonrelatives only[1] ...	110	29	81	4.9	3.8	5.5

Source; Marital Status and Living Arrangements: March 1990, Bureau of the Census, (WDC, 1991)

group: 71 percent of men lived with their spouse, compared to less than 28 percent of women. By the age of 85, 47 percent of men lived with their spouses; only 10 percent of women did.

LIVING WITH OTHER RELATIVES

Almost 15 percent (over 4.4 million) of people over age 65 lived with a relative other than a spouse in 1989 (Figure 3.1). Again, the difference between men and women is significant; well over twice as many women (16.1 percent) as men (7.7 percent) lived with a relative other than their spouse (Table 3.1).

26

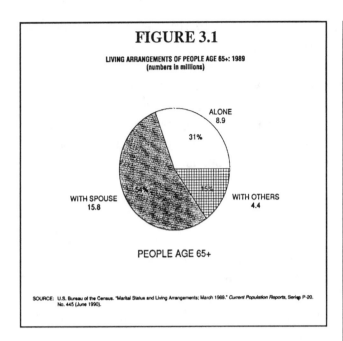

FIGURE 3.1

LIVING ARRANGEMENTS OF PEOPLE AGE 65+: 1989
(numbers in millions)

ALONE
8.9
31%

WITH SPOUSE
15.8
54%

WITH OTHERS
4.4
15%

PEOPLE AGE 65+

SOURCE: U.S. Bureau of the Census. "Marital Status and Living Arrangements: March 1989." *Current Population Reports*, Series P-20. No. 445 (June 1990).

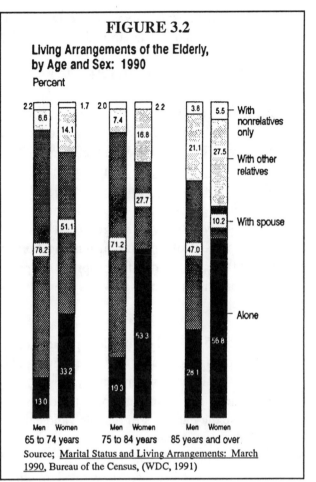

FIGURE 3.2

Living Arrangements of the Elderly, by Age and Sex: 1990

Percent

With nonrelatives only

With other relatives

With spouse

Alone

	Men	Women
65 to 74 years		
75 to 84 years		
85 years and over		

Source; <u>Marital Status and Living Arrangements: March 1990</u>, Bureau of the Census, (WDC, 1991)

LIVING ALONE

Most elderly people who live alone have outlived their spouses, and in some cases, their children and siblings. The percentage of persons living alone therefore increases with age. More than 33 percent of all women between 65 and 74, 53 percent of those 75 to 84, and nearly 57 percent of women 75 and over lived alone in 1990 (Figure 3.2). By contrast, 13 percent of 65 to 74 year-old men, 19 percent of men 75 to 84, and 28 percent of men over age 85 lived alone. These figures reflect the fact that women generally live longer than men, are more likely to be widowed, and are less likely to remarry.

Differing Views on Living Alone

Are those who live alone independent and proud of it, do they enjoy the freedom and lack of responsibility for others, or are they a sad, lonely group isolated from the rest of the community? Certainly one will find examples of all views. For those who are socially active and in good health, living alone is not a problematic. However, that is not the case with the majority of those who live alone. On the average, they have lower incomes than older couples, particularly if they are female, members of a minority group, or over the age of 85. In addition, a very high proportion of elderly who live alone suffer from chronic health problems and report their health to be fair or poor. The combination of poor health, poverty, and solitude is not a formula for happy living. Substantial numbers of elderly persons living alone experience loneliness and fear. Fewer of them consider themselves happy than do those who live with others, and they are generally less satisfied with life. They frequently say that if they needed help, they would have no one to call on for a period of days, perhaps even weeks. This is an enormous challenge to the nation's long-term care system.

A Transitional Stage

Living alone is often a transitional stage between living with a spouse or other relative and, as health deteriorates, living in a nursing home or institution. Most older people prefer to remain independent as long as possible. While some have the physical and financial resources to live alone comfortably, others, especially very elderly women, are extremely poor and isolated from the community.

LIVING IN A NURSING HOME

One of the main reasons for entering a nursing home or similar long-term care facility is to receive medical care. However, L. Heumann, in A Cost Comparison of Congregate Housing and Long-Term Care Facilities in the Mid-West (1985, Urbana, Illinois: Housing Research and Development Program, University of Illinois), suggests that between 12 and 60 percent of persons in nursing homes could live in the community if appropriate supportive (primarily nonmedical) services were available.

Only about 5 percent of the older population is living in nursing homes at any one time. The average nursing home resident is very old, female, and unmarried. Most nursing home residents are there because they are sick or disabled and cannot obtain adequate care in the community. However, health policy experts agree that many people live in nursing homes not because they need medical attention but because that is the most available (and most likely to be financed) option. (See Chapter IX for a further discussion of nursing homes.)

Respite Care

A concept known as "respite care" offers hope for the disabled elderly and their families. Such care involves short-term stays in nursing homes or hospitals. Reasons for choosing temporary care in an institution include vacation needs for adult caregivers, brief medical or therapeutic needs of the elderly person, and relief for both parties from the caregiver/receiver relationship. Despite the growing need, the number of institutions (hospitals and nursing homes) offering such short-term stays is relatively small (according to a 1989 study, 30 percent of nursing homes and 10 percent of hospitals). Respite care averages approximately $100 a day, depending on the institution and the level of care, and the cost is normally not reimbursable under private or federal insurance programs or Medicare. A bill (HR 2967) passed in September, 1991 by the House of Representatives proposes funding for respite care. That bill, if it were to become law, would also appropriate funds for in-home care for the elderly who are unable to perform such chores as shopping or cleaning as well as for home-delivered and "congregate meals" served in senior citizens' centers. (See also Chapter IX.)

LIVING HOMELESS

Very little research has been conducted on the homeless elderly. Estimates range from 6 to 20 percent. However, with approximately 12 percent of the population of the U. S. over 65, only 3 percent of homeless people who have sought care were elderly. The relatively low proportion of elderly homeless suggested by this figure may be explained by their access to benefits (Social Security, Medicare, housing), by high death rates once they enter street life, or by their avoidance of high visibility shelters and programs which they fear may be dangerous. (For further information, see Homeless in America, Information Plus, Wylie, Texas, 1991.)

ALTERNATIVE LIVING ARRANGEMENTS

For those who have the option of selecting where and how they live, several alternatives to the single-family house have emerged in recent years. There is no perfect alternative; each type of arrangement has its own particular problems and benefits.

Life-Care Communities

Life-care communities provide their residents with housing, personal care, nursing home care, and a variety of social and recreational activities. Typically, residents enter into a lifetime contractual arrangement with the facility in which they pay an entrance fee and a set monthly fee in return for services and benefits. Most facilities are operated by private, non-profit, and/or religious organizations.

According to government findings, entrance fees in these communities can vary substantially, from $20,000 to $200,000, and monthly fees range from $500 to $2,000 depending on the size of the facility and the quality and number of services. Services usually do not include acute health care needs such as doctor visits and hospitalization.

There were approximately 680 life-care communities in the United States in 1987, the last year for which figures are available, with an average of 245 residents each. The American Association of Retired Persons estimates that the number of these facilities has doubled in the past 10 years and will more than double from present levels before the turn of the century.

While life-care communities insure their residents against rising health care costs and assure daily care, they have come under criticism in several areas. Sometimes fee calculations are not based on sound actuarial data, so that a facility may find itself without adequate financial resources, or residents may be paying more than necessary for care received. Residents sometimes find that if they decide to leave the community, none of their fees will be refunded.

Only 13 states currently regulate life-care communities, and there is little standardization in regulations between states. New York State forbids prepaid nursing home care, which effectively bans life-care facilities.

Shared Housing

Some elderly persons share living quarters (and expenses) to reduce costs and responsibilities and also for companionship. Many elderly live in the same homes in which they raised their families. These houses may be too large for the needs of one or two persons. Shared housing is very cost effective for those who wish to remain in their own homes and for those who cannot afford a home of their own or the expense of a retirement community. Census statistics show that in 1990, approximately 653,000 people over 65 share housing with nonrelatives, a 57 percent increase over the last 10 years.

Unfortunately, the elderly poor who desire to share housing may lose some of their already meager incomes. Under government rulings, supplemental Social Security eligibility and benefits are computed on the basis of the income of the entire household rather than the individual residents. Savings in living expenses may be more than offset by a reduction in benefits and money for food and medicine. Another barrier to shared housing is zoning restrictions. Some cities restrict people who are not related from sharing living quarters.

ECHO Units or "Granny Flats"

Elder Cottage Housing Opportunity units (ECHO) or "granny flats" are small, free-standing, removable housing units that are located on the same lot as a single-family house. Another term used in local zoning is "accessory apartments or units." Generally, they are constructed by a family for an elderly parent or grandparent so that they can be close while each party maintains a degree of independence. Zoning laws and concerns about property values and traffic patterns are major obstacles to granny flats, although as the elderly survive longer and nursing home costs increase, this concept may continue to gain support.

Retirement Communities

A few developers have experimented with constructing entire cities just for the elderly. Two examples are Sun City (population 46,000) and Sun City West (expected population 25,000) in Arizona. Opened in the 1960s, they cover 25 square miles with homes available only to those families in which at least one member is 55 or older. Sun City offers more than 400 clubs and social organizations and 10 recreational complexes. Sun City is not for the poor. Forty percent of its residents have a net worth of $300,000, and 35 percent are worth $400,000 or more. About 60 percent have had at least some college education,

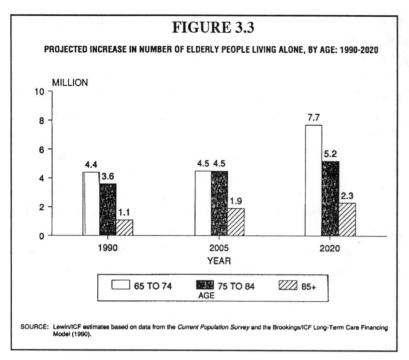

FIGURE 3.3

PROJECTED INCREASE IN NUMBER OF ELDERLY PEOPLE LIVING ALONE, BY AGE: 1990-2020

SOURCE: Lewin/ICF estimates based on data from the *Current Population Survey* and the Brookings/ICF Long-Term Care Financing Model (1990).

compared with 20 percent of all adults aged 65 and older.

While cities devoted to the needs and interests of the elderly may seem ideal, they have a unique problem: everyone is getting older. By the year 2000, the demand for social and health services for 75,000 people with a median age of 80 may prove overwhelming.

"Board and Care" Facilities

The Subcommittee on Health and Long-term Care of the Select Committee on Aging of the House of Representatives defines a board and care facility as one that "provide[s] shelter, food and protection to frail and disabled individuals." While the concept is praiseworthy, in actuality, the board and care business is riddled with fraud and abuses. Totally unregulated in many states, these facilities have frequently become dumping grounds for the old, the ill, the mentally retarded, and the disabled.

In its report <u>Board and Care Homes in American: A National Tragedy</u> (1989, Washington, DC), the Subcommittee estimated that one million persons, two-thirds of whom are elderly and female, now reside in 68,000 facilities nationwide. Supple-

mental Social Security (SSI) is the only form of income for 72 percent of these residents. Federal and State support for board and care residents now exceeds $7 billion each year. It is not uncommon for a resident to turn over his or her entire SSI check to the facility's manager and receive less than minimal care in return.

In an attempt to stem abuses, the federal government passed the Keys Amendment in 1978. Under this amendment, residents in board and care facilities that do not provide adequate care are subject to reduced SSI income. The facility's owners would then suffer economically as a result of their tenants' reduced income. In fact, the only ones who have suffered (even more than before) are the residents. Board and care facilities do provide an alternative living arrangement for the elderly, but it is one that, given the choice, probably very few would choose.

FUTURE TRENDS

There has been a marked increase in the number of elderly persons living independently. The trend toward independent living is expected to continue into the next century (Figure 3.3). Those now approaching retirement age are more health-conscious than their parents were, and they generally had a higher personal income during their working years. While many people still fail to plan adequately for their later years, the importance of such planning is being widely publicized by government agencies and private organizations. The "young-old" can still take steps to ensure a financially comfortable old age.

The declining birth rate after the "baby boom" means that there are fewer children with whom the future elderly can share housing. Because the extended family will become even less common than it is now, older people living alone will rely more on community services, that is, senior citizen

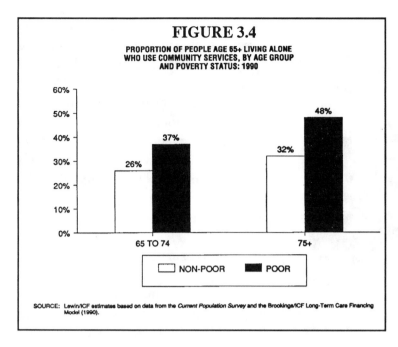

FIGURE 3.4

PROPORTION OF PEOPLE AGE 65+ LIVING ALONE
WHO USE COMMUNITY SERVICES, BY AGE GROUP
AND POVERTY STATUS: 1990

SOURCE: Lewin/ICF estimates based on data from the *Current Population Survey* and the Brookings/ICF Long-Term Care Financing Model (1990).

centers, special transportation, meals, visiting nurses or day care. A greater proportion of the elderly living alone use community services, a situation that is especially true of the poor (Figure 3.4).

While the number of elderly living independently will increase, so will the number of those who will become nursing home residents. Since 1980 the number of older Americans in need of long-term care has grown 14 percent, and the number is expected to increase steadily during the 1990s and double by 2020.

The near-universal desire of even the frail and chronically ill elderly to remain at home has fostered a number of alternatives that will enable them to stay in familiar surroundings with control of their lives, when possible. Among these approaches are adult day care, home repair services, and housekeeping and visiting nurse programs. Telephone reassurance programs are designed for workers to telephone the frail person daily to check their status. Technology also plays a part; electronic alarm systems and remote control appliances are now marketed to the aging population. Foster families for the elderly have emerged. The goal of all of these programs is to enable the elderly to remain independent, in their own homes, out of institutions, for as long and as often as possible. (For further discussion of health care, see Chapter IX.)

THE HIGH COST OF LIVING ARRANGEMENTS

Owning a Home - the American Dream?

In 1985, the latest year for which figures have been prepared, 21 percent of householders 65 or over who still had a mortgage on their homes paid 50 percent or more of their income on housing, compared to 7 percent of those under 65 (Table 3.2). Eight percent of those 65 and over who did not have a mortgage spent over 50 percent of their income on housing costs. The median amount spent on housing by the householder 65 or older with a mortgage was 28 percent of income, and without a mortgage, 18 percent. In addition, even where there is no mortgage remaining on the home, the homeowner must still pay taxes, insurance, utility bills, and often high repair costs for what is most likely an older home. Failing health and physical ability, often accompanied by reduced or fixed income, can make home ownership a burden. The result is that the proportion of elderly who own their own homes begins to decline at age 65 (Figure 3.5).

TABLE 3.2

—HOUSING COSTS AS A PERCENTAGE OF INCOME, BY AGE OF HOUSEHOLDER, TENURE, AND MORTGAGE STATUS: 1985

Tenure and mortgage status	Median percent of income spent on housing		Percent of households spending 50 percent or more of income on housing	
	Householder under 65	Householder 65 plus	Householder under 65	Householder 65 plus
Owned, without mortgage	10	18	4	8
Owned, with mortgage	21	28	7	21
Rented	26	35	19	29

Note.—Rental units exclude one-unit structures on 10 acres or more.

Source: U.S. Bureau of the Census and U.S. Department of Housing and Urban Development, "American Housing Survey for the United States in 1985," Current Housing Reports, Series H-150-85 (December 1988).

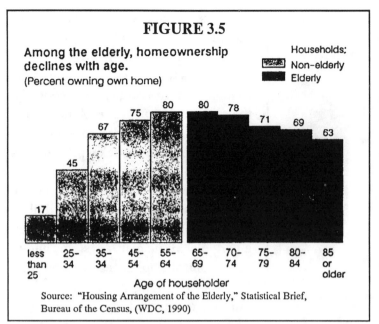

FIGURE 3.5

Among the elderly, homeownership declines with age.
(Percent owning own home)

Households:
Non-elderly
Elderly

Age of householder

Source: "Housing Arrangement of the Elderly," Statistical Brief, Bureau of the Census, (WDC, 1990)

Renting is Even More Expensive

About one-third of elderly households reside in rented facilities. As shown in Table 3.2, renters pay a higher percentage of their incomes for housing than do homeowners. Renters are faced with an additional difficulty: mortgage payments generally remain the same over a period of years (often until the entire mortgage is paid off), but rents may increase each year while the renter remains on a fixed income. Also, homeowners have the equity in their homes to fall back on in times of financial crisis; the renter makes out a monthly check, but none of the money is ever returned as a tangible asset.

ADDITIONAL HOUSING PROBLEMS OF THE ELDERLY

Older Houses

Most older people live in older houses. A Population Reference Bureau, Inc. study (Soldo, Beth J. and Agree, Emily M., September 1988, America's Elderly, Population Bulletin, Vol. 43, No. 3) indicates that more than two-thirds of older persons live in houses built more than 40 years ago, over one-third of them before World War II. While the age of a house does not necessarily reflect its physical condition, older houses typically need more frequent and more expensive repairs. Building materials become stressed with age. Older houses may be poorly insulated. The Bureau of the Census' 1985 Annual Housing Survey found that 8 percent of housing units occupied by persons 65 or older had "physical problems," that is, a flaw in one or more of six areas: plumbing, kitchen, maintenance of physical structure, public hall/common area, heating, and electrical systems.

Physical Hazards

Features considered desirable by younger householders may be handicaps to the elderly. For example, the staircase in a two story house may become a formidable obstacle to someone with osteoporosis or a neuromuscular problem. Narrow halls and doorways cannot be navigated in a wheelchair. High cabinets and shelves may be beyond the reach of an arthritis sufferer. Houses can be modified to meet the physical needs of the elderly, but not all older houses can be remodeled to accept such modifications, and installing them may be more costly than some elderly can afford.

Anticipating the increase in the elderly population within the next 20 to 30 years, some real estate developers are manufacturing experimental houses designed to meet the needs of the elderly and thus prolong independent living. The Middletown House, developed by William K. Wasch Associates (Middletown, Connecticut) and the A-factor Home, developed by Aging and Adult Services of the Florida Department of Health, are projects consisting of single-family, single-story houses. The houses include non-skid flooring, walls strong enough to support grab bars, light plugs at convenient heights, levers instead of knobs on doors and plumbing fixtures, and wide doors and hallways.

Lack of Transportation

When an elderly person's vision and physical reflexes decline, driving a car can be difficult and perilous. Older people whose homes are far from shopping centers or public transportation may have to depend on others for transportation or delivery of the basic necessities, or they may simply have to do without. This is a particularly acute problem for the approximately 25 percent of the U.S. elderly population who live in rural areas. The rural elderly may be isolated not only from food and clothing stores, but from health and social services as well.

THE ROLE OF THE FEDERAL GOVERNMENT

In 1937, Congress passed the United States Housing Act of 1937 (PL 75-412) to create low-income public housing. Prior to 1956, only 10 percent of available units were occupied by persons 65 or older; by 1988, the elderly occupied 44 percent of available units.

The federal government makes direct loans to private, non-profit developers to build housing designed specifically for the elderly and the handicapped. About one-half of the nation's 10,000 low-income housing units are now more than 20 years old. Many were built during the 1930s and 1940s and are in need of major renovation.

From the days of early legislation through 1981, the federal government progressively in-creased its involvement in meeting the housing needs of the low-income elderly. During the Reagan Administration, housing assistance programs were cut by 77 percent. The Reagan Administration offered a "voucher" system whereby low-income families received a voucher worth the difference between 30 percent of the family's income and the fair market rent of a suitable-sized unit. In practice, this system does little to assist the elderly in initially finding suitable housing and does not address the fact that the only suitable units available may be renting at far above their fair market value.

Despite federal programs to provide decent, affordable housing, it is still beyond the reach of many millions of elderly. According to the National Council of Senior Citizens (a private advocacy group), the average time on a waiting list for elderly housing is three to five years, and only one in seven elderly poor receives federal housing assistance.

How future administrations will respond to this need is uncertain. An apparent reluctance to redirect federal funds makes it unlikely that new or existing programs will receive additional funding. On the other hand, the elderly are becoming a more numerous, more informed, and more aggressive voting bloc.

CHAPTER IV

WORKING - PAID AND UNPAID CONTRIBUTIONS

Productivity is not the exclusive domain of the young. Genius, creativity, and dedication do not end on a person's 65th birthday. Older people have made, and continue to make, significant contributions in all areas. Benjamin Franklin - writer, scientist, inventor, and statesman - helped draft the Declaration of Independence at the age of 70. Golda Meir was elected Prime Minister of Israel when she was 71. Thomas Alva Edison worked on such inventions as the light bulb, the microphone, and the phonograph until his death at the age of 81. Rear Admiral (Ret.) Grace Hooper, one of the early computer scientists and co-creator of the computer language COBOL, maintained an active speaking and consulting schedule up until her recent death in her 80s. Margaret Mead, the noted anthropologist, returned to New Guinea when she was 72 and exhausted a much younger television filming crew as they tried to keep up with her. Albert Einstein, who formulated the theory of relativity, was working on a unifying theory of the universe when he died at age 76. Pablo Picasso and Georgia O'Keefe created masterful paintings when they were each past 80 years of age.

A CHANGING ECONOMY AND CHANGING ROLES

From Agricultural ...

In early America, there was little correlation between age and work. In that agricultural society, youngsters were put to work as soon as possible to contribute to the family upkeep. At the other end of the age scale, workers did not retire; they worked as long as physically able to do so. Then they were cared for by the younger members of the family. Older people were valued and respected for their accumulated knowledge and experience. They were an integral part of the interconnected family and labor systems.

... to Industrial

The Industrial Revolution took men away from the farm and into manufacturing jobs. The work was physically demanding, the hours long, and the tasks strictly structured. Women labored in factories and at home caring for the home and children. Older people found themselves without a place in the workforce. Their skills and experience were not relevant to new technologies, nor could they physically compete with the large number of young workers eager to take advantage of new economic opportunities.

As industrial workers matured, some of them were promoted to positions as supervisors, managers, and CEOs (chief executive officers). Labor unions provided some job security through the seniority system (first hired, last fired) for older workers who had been with the same company for many years. However, in an increasingly youth-oriented society, older workers were often pushed aside to make way for younger workers. The problem became so severe that Congress passed the Age Discrimination Act (PL 90-202) in 1967 and the Age Discrimination Act Amendment (PL 95-256) in 1978 prohibiting differential treatment of workers based solely on age. In 1986, Congress passed further legislation abolishing age-based mandatory retirement for most workers in the private sector as well as those in government employment (see AGE DISCRIMINATION, below).

... to Service

The American economy is again in a state of dramatic change. It is shifting away from manufacturing and toward the service sector. According to the U.S. Bureau of Labor Statistics (BLS), for every one manufacturing job, there are three service jobs. Doctors, gardeners, travel agents, auto mechanics, and teachers far outnumber coal miners, carpenters, and pipefitters.

Many service jobs are ideally suited for older workers. They usually do not require heavy labor, and the cumulative experience of years of work is an advantage in almost all professional fields. More than one-third of the jobs of older workers are in the service sector. Nonetheless, bias against older workers is still prevalent.

PERCEPTIONS OF OLDER WORKERS ... AND THE REALITY

Often, older workers are stereotyped by the common assumption that performance declines with age. Performance studies, however, show that older workers perform intellectually as well or better than workers 30 or 40 years younger. They maintain their IQ levels, vocabulary, and creative thinking skills well into their sixties and sometimes beyond.

Many of today's jobs do not require physical stamina or strength, yet older people are often seen as too frail or sickly to work. But corporate studies indicate that older workers have better attendance records and do as much work as younger employees, and that poor health is cited as a reason for leaving a job in only a small number of workers over 50.

A misconception of high health insurance costs coupled with the notion of an older person's low productivity may lead an employer to believe that it is not cost-effective to hire or retain older employees. However, in the majority of cases, this is not true. Very small companies may see higher insurance and benefit costs for older workers, but lower turnover rates, specialized skills, and job experience may more than offset these costs. Employee turnover is very costly for a company because the company puts time and money into training each new employee, and there is a learning period before a new employee becomes fully productive.

A major 1991 study, "America Over 55 at Work Program," commissioned by the Commonwealth Fund of major businesses, concluded that older workers are good investments for employers. The older worker was found to have a rate of absenteeism 39 percent below younger employees, a turnover 6 times lower, half the loss in theft and damage, and an 18 percent higher profit. The study also found that older workers can be trained in new technologies and are often better salespeople than younger workers. The report concluded that the employment of older people makes good business sense.

PARTICIPATION IN THE LABOR FORCE

Approximately 3.5 million men and women over age 65 participated in the labor force (either by actively working or actively seeking work) in 1991, compared to almost 7 million people aged 55 to 59, and nearly 5 million aged 60 to 64. Workers over age 65 were nearly 3 percent of the total U.S. labor force.

Table 4.1 shows the percentage of men and women in various age groups by labor force participation in 1991. Although older women outnumber older men in the general population, a greater percentage of men than women were in the labor force. The majority of men (67 percent) aged 55 to 64 were participants; by age 65, only 16 percent participated. Forty-six percent of women aged 55 to 64 were in the labor force; by age 65 the percentage dropped to 9 percent.

TABLE 4.1

Employment status of the civilian noninstitutional population by age and sex

(Numbers in thousands)

Age, sex, and race	October 1991										
	Civilian noninstitutional population	Civilian labor force					Not in labor force				
		Total	Percent of population	Employed	Unemployed		Total	Keeping house	Going to school	Unable to work	Other reasons
					Number	Percent of labor force					
TOTAL											
16 years and over	190,289	125,568	66.0	117,555	8,013	6.4	64,721	25,810	9,107	3,818	25,986
16 to 19 years	13,263	6,543	49.3	5,312	1,232	18.8	6,719	467	5,785	21	446
16 to 17 years	6,599	2,581	39.1	2,032	549	21.3	4,018	103	3,750	10	155
18 to 19 years	6,663	3,962	59.5	3,280	683	17.2	2,701	364	2,035	11	291
20 to 24 years	17,910	13,645	76.2	12,175	1,470	10.8	4,265	1,451	2,044	93	677
25 to 54 years	107,625	90,083	83.7	85,301	4,783	5.3	17,541	11,306	1,219	1,668	3,348
25 to 34 years	42,254	35,387	83.7	33,081	2,306	6.5	6,867	4,636	809	358	1,064
25 to 29 years	20,083	16,687	83.1	15,479	1,209	7.2	3,395	2,228	527	137	503
30 to 34 years	22,171	18,700	84.3	17,602	1,098	5.9	3,471	2,409	282	220	561
35 to 44 years	38,961	33,254	85.4	31,716	1,538	4.6	5,707	3,734	303	594	1,077
35 to 39 years	20,519	17,434	85.0	16,581	853	4.9	3,085	2,023	192	281	589
40 to 44 years	18,442	15,819	85.8	15,135	685	4.3	2,623	1,711	110	313	488
45 to 54 years	26,409	21,443	81.2	20,504	938	4.4	4,967	2,936	108	717	1,207
45 to 49 years	14,528	12,212	84.1	11,673	540	4.4	2,316	1,410	71	323	511
50 to 54 years	11,881	9,230	77.7	8,832	398	4.3	2,651	1,526	36	393	696
55 to 64 years	21,148	11,791	55.8	11,362	429	3.6	9,357	4,083	33	838	4,404
55 to 59 years	10,558	6,987	66.2	6,739	248	3.5	3,571	1,799	16	407	1,348
60 to 64 years	10,590	4,804	45.4	4,623	181	3.8	5,786	2,284	17	431	3,055
65 years and over	30,343	3,505	11.6	3,406	99	2.8	26,838	8,504	27	1,197	17,110
65 to 69 years	10,032	2,071	20.6	2,002	69	3.3	7,961	2,666	6	262	5,027
70 to 74 years	8,207	925	11.3	907	18	1.9	7,282	2,320	2	241	4,719
75 years and over	12,104	509	4.2	497	13	2.5	11,595	3,517	19	695	7,364
Men											
16 years and over	90,830	68,255	75.1	63,921	4,334	6.3	22,575	608	4,587	2,126	15,254
16 to 19 years	6,678	3,361	50.3	2,721	640	19.0	3,318	26	3,016	12	263
16 to 17 years	3,372	1,302	38.6	1,015	287	22.1	2,070	7	1,970	6	87
18 to 19 years	3,306	2,059	62.3	1,706	353	17.1	1,248	19	1,046	7	175
20 to 24 years	8,729	7,173	82.2	6,378	795	11.1	1,557	34	1,074	60	389
25 to 54 years	52,743	49,078	93.1	46,497	2,581	5.3	3,665	300	480	1,091	1,793
25 to 34 years	20,813	19,574	94.0	18,382	1,191	6.1	1,239	108	360	255	517
25 to 29 years	9,870	9,231	93.5	8,581	650	7.0	639	46	254	101	238
30 to 34 years	10,943	10,342	94.5	9,801	541	5.2	601	62	106	154	279
35 to 44 years	19,107	17,945	93.9	17,049	896	5.0	1,163	117	94	371	580
35 to 39 years	10,098	9,489	94.0	8,991	499	5.3	609	60	56	169	324
40 to 44 years	9,009	8,455	93.9	8,058	397	4.7	554	58	38	202	255
45 to 54 years	12,822	11,559	90.2	11,066	493	4.3	1,263	75	26	465	697
45 to 49 years	7,087	6,556	92.5	6,288	268	4.1	531	29	16	219	267
50 to 54 years	5,735	5,003	87.2	4,778	225	4.5	732	46	10	246	429
55 to 64 years	10,004	6,675	66.7	6,412	263	3.9	3,329	98	14	490	2,728
55 to 59 years	5,035	3,935	78.2	3,799	136	3.5	1,100	41	8	243	807
60 to 64 years	4,970	2,740	55.1	2,614	127	4.6	2,229	57	6	246	1,920
65 years and over	12,675	1,968	15.5	1,912	56	2.8	10,707	150	2	473	10,082
65 to 69 years	4,551	1,105	24.3	1,062	43	3.9	3,446	36	2	149	3,259
70 to 74 years	3,606	560	15.5	553	7	1.3	3,046	33	–	110	2,903
75 years and over	4,518	302	6.7	297	5	1.7	4,215	81	–	214	3,920
Women											
16 years and over	99,459	57,313	57.6	53,635	3,678	6.4	42,146	25,202	4,520	1,692	10,731
16 to 19 years	6,584	3,183	48.3	2,591	592	18.6	3,402	441	2,769	9	184
16 to 17 years	3,227	1,279	39.6	1,017	262	20.5	1,948	95	1,780	5	68
18 to 19 years	3,357	1,904	56.7	1,573	330	17.3	1,454	345	988	4	116
20 to 24 years	9,181	6,472	70.5	5,796	676	10.4	2,709	1,417	970	33	289
25 to 54 years	54,882	41,006	74.7	38,804	2,202	5.4	13,876	11,006	739	577	1,555
25 to 34 years	21,441	15,813	73.8	14,698	1,115	7.1	5,627	4,529	449	103	547
25 to 29 years	10,213	7,456	73.0	6,897	559	7.5	2,757	2,182	273	37	265
30 to 34 years	11,228	8,357	74.4	7,801	556	6.7	2,871	2,347	176	66	282
35 to 44 years	19,854	15,309	77.1	14,667	642	4.2	4,545	3,616	208	223	497
35 to 39 years	10,421	7,945	76.2	7,590	355	4.5	2,476	1,963	136	112	265
40 to 44 years	9,433	7,364	78.1	7,077	287	3.9	2,069	1,653	72	111	233
45 to 54 years	13,587	9,883	72.7	9,438	445	4.5	3,704	2,861	81	252	510
45 to 49 years	7,441	5,656	76.0	5,385	271	4.8	1,785	1,381	56	104	244
50 to 54 years	6,146	4,227	68.8	4,054	173	4.1	1,919	1,479	26	147	267
55 to 64 years	11,144	5,116	45.9	4,950	166	3.2	6,028	3,985	19	349	1,676
55 to 59 years	5,523	3,052	55.3	2,940	112	3.7	2,471	1,758	8	164	541
60 to 64 years	5,621	2,064	36.7	2,009	54	2.6	3,557	2,227	11	184	1,135
65 years and over	17,668	1,537	8.7	1,494	43	2.8	16,131	8,353	25	724	7,028
65 to 69 years	5,481	966	17.6	940	25	2.6	4,515	2,630	4	113	1,768
70 to 74 years	4,601	365	7.9	355	10	2.9	4,236	2,287	2	131	1,816
75 years and over	7,586	207	2.7	199	8	3.7	7,380	3,436	19	480	3,444

Source: Bureau of Labor Statistics

TABLE 4.2

Persons at work in nonagricultural industries by sex, age, race, marital status, and full- or part-time status

(Numbers in thousands)

Sex, age, race, and marital status	Total at work	On part time for economic reasons	On voluntary part time	On full-time schedules			Average hours, total at work	Average hours, workers on full-time schedules
				Total	40 hours or less	41 hours or more		
TOTAL								
Total, 16 years and over	109,878	5,639	15,396	88,844	56,115	32,729	39.3	43.8
16 to 19 years	5,023	387	3,332	1,304	1,016	288	22.9	40.2
16 to 17 years	1,878	46	1,722	110	87	23	16.2	38.9
18 to 19 years	3,145	341	1,610	1,194	929	265	26.9	40.4
20 years and over	104,855	5,252	12,064	87,539	55,099	32,441	40.1	43.9
20 to 24 years	11,565	903	2,513	8,149	5,756	2,393	36.0	42.5
25 years and over	93,290	4,349	9,551	79,391	49,343	30,048	40.6	44.0
25 to 44 years	60,992	2,928	5,183	52,881	32,489	20,392	41.1	44.1
45 to 64 years	29,431	1,284	2,948	25,199	15,947	9,252	40.7	44.0
65 years and over	2,867	136	1,420	1,312	907	405	29.4	43.4
Men, 16 years and over	59,136	2,715	4,599	51,822	29,062	22,759	42.2	45.3
16 to 19 years	2,529	211	1,559	759	550	210	24.6	42.1
16 to 17 years	917	21	824	72	52	19	17.1	(¹)
18 to 19 years	1,612	190	735	687	497	190	28.9	42.1
20 years and over	56,607	2,505	3,041	51,062	28,513	22,549	43.0	45.4
20 to 24 years	6,010	464	1,088	4,457	2,914	1,543	37.7	43.5
25 years and over	50,598	2,041	1,952	46,605	25,599	21,007	43.6	45.6
25 to 44 years	33,162	1,422	708	31,032	16,739	14,293	44.1	45.6
45 to 64 years	15,912	556	575	14,781	8,334	6,447	43.8	45.5
65 years and over	1,523	62	669	792	527	265	31.5	44.2
Women, 16 years and over	50,742	2,923	10,797	37,022	27,053	9,969	35.9	41.8
16 to 19 years	2,494	176	1,773	545	467	78	21.2	37.7
16 to 17 years	962	25	898	39	36	4	15.3	(¹)
18 to 19 years	1,533	151	875	506	432	75	24.8	37.9
20 years and over	48,248	2,747	9,023	36,477	26,586	9,891	36.7	41.8
20 to 24 years	5,555	438	1,425	3,692	2,842	850	34.1	41.2
25 years and over	42,693	2,309	7,598	32,785	23,744	9,041	37.1	41.9
25 to 44 years	27,830	1,506	4,475	21,849	15,751	6,098	37.5	41.9
45 to 64 years	13,518	729	2,373	10,416	7,611	2,805	37.1	41.9
65 years and over	1,344	74	751	520	380	139	27.1	42.2
RACE								
White, 16 years and over	94,782	4,544	13,760	76,477	46,840	29,637	39.5	44.1
Men	51,501	2,171	4,022	45,308	24,621	20,687	42.5	45.6
Women	43,281	2,373	9,739	31,169	22,219	8,950	35.8	41.9
Black, 16 years and over	11,273	936	1,077	9,260	7,140	2,120	38.4	42.0
Men	5,558	459	374	4,725	3,314	1,411	40.0	43.2
Women	5,715	477	703	4,535	3,826	708	36.7	40.7
MARITAL STATUS								
Men, 16 years and over:								
Married, spouse present	37,752	1,160	1,372	35,220	18,844	16,377	44.1	45.8
Widowed, divorced, or separated	6,222	403	256	5,563	3,174	2,390	42.9	45.4
Single (never married)	15,162	1,152	2,972	11,038	7,045	3,993	37.3	44.0
Women, 16 years and over:								
Married, spouse present	28,334	1,409	6,201	20,725	15,410	5,315	36.0	41.5
Widowed, divorced, or separated	10,332	692	1,300	8,340	5,765	2,574	38.3	42.5
Single (never married)	12,076	822	3,296	7,958	5,878	2,080	33.9	41.7

¹ Data not shown where base is less than 75,000.

Source: Bureau of Labor Statistics

Part-Time Work

Older people who are forced to abandon a lifetime of labor sometimes feel unproductive and worthless. They may suffer emotional as well as financial hardship or become bored or lonely. It is increasingly common to find retired workers re-entering the workforce through part-time jobs. In 1991, 48 percent of men and 61 percent of women 65 and older were part-time, as compared to 30 percent of men and 44 percent of women 65+ in 1960 (Tables 4.2 and 4.3).

For employers, hiring part-time older workers is often an attractive alternative to hiring younger, full-time workers, partly because of older workers' dependability and experience. Unfortunately, companies often pay older workers lower wages and do not provide benefits such as health insurance, pensions, profit-sharing, etc.

Older persons who are receiving Social Security benefits may choose part-time work to supplement their incomes, yet they lose part of their Social Security benefits if their earnings are too great. In 1990, the threshold for benefits retention for 62 to 64-year-old workers was raised to $8,640 (after which they lose $1 for every $2 they earn), and to $9,360 for workers 65 and older (after which they lose $1 for every $3 they earn).

RETIREMENT

Increasing longevity means that people spend more time in <u>all</u> phases of their lives - education, work, and retirement. According to <u>Aging America</u>, in 1900 the average man spent only 1.2 years in retirement; by 1980, he was retired 13.6 years. This represents an increase from 3 percent to 19 percent of one's life span. Retirement, therefore, has become an institution in the life span of the American citizen.

The age of 65 has been considered "normal retirement age" since the Social Security legislation of 1935 set that age for receipt of Social Security benefits.

TABLE 4.3

FULL- OR PART-TIME STATUS OF WORKERS 45+ IN NONAGRICULTURAL INDUSTRIES, BY SEX AND AGE: SELECTED YEARS, 1960 TO 1989

Sex and age	1960		1970		1982		1989	
	Full-time	Part-time	Full-time	Part-time	Full-time	Part-time	Full-time	Part-time
Men:								
45 to 64	94	6	96	4	93	7	93	7
65+	70	30	62	38	52	48	52	48
Women:								
45 to 64	78	22	77	23	74	26	76	24
65+	56	44	50	50	40	60	41	59

SOURCES: U.S. Department of Labor, Bureau of Labor Statistics. *Employment and Earnings* Vol. 37, No. 1 (January 1990); Vol. 30, No. 1 (January 1983); Vol. 17, No. 7 (January 1971).

U.S. Department of Labor, Bureau of Labor Statistics. *Labor Force and Employment in 1960* Special Labor Force Report No. 14 (April 1961).

However, many persons choose to exit the labor force before that time for a variety of reasons - health, the retirement of a spouse, the availability of Social Security or pension benefits, or the opportunity for leisure activities. Downturns in the economy, mergers, layoffs, and bankruptcies can also result in unplanned early retirement. Some companies have reduced staff by offering attractive retirement packages.

Some labor economists feel that early retirements deprive the nation of skilled workers needed for robust growth. The government also loses the revenue that those workers would have contributed in income and payroll taxes. For those elderly who must work for economic reasons, forced retirement and unemployment are serious problems. Older workers often experience difficulty being re-hired, and the duration of their unemployment is longer.

AGE DISCRIMINATION

The Age Discrimination in Employment Act (PL 90-202, 1967) and an amendment in 1978 were intended to promote the employment of older workers based on their ability and ban discrimination against workers between 40 and 65 years of age. The law made it illegal for employers to discriminate because of age in hiring, discharging, and compensating employees. It also prohibited companies from coercing older workers into accepting incentives to early retirement. In 1987 the Act was amended to lift the 65-year-old limit, making it illegal to discriminate against any worker over 40 years of age and eliminating mandatory retirement at any age.

Although age discrimination in the workplace is against the law, it still exists. Some workers begin to experience negative attitudes about their age when they are still in their 50s, and by the time they reach their 60s, age discrimination may be obvious. Despite the fact that age discrimination in the workplace is illegal, there are many ways an employer (and fellow employees) can exert pressure on an older employee to retire or simply quit. Age discrimination may be overt, but it may also be subtle, even unintentional.

The Pressure to Retire

Corporations base employment decisions not only on how much an employee contributes to the company, but on how much salary and benefits the company must pay the employee. Since salary tends to increase with longevity on the job, older workers usually receive higher wages than younger ones. Thus, if two employees are equally productive, but the older one has a higher salary, a company has an economic incentive to encourage the older worker to take early retirement.

Employees in this situation find themselves in a difficult position. Early retirement benefits are almost always less than regular retirement benefits, and they may not provide enough financial support to allow a retiree to live comfortably without working. Finding a new job is more difficult for an older person than for a younger one, and older persons are usually unemployed for longer periods of time than are younger ones. If they refuse to accept early retirement, they may find themselves without a job at all, perhaps with no pension and no severance pay to fall back on.

Suing the Company

Anyone choosing to file an age discrimination suit can expect to face extensive legal fees. In addition, employers are reluctant to hire someone who has filed a discrimination suit against a former employer. Workers caught in this no-win battle can suffer emotional and financial damage which may adversely affect them for the rest of their lives.

Nonetheless, more older workers are choosing to sue their employers. Three main classes of issues affecting older workers remain unsolved, (1) whether "over-qualification" can be grounds (or pretexts) for refusing to hire an older person, (2) whether a senior worker's higher salary can be used as a basis for discharge, and (3) under what conditions binding arbitration may be used as a condition for employment (for example, hiring an older worker with special exemptions from benefits).

TABLE 4.4
CIVILIAN LABOR FORCE PARTICIPATION RATES FOR OLDER PEOPLE, BY AGE AND SEX: 1950-1989
(annual averages)

Year	Men		Women		Total	
	55 to 64	65+	55 to 64	65+	55 to 64	65+
1950	86.9	45.8	27.0	9.7	56.7	26.7
1955	87.9	39.6	32.5	10.6	59.5	24.1
1960	86.8	33.1	37.2	10.8	60.9	20.8
1965	84.6	27.9	41.1	10.0	61.9	17.8
1970	83.0	26.8	43.0	9.7	61.8	17.0
1975	75.6	21.6	40.9	8.2	57.2	13.7
1980	72.1	19.0	41.3	8.1	55.7	12.5
1985	67.9	15.8	42.0	7.3	54.2	10.8
1989	67.2	16.6	45.0	8.4	55.5	11.8

SOURCES: 1950-1980 data: U.S. Department of Labor, Bureau of Labor Statistics. *Handbook of Labor Statistics* Bulletin 2217 (June 1985).

1985 data: U.S. Department of Labor, Bureau of Labor Statistics. *Employment and Earnings* Vol. 33, No.1 (January 1986).

1989 data: U.S. Department of Labor, Bureau of Labor Statistics. *Employment and Earnings* Vol. 37, No. 1 (January 1990).

HISTORICAL TRENDS AND THE FUTURE OF OLDER WORKERS

The number of men aged 55 and older participating in the civilian (non-military) labor force has declined in recent years. Table 4.4 and Figure 4.1 show that in 1950, 86.9 percent of men aged 55 to 64 and over 45 percent of those aged 65 and older participated; by 1991, the percentages dropped to 66.7 percent and 15.5 percent, respectively.

On the other hand, the number of women between the ages of 55 and 64 in the labor force increased substantially during the same period, from about 27 percent to 46.9 percent. The number of women 65 years and older who worked dropped from 9.7 percent in 1950 to 8.7 percent in 1991.

The U.S. Bureau of Labor Statistics estimates that as America's general population grows older, so will its workforce. By the end of the century, the median age of the labor force will increase from about 36 to 39 years. Between now and the year 2000, the number of workers over age 55 will slowly increase, but during the early years of the 21st century, as the baby boomers mature, it will increase dramatically. At the same time, the number of workers between the ages of 16 and 24 will decline.

The role of the older worker in America's future is difficult to predict. As fewer young people enter the labor force, industry may have no choice but to retain or hire older workers. There is a general feeling that today's young workers are less skilled and less well educated than their mature counterparts, making older workers more desirable employees.

On the other hand, many older persons have worked most of their adult lives and are ready for a period of leisure and freedom. Social Security benefits, pensions, savings, and investments make retirement possible for ever-larger numbers of older people who wish to quit working when they reach retirement age.

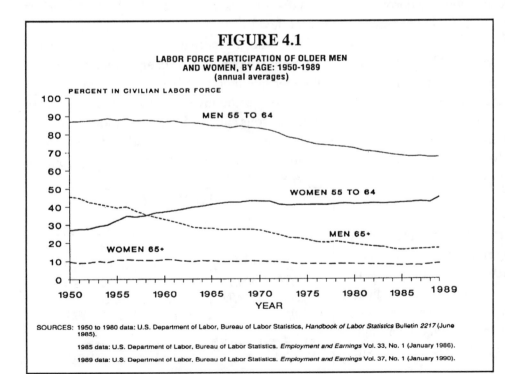

FIGURE 4.1
LABOR FORCE PARTICIPATION OF OLDER MEN AND WOMEN, BY AGE: 1950-1989
(annual averages)

SOURCES: 1950 to 1980 data: U.S. Department of Labor, Bureau of Labor Statistics, *Handbook of Labor Statistics* Bulletin 2217 (June 1985).

1985 data: U.S. Department of Labor, Bureau of Labor Statistics. *Employment and Earnings* Vol. 33, No. 1 (January 1986).

1989 data: U.S. Department of Labor, Bureau of Labor Statistics. *Employment and Earnings* Vol. 37, No. 1 (January 1990).

VOLUNTEERING - THE UNPAID CONTRIBUTION

One of the reasons older people may get depressed and frustrated when they retire from the workforce is the sense that they are no longer making a meaningful contribution, that they are not an important part of society. But every day, millions of older Americans participate through volunteer work. In 1989, approximately 13 percent (almost 5 million persons) of the volunteers were age 65 and older (Table 4.5). Not only does volunteer work benefit society, it also gives the volunteer worker a sense of worth and purpose.

Older persons make ideal volunteers. They have time in a world where time is at a premium; they have wisdom and experience that years of living can bring; they have compassion from having encountered the same problems they are helping others cope with.

Volunteering by older people is a relatively new phenomenon. Historically, the elderly were seen as the segment of society most in need of care and support. However, as medical technology enables people to live longer, healthier lives, and stereotypes about aging crumble, the elderly are now recognized as a valuable asset for every type of volunteer activity. Increased education and affluence among the elderly suggest they may be more able and available for volunteer work.

The Elderly Volunteer

Older people do not usually do volunteer work because they have nothing else to do. The strongest influence on volunteer activity is a person's general activity. People with higher levels of education (and consequently, a higher income) are more likely to be volunteers at all ages, including old age, as are those who report general satisfaction with their lives. Retired women are more involved in volunteer activities than are retired men.

A factor closely linked to volunteer work is income level (Table 4.6). In general, the higher one's income, the more likely he or she is to engage in volunteer work. As the chart demonstrates, the volunteer rate increases from 9.2 percent of those below the income level of $10,000 to 27 percent among persons earning $50,000 or more. Well-off persons are more able to donate their time because volunteering often requires some out-of-pocket

TABLE 4.5

Persons who performed unpaid volunteer work at some time during the year ended May 1989, by sex and selected characteristics

[Numbers in thousands]

Characteristic	Both sexes		Men		Women	
	Volunteer workers	Volunteers as percent of population	Volunteer workers	Volunteers as percent of population	Volunteer workers	Volunteers as percent of population
Total	38,042	20.4	16,681	18.8	21,361	21.9
Age						
16 to 24 years old	3,966	12.3	1,814	11.4	2,152	13.1
16 to 19	1,902	13.4	879	12.3	1,023	14.4
20 to 24	2,064	11.4	935	10.6	1,129	12.1
25 to 34 years old	8,680	20.2	3,678	17.4	5,002	23.0
35 to 44 years old	10,337	28.9	4,683	26.8	5,655	30.9
45 to 54 years old	5,670	23.0	2,601	21.8	3,069	24.1
55 to 64 years old	4,455	20.8	1,987	19.8	2,468	21.8
65 years old and over	4,934	16.9	1,917	15.8	3,016	17.7
Race and Hispanic origin						
White	34,823	21.9	15,273	20.0	19,550	23.6
Black	2,505	11.9	1,082	11.5	1,423	12.3
Hispanic origin	1,289	9.4	587	8.6	702	10.1
Marital status						
Never married	6,327	13.7	3,102	12.4	3,225	15.3
Married, spouse present	26,344	24.8	12,131	22.8	14,213	26.9
Married, spouse absent	765	13.2	275	12.1	489	14.0
Divorced	2,510	17.3	908	15.3	1,602	18.6
Widowed	2,096	15.3	266	11.9	1,831	16.0
Years of school completed by persons 25 years old and over						
0 to 11 years	2,939	8.3	1,295	7.8	1,644	8.8
12 years only	11,105	18.8	4,120	16.0	6,985	20.9
13 to 15 years	7,572	28.1	3,042	24.0	4,531	31.6
16 years or more	12,459	38.4	6,410	36.0	6,049	41.4
Employment status						
In labor force	27,284	22.1	14,094	20.9	13,190	23.6
Employed	26,439	22.6	13,734	21.4	12,705	24.0
Full time	21,182	21.9	12,541	21.8	8,641	22.0
Part time	5,257	26.0	1,193	18.0	4,064	29.9
Unemployed	845	13.8	360	11.1	485	16.8
Not in labor force	10,758	17.1	2,587	12.2	8,171	19.6

Source: "Volunteers in the U.S.: who donates their time?" Monthly Labor Review, Vol 114, No.2, February 1991, (WDC)

TABLE 4.6

Income	Volunteer rate		
	Total	Men	Women
Under $10,000	9.2	7.5	10.0
$10,000 to $29,999	15.6	12.9	18.0
$30,000 to $49,999	23.4	20.9	26.0
$50,000 or more	27.0	25.1	29.1

Source: "Volunteers in the U.S.: who donates their time?" Monthly Labor Review, Vol 114, No.2, February 1991, (WDC)

TABLE 4.7

Percent of Adult Population Doing Volunteer Work: 1989

[For year ending in May. Covers civilian noninstitutional population, 16 years old and over. A volunteer is a person who performed unpaid work for an organization such as a church, the Boy or Girl Scouts, a school, Little League, etc. during the year. Persons who did work on their own such as helping out neighbors or relatives are excluded. Based on Current Population Survey; see text, section 1 and Appendix III]

CHARACTERISTIC	VOLUNTEER WORKERS		PERCENT DISTRIBUTION OF VOLUNTEERS, BY TYPE OF ORGANIZATION [1]							
	Number (1,000)	Per- cent of popu- lation	Total	Churches, other religious organi- zations	Schools, educa- tional insti- tutions	Civic or political organi- zations	Hospi- tals, other health organi- zations	Social or welfare organi- zations	Sport or recrea- tional organi- zations	Other organi- zations
Total [2]	38,042	20.4	100.0	37.4	15.1	13.2	10.4	9.9	7.8	6.3
16-19 years old	1,902	13.4	100.0	34.4	26.8	8.9	9.2	7.0	8.2	5.5
20-24 years old	2,064	11.4	100.0	30.5	18.5	12.7	11.9	11.6	8.0	6.8
25-34 years old	8,680	20.2	100.0	34.9	18.3	13.3	9.1	9.3	8.9	6.1
35-44 years old	10,337	28.9	100.0	33.1	20.3	12.6	7.4	8.5	12.1	6.1
45-54 years old	5,670	23.0	100.0	40.8	11.8	15.1	10.1	8.8	7.1	6.3
55-64 years old	4,455	20.8	100.0	45.7	6.7	16.1	12.4	10.9	2.5	5.7
65 years old and over......	4,934	16.9	100.0	43.3	4.3	11.1	17.8	14.5	1.8	7.2
Male	16,681	18.8	100.0	35.9	10.5	17.2	7.0	10.1	11.8	7.5
Female.................	21,361	21.9	100.0	38.5	18.8	10.1	13.1	9.7	4.6	5.3
White.................	34,823	21.9	100.0	36.6	15.1	13.5	10.7	9.8	8.0	6.3
Black.................	2,505	11.9	100.0	50.4	12.4	9.6	7.0	10.4	4.6	5.6
Hispanic origin [3]	1,289	9.4	100.0	42.2	18.3	9.6	8.5	8.9	6.9	5.6
Educational attainment: [4] Less than 4 years of high school	2,939	8.3	100.0	48.4	6.6	10.0	10.0	13.1	4.8	7.0
4 years of high school	11,105	18.8	100.0	41.5	12.5	11.2	11.1	8.8	8.2	6.7
1 to 3 years of college....	7,572	28.1	100.0	36.8	14.7	13.3	10.8	10.8	8.0	6.3
4 years of college or more .	12,459	38.4	100.0	32.9	17.4	16.4	9.7	10.1	7.8	5.7

[1] Organization for which most of the work was done. [2] Includes other races, not shown separately. [3] Persons of Hispanic origin may be of any race. [4] Persons 25 years old and over.

Source: U.S. Bureau of Labor Statistics, *News*, USDL 90-154, March 29, 1990.

phone hot lines, and staff food banks. Many volunteers take the opportunity to share the knowledge they have gained during their professional careers, and others pick an assignment - directing a theatrical production, for example - that allows them to pursue an avocation while helping others. Although RSVP volunteers receive no pay, they are covered by accident and liability insurance and may receive money for incidental expenses such as transportation.

The Foster Grandparent Program

expenses that the poorer person cannot afford. In the future, the increasing number of baby boom elderly with greater discretionary income will likely lead to a rise in the participation of the elderly in volunteerism.

Volunteer Programs

Volunteer activities take many forms. Many older volunteers work through their churches and community centers or help friends and neighbors on a regular basis (Table 4.7). Others work with established government and private programs. More than 400,000 people over the age of 60 participate in ACTION, a group of volunteer agencies supported by the federal government; there are more than 250,000 volunteers in American Association of Retired Persons (AARP) programs.

RSVP

The Retired Senior Volunteer Program (RSVP) is part of ACTION. It has over one-half million retired volunteers who serve through 51,000 local organizations. Along with many other activities, RSVP volunteers help young people acquire job skills, teach English to refugee children, man tele-

The Foster Grandparent Program is also sponsored by ACTION and is open to low-income persons 60 years old and over. Foster grandparents bring their love and nurturing skills to children in institutions and hospitals for retarded, disturbed, and handicapped children. In San Antonio, Texas, a pilot program enables foster grandparents to address the problem of abused and neglected children in the children's own homes. Volunteers in the Foster Grandparent Program receive a small, tax-free stipend for their services, a transportation allowance, hot meals while in service, accident insurance, and annual physical examinations. These benefits allow elderly people to participate in the program who otherwise might not be able to do so.

The Peace Corps

In 1992, approximately 670 Americans aged 50 and older (11 percent of the total number of Peace Corps volunteers) are serving as Peace Corps volunteers in 85 countries throughout the world. Senior volunteers' assignments are similar to those of younger volunteers. Age is no handicap to bringing assistance and new knowledge to needy people wherever they may be.

41

Private Programs

As mentioned above, thousands of senior citizens provide volunteer service through national and local non-government programs such as those offered by AARP, the Family Friends Program (developed by the National Council on Aging), and the National Executive Service Corps. In Florida, retired physicians and nurses donate their time to run the 24 clinics of the Senior Friendship Centers Health Service. Senior volunteers are helping the City of Virginia Beach's police department expand its services by maintaining and purging files, checking suspects through the national Crime Information Center, and collecting, collating, and coding reports.

"Service Credits"

Seven metropolitan communities around the country and the state of Missouri have implemented model programs in which senior citizens earn credit for volunteer work. These service credits are earned by performing services for others, ranging from child care to hospital visits. Credits are redeemed when the volunteer her(him)self needs assistance, which is provided by another volunteer (who in turn receives service credits). Volunteers are thus rewarded for their service, yet there is no expense for either government or private agencies.

The service credit program faces some difficulties, such as keeping track of the credits, repaying them in kind, and dealing with a "run on the bank" where many volunteers may need to redeem their credits at the same time. Others worry that the very spirit of volunteerism is violated by "paying" for good deeds. Nonetheless, the program has attracted serious attention from many countries including England, Israel, and Japan. As for the spirit of volunteerism, many volunteers never claim their service credits at all. Knowing that their work is recognized is payment enough.

The Future of Senior Volunteering

Older volunteers make up more than 20 percent of the elderly population in the U.S. The National Academy of Sciences estimates that for every five senior volunteers working today, there are another two who would like to volunteer but are unaware of volunteer activities in which they could participate. Some cannot afford the minimal cost associated with volunteering, even with the reimbursement for expenses offered by some programs. As the value of older volunteers receives wider recognition, perhaps resources will become available to help more of them in their desire to help others.

CHAPTER V

EDUCATION AND VOTING BEHAVIOR

EDUCATION LEVELS OF OLDER AMERICANS

At the turn of the last century, most children were not educated beyond the eighth grade. Today's elderly who are over age 85 reflect the limited educational opportunities of children born and reared during the early 1900s. After World War I, the number of young people graduating from high school began to increase. This change is reflected in the education level of today's elderly. Tomorrow's elderly will mirror the rapid growth in education that occurred after World War II.

More than 33 percent of Americans who were 65 or older in 1989 had completed four years of high school, compared to 41.7 percent of people in the 25 to 29 age group (Table 5.1). Only 11 percent of older Americans had completed four or more years of college, considerably less that the 23.4 percent of the 25 to 29 age group.

Only 15.8 percent of blacks 65 or older had a high school degree in 1989. However, blacks in the 25 to 29 year age group had a higher percentage (47.6) of high school graduates than did whites of the same age. Barely 5 percent of older blacks had college degrees. Slightly more than 17 percent of older Hispanics had high school diplomas in 1989, while 5.9 percent had four or more years of college.

The education gap between older and younger people is closing (Figure 5.1 and Table 5.2). From 1950 to 1989, the median number of school years for people over age 65 increased from 8.3 to 12.1 years. For those younger, the number of years increased from 9.3 to 12.7. By the year 2000, people over age 65 are expected to have completed 12.4 years of school compared to 12.8 years for younger persons.

Continuing to Learn

Recent years have shown a new trend in education among the elderly (See also Chapter XI). A "graying of the campus" has occurred. Retired people were the active participants in what was once termed "adult education," that is, in courses that did not lead to a formal degree. In 1984, the last year for which figures are available, nearly six percent

TABLE 5.1

Years of School Completed, by Age, Race, and Hispanic Origin: 1989

(Persons 25 years old and over. As of March 1989. See headnote, table 223. For definition of median, see Guide to Tabular Presentation)

SEX, AGE, RACE, AND HISPANIC ORIGIN	Population (1,000)	PERCENT OF POPULATION COMPLETING—							Median years of school completed
		Elementary school			High school		College		
		1 to 4 years	5 to 7 years	8 years	1 to 3 years	4 years	1 to 3 years	4 years or more	
Total persons	154,155	2.5	4.1	5.0	11.5	38.5	17.3	21.1	12.7
Male	73,225	2.8	4.3	4.8	11.0	35.4	17.4	24.5	12.8
Female	80,930	2.4	4.0	5.2	11.9	41.3	17.2	18.1	12.6
25 to 29 years old	21,478	1.0	1.5	1.6	10.4	41.7	20.4	23.4	12.9
30 to 34 years old	21,762	1.1	1.8	1.4	8.1	41.1	21.5	25.0	12.9
35 to 44 years old	35,873	1.4	2.1	1.9	7.9	37.3	21.5	27.9	13.0
45 to 54 years old	24,622	2.0	3.7	3.9	12.0	40.5	15.9	22.0	12.7
55 to 64 years old	21,399	3.5	5.5	6.6	15.3	39.6	13.3	16.2	12.5
65 years old and over	29,022	5.8	9.6	13.8	15.9	33.2	10.6	11.1	12.1
White	132,903	2.0	3.7	5.0	10.8	39.1	17.5	21.8	12.7
25 to 29 years old	17,973	0.9	1.7	1.5	9.9	41.2	20.4	24.4	12.9
30 to 34 years old	18,298	1.0	1.8	1.3	7.5	41.3	21.2	25.8	12.9
35 to 44 years old	30,687	1.4	1.9	1.8	7.0	37.3	21.9	28.8	13.1
45 to 54 years old	21,127	1.7	3.1	3.7	10.8	41.7	16.5	22.5	12.7
55 to 64 years old	18,818	2.7	4.7	6.6	14.2	41.1	13.7	17.1	12.5
65 years old and over	26,001	4.0	8.4	13.9	15.9	34.9	11.3	11.7	12.2
Black	16,395	5.3	7.1	4.9	18.1	36.5	16.3	11.8	12.4
25 to 29 years old	2,726	0.5	0.5	1.8	14.9	47.6	21.9	12.7	12.7
30 to 34 years old	2,662	0.8	0.9	1.4	13.8	44.1	25.0	13.9	12.7
35 to 44 years old	3,900	0.6	3.1	2.4	15.7	41.3	20.3	16.7	12.7
45 to 54 years old	2,565	2.9	8.1	6.0	22.9	35.9	12.4	11.8	12.3
55 to 64 years old	2,105	9.4	12.8	6.8	25.8	28.5	9.8	6.9	11.4
65 years old and over	2,436	21.8	22.0	13.5	18.1	15.8	4.1	4.6	8.5
Hispanic origin [1]	10,438	12.2	15.1	7.1	14.7	27.9	13.2	9.9	12.0
25 to 29 years old	2,152	5.4	10.9	4.4	18.4	34.0	17.0	10.1	12.3
30 to 34 years old	1,816	6.9	14.0	5.7	14.8	29.2	17.6	11.8	12.3
35 to 44 years old	2,669	10.8	14.1	6.1	12.9	30.2	14.9	10.9	12.2
45 to 54 years old	1,645	14.4	17.2	7.3	16.5	25.0	9.7	10.0	11.0
55 to 64 years old	1,151	20.0	17.2	10.7	15.4	22.2	7.4	7.2	9.4
65 years old and over	1,005	27.4	22.2	14.3	8.4	17.4	4.5	5.9	8.0

[1] Persons of Hispanic origin may be of any race.

Source: U.S. Bureau of the Census, unpublished data.

FIGURE 5.1

MEDIAN YEARS OF SCHOOL FOR PEOPLE
25+ AND 65+: 1950-1989

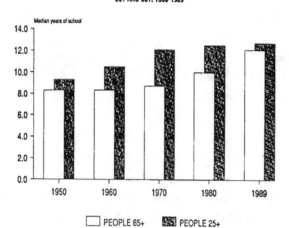

SOURCES: U. S. Bureau of the Census. Unpublished data from the March 1989 Current Population Survey.

U.S. Bureau of the Census. "Detailed Population Characteristics." *1980 Census of Population* PC80-1-D1, United States Summary (March 1984).

U.S. Bureau of the Census. "Detailed Characteristics." *1970 Census of Population* PC (1)-D1, United States Summary (February 1973).

U.S. Bureau of the Census. "Characteristics of the Population." *1960 Census of Population* Volume 1, Part 1, United States Summary, Chapter D (1964).

TABLE 5.2

SELECTED MEASURES OF EDUCATIONAL ATTAINMENT
FOR PEOPLE AGE 25+ AND 65+: 1950-1989

Year and age group	Percent with:		Median years of school
	High school education	Four or more years of college	
1989*			
25+ years	76.9	21.1	12.7
65+ years	54.9	11.1	12.1
1980			
25+ years	66.5	16.2	12.5
65+ years	38.8	8.2	10.0
1970			
25+ years	52.3	10.7	12.1
65+ years	27.1	5.5	8.7
1960			
25+ years	41.1	7.7	10.5
65+ years	19.1	3.7	8.3
1950			
25+ years	33.4	6.0	9.3
65+ years	17.0	3.4	8.3

SOURCES: U.S. Bureau of the Census. Unpublished data from the March 1989 Current Population Survey.

U.S. Bureau of the Census. "Detailed Population Characteristics." *1980 Census of Population* PC80-1-D1, United States Summary (March 1984).

U.S. Bureau of the Census. "Detailed Characteristics." *1970 Census of Population* PC(1)-D1, United States Summary (February 1973).

U.S. Bureau of the Census. "Characteristics of the Population." *1960 Census of Population* Volume 1, Part 1, United States Summary, Chapter D (1964).

TABLE 5.3

—Selected characteristics of participants in adult education: 1984

[Numbers in thousands]

Characteristics of participants	Number of adults in population [1]	Participants in adult education [2]					
		Total		Full-time students in high school or college degree programs [3]		Not full-time students in high school or college degree programs [3]	
		Number	Percent	Number	Percent	Number	Percent
1	2	3	4	5	6	7	8
Total	172,583	23,303	13.5	1,118	0.6	22,184	12.9
Age							
17 to 34 years	71,891	11,704	16.3	948	1.3	10,756	15.0
35 to 54 years	52,303	8,864	16.9	152	0.3	8,712	16.7
55 years and over	48,388	2,735	5.7	18	(*)	2,717	5.6
Sex							
Men	81,700	10,446	12.8	485	0.6	9,961	12.2
Women	90,883	12,857	14.1	634	0.7	12,224	13.5
Racial/ethnic group							
White, non-Hispanic	139,777	20,429	14.6	939	0.7	19,491	13.9
Black, non-Hispanic	18,628	1,506	8.1	88	0.5	1,418	7.6
Hispanic	9,706	796	8.2	63	0.6	733	7.6
Other	4,472	571	12.8	28	0.6	543	12.1
Highest level of education completed							
Less than 4 years of high school	47,297	1,890	4.0	315	0.7	1,574	3.3
4 years of high school	66,224	6,991	10.6	193	0.3	6,799	10.3
1 to 3 years of college	30,267	6,022	19.9	394	1.3	5,628	18.6
4 or more years of college	28,775	8,400	29.2	217	0.8	8,184	28.4
Labor force status							
In labor force	112,441	19,788	17.6	740	0.7	19,047	16.9
Employed	104,464	18,929	18.1	654	0.6	18,275	17.5
Unemployed	7,977	859	10.8	86	1.1	772	9.7
Not in labor force	60,141	3,515	5.8	378	0.6	3,137	5.2
Keeping house	31,131	2,178	7.0	22	0.1	2,156	6.9
Going to school	6,866	524	7.6	330	4.8	195	2.8
Other	22,144	813	3.7	26	0.1	786	3.5
Annual family income							
Under $5,000	13,016	797	6.1	85	0.7	712	5.5
$5,000 to $7,499	11,562	712	6.2	69	0.6	643	5.6
$7,500 to $9,999	10,306	742	7.2	44	0.4	698	6.8
$10,000 to $12,499	12,079	1,089	9.0	54	0.4	1,035	8.6
$12,500 to $14,999	10,509	1,026	9.8	39	0.4	988	9.4
$15,000 to $17,499	10,353	1,253	12.1	61	0.6	1,192	11.5
$17,500 to $19,999	9,422	1,255	13.3	53	0.6	1,202	12.8
$20,000 to $24,999	17,431	2,625	15.1	116	0.7	2,509	14.4
$25,000 to $29,999	15,090	2,503	16.6	106	0.7	2,397	15.9
$30,000 to $34,999	13,839	2,505	18.1	110	0.8	2,395	17.3
$35,000 to $39,999	10,267	1,919	18.7	76	0.7	1,843	17.9
$40,000 to $49,999	12,643	2,626	20.8	103	0.8	2,522	19.9
$50,000 to $74,999	11,961	2,543	21.2	123	1.0	2,420	20.2
$75,000 or more	5,112	1,011	19.8	48	0.9	963	18.8
Not reported	8,951	695	7.8	32	0.4	664	7.4

[1] Persons 17 years of age and over on the date of the survey.
[2] Data are for the year ending in May 1984.
[3] On the date of the survey. Includes part-time undergraduate and graduate students who indicated that they were also adult education participants.
(*) Less than .05 percent.

NOTE.—Data are based upon a sample survey of the civilian noninstitutional population. Because of rounding, details may not add to totals.

SOURCE: U.S. Department of Education, National Center for Education Statistics, *Participation in Adult Education*, May 1984. (This table was prepared June 1986.)

participated in adult education (Table 5.3). Since that time, a broadening has also occurred in the term "adult education." Increasingly, the elderly are attending two and four year universities for degrees as well as auditing courses for non-credit. In addition, numerous courses are sponsored by community and recreation facilities.

The reasons for returning for additional schooling have changed as well. While the elderly once might have taken courses for "pleasure," today's older students may be in school for more practical reasons as well as for enjoyment. Many older people are "retraining" for new careers or in order to remain competitive in existing occupations. Homemakers who have been "displaced" by divorce or widowhood are often seeking careers. A number of the elderly now have the time and funds to seek learning for personal and social reasons. Some universities even allow the elderly to audit courses without charge.

VOTING BEHAVIOR

Americans tend to vote more often as they get older. Retirement often means more leisure time to devote to community affairs such as politics. In addition, dependence on Social Security funds by many older people gives them a major personal stake in how the government is run. Almost 40 percent of Americans aged 50 and over are members of the American Association of Retired Persons (AARP), sometimes considered the most powerful lobby on Capitol Hill because of its forceful, non-partisan political activities. AARP does not endorse any particular candidate but questions all candidates on issues such as health care, Social Security and Medicare, long-term care, pension reform, and age discrimination. A candidate's position on each issue is made available to members of AARP, making these older citizens an informed and potentially formidable force in the candidate's bid for election.

TABLE 5.4

Voting-Age Population, and Percent Reporting Registered and Voted: 1974 to 1988

[As of November. Covers civilian noninstitutional population 18 years old and over. Includes aliens. Figures are based on Current Population Survey (see text, section 1, and Appendix III) and differ from those in table 453 based on population estimates and official vote counts]

| CHARACTERISTIC | VOTING-AGE POPULATION (mil.) | | | | | | | | PERCENT REPORTING THEY REGISTERED | | | | | | | | PERCENT REPORTING THEY VOTED | | | | | | | |
| | | | | | | | | | Presidential election years | | | | Congressional election years | | | | Presidential election years | | | | Congressional election years | | | |
	1974	1976	1978	1980	1982	1984	1986	1988	1976	1980	1984	1988	1974	1978	1982	1986	1976	1980	1984	1988	1974	1978	1982	1986
Total [1]	141.3	146.5	151.6	157.1	165.5	170.0	173.9	178.1	66.7	66.9	68.3	66.6	62.2	62.6	64.1	64.3	59.2	59.2	59.9	57.4	44.7	45.9	48.5	46.0
18-20 years old	11.6	12.1	12.2	12.3	12.1	11.2	10.7	10.7	47.1	44.7	47.0	44.9	36.4	34.7	35.0	35.4	38.0	35.7	36.7	33.2	20.8	20.1	19.8	18.6
21-24 years old	14.1	14.8	15.5	15.9	16.7	16.7	15.7	14.8	54.8	52.7	54.3	50.6	45.3	45.1	47.8	46.6	45.6	43.1	43.5	38.3	26.4	26.2	28.4	24.2
25-34 years old	29.3	31.7	33.4	35.7	38.8	40.3	41.9	42.7	62.3	62.0	63.3	57.8	54.7	55.5	57.1	55.8	55.4	54.6	54.5	48.0	37.0	38.0	40.4	35.1
35-44 years old	22.4	22.8	24.2	25.6	28.1	30.7	33.0	35.2	69.8	70.6	70.9	69.3	66.7	66.7	67.5	67.9	63.3	64.4	63.5	61.3	49.1	50.1	52.2	49.3
45-64 years old	43.0	43.3	43.4	43.6	44.2	44.3	44.8	45.9	75.5	75.8	76.6	75.5	73.6	74.3	75.6	74.8	68.7	69.3	69.8	67.9	56.9	58.5	62.2	58.7
65 years old and over	21.0	22.0	23.0	24.1	25.6	26.7	27.7	28.8	71.4	74.6	76.9	78.4	70.2	72.8	75.2	76.9	62.2	65.1	67.7	68.8	51.4	55.9	59.9	60.9
Male	66.4	69.0	71.5	74.1	78.0	80.3	82.4	84.5	67.1	66.6	67.3	65.2	62.8	62.6	63.7	63.4	59.6	59.1	59.0	56.4	46.2	46.6	48.7	45.8
Female	74.9	77.6	80.2	83.0	87.4	89.6	91.5	93.6	66.4	67.1	69.3	67.8	61.7	62.5	64.4	65.0	58.8	59.4	60.8	58.3	43.4	45.3	48.4	46.1
White	125.1	129.3	133.4	137.7	143.6	146.8	149.9	152.9	68.3	68.4	69.6	67.9	63.5	63.8	65.6	65.3	60.9	60.9	61.4	59.1	46.3	47.3	49.9	47.0
Black	14.2	14.9	15.6	16.4	17.6	18.4	19.0	19.7	58.5	60.0	66.3	64.5	54.9	57.1	59.1	64.0	48.7	50.5	55.8	51.5	33.8	37.2	43.0	43.2
Hispanic [2]	6.1	6.6	6.8	8.2	8.8	9.5	11.8	12.9	37.8	36.3	40.1	35.5	34.9	32.9	35.3	35.9	31.8	29.9	32.6	28.8	22.9	23.5	25.3	24.2
Region:																								
Northeast	33.3	33.9	35.1	35.5	36.4	36.9	37.3	37.9	65.9	64.8	66.6	64.8	62.2	62.3	62.5	62.0	59.5	58.5	59.7	57.4	48.7	48.1	49.8	44.4
Midwest	38.1	39.2	40.3	41.5	41.9	42.1	42.8	43.3	72.3	73.8	74.6	72.5	66.6	68.2	71.1	70.7	65.1	65.8	65.7	62.9	49.3	50.5	54.7	49.5
South	44.8	47.1	48.8	50.6	55.4	57.6	59.2	60.7	64.6	64.8	66.9	65.6	59.8	60.1	61.7	63.0	54.9	55.6	56.8	54.5	36.0	39.6	41.8	43.0
West	25.0	26.2	27.5	29.5	31.9	33.4	34.6	36.2	63.2	63.3	64.7	63.0	59.8	59.1	60.6	60.8	57.5	57.2	58.5	55.6	48.1	47.5	50.7	48.4
School years completed:																								
8 years or less	24.4	24.9	23.6	22.7	22.4	20.6	19.6	19.1	54.4	53.0	53.4	47.5	54.1	53.2	52.3	50.5	44.1	42.6	42.9	36.7	34.4	34.6	35.7	32.7
High school:																								
1-3 years	21.7	22.2	22.3	22.5	22.3	22.1	21.4	21.1	55.6	54.6	54.9	52.8	54.3	52.9	53.3	52.4	47.2	45.6	44.4	41.3	35.9	35.1	37.7	33.8
4 years	51.7	55.7	58.4	61.2	65.2	67.8	68.6	70.0	66.9	66.4	67.3	64.6	61.9	62.0	62.9	62.9	59.4	58.9	58.7	54.7	44.7	45.3	47.1	44.1
College:																								
1-3 years	23.7	23.6	25.1	26.7	28.8	30.9	33.0	34.3	75.2	74.4	75.7	73.5	66.9	68.7	70.0	70.0	68.1	67.2	67.5	64.5	49.6	51.5	53.3	49.9
4 years or more	19.8	20.2	22.2	24.0	26.9	28.6	31.3	33.6	83.7	84.3	83.8	83.1	76.0	76.9	79.4	77.8	79.8	79.9	79.1	77.6	61.3	63.9	66.5	62.5
Employed	83.1	86.0	93.2	95.0	97.2	104.2	108.5	113.8	68.8	68.7	69.4	67.1	63.8	63.0	65.5	64.4	62.0	61.8	61.6	58.4	46.8	46.7	50.0	45.7
Unemployed	5.0	6.4	4.9	6.9	10.8	7.4	6.6	5.8	52.1	50.3	54.3	50.4	44.4	44.1	49.8	50.6	43.7	41.2	44.0	38.6	28.8	27.4	34.1	31.2
Not in labor force	53.2	54.1	53.5	55.2	57.5	58.4	58.8	58.5	65.2	65.8	68.1	67.2	61.3	63.4	64.3	65.4	56.5	57.0	58.9	57.3	43.0	46.2	48.7	48.2

[1] Includes other races not shown separately.　[2] Hispanic persons may be of any race.

Source: U.S. Bureau of the Census, Current Population Reports, series P-20, No. 440 and earlier reports.

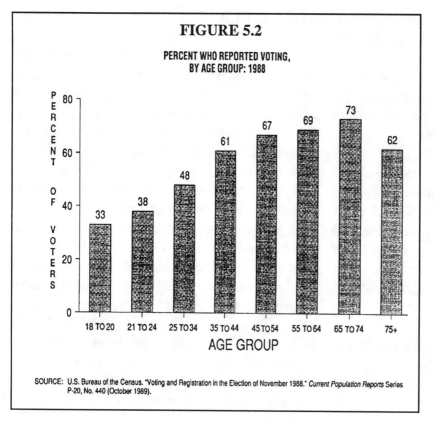

FIGURE 5.2

PERCENT WHO REPORTED VOTING,
BY AGE GROUP: 1988

SOURCE: U.S. Bureau of the Census. "Voting and Registration in the Election of November 1988." *Current Population Reports* Series
P-20, No. 440 (October 1989).

participation will increase. They are expected to become an even more powerful voting bloc as the aging population swells.

The Center for Political Studies has found differences in political party affiliation based on age . Those persons 62 years and older show a firmer identification with the two major American political parties, the Democratic and the Republican. Only half of those younger than 62 report attachment to one of those two parties and greater numbers of voters who consider themselves "independent." Among the older citizens, fully three-quarters consider themselves either Democrat or Republican. This may reflect a greater flexibility among younger voters or less firmly decided minds and histories regarding their vote. It may, however, indicate a true shift in political party support among American voters. In other words, the elderly may become more "decided" regarding political affiliation as they age, simply due to maturation. On the other hand, the younger voters being raised today may simply have different values that will remain intact, that is, as they age, they may remain less connected to the two major political parties. That could have important political implications.

The U.S. Census Bureau found that in the 1988 Presidential election, among those 18 to 20 years old, 35.4 percent reported voting. Among the 35 to 44 group, 61 percent reported voting, and almost 69 percent of the 65+ segment voted, twice the participation rate of the youngest voters (Table 5.4). Comparisons between those figures are shown in Figure 5.2.

With the increasingly large number of elderly and their advancing education and financial resources, it is expected that their already high voting

CHAPTER VI

GENERAL HEALTH AND HEALTH PROBLEMS

One of the reasons people sometimes fear growing older is having to face the loss of mental and physical abilities. Although the human body progressively declines with age, the rate and amount of decline is an individual process. One person may be afflicted with arthritis and senility at age 65 while another is vigorous and active at 80. It is true, however, that older people have more health problems and require more health care than younger ones.

GENERAL HEALTH OF OLDER AMERICANS

The U.S. Department of Health and Human Services, in Aging America - Trends and Projections, 1991 Edition, reported that 71 percent of noninstitutionalized elderly people describe their health as good or excellent compared to others their age; only 29 percent thought their health was fair or poor (Table 6.1).

The same source indicates that one quarter of all elderly persons and one-half of the oldest old (over 85 years) have at least a mild degree of functional disability. More than four out of five persons 65 and over have at least one chronic (long-lasting or often recurring) illness, and many have multiple chronic conditions.

Chronic conditions are the burden of old age. At the turn of the century, acute conditions (severe illnesses of limited duration, such as infections) were predominant. With the development of antibiotics and cures for many acute infectious diseases, chronic conditions are now the prevalent health problem for the elderly. Because people are now living to an older age, they have more years in which to suffer a chronic condition.

The leading chronic conditions of the elderly are arthritis, hypertension, hearing impairments, and heart disease (Figure 6.1 and Table 6.2). In most cases, the likelihood for disease increases with age. Older men are more likely than women to have acute illnesses that are life threatening, while older women are more likely to have chronic conditions that cause physical limitation.

TABLE 6.1
NUMBER OF ELDERLY PEOPLE AND PERCENT DISTRIBUTION BY RESPONDENT-ASSESSED HEALTH STATUS, BY SEX AND FAMILY INCOME, 1989

Characteristic	All persons[1] (000s)	Respondent-assessed health status[2]					
		All health status[3]	Excellent	Very good	Good	Fair	Poor
All persons 65+[4]	29,219	100.0	16.4	23.1	31.9	19.3	9.2
Sex:							
Men	12,143	100.0	16.9	23.2	30.8	18.4	10.7
Women	17,076	100.0	16.1	23.0	32.8	20.0	8.1
Family income:							
Under $10,000	5,612	100.0	10.3	19.4	29.7	25.0	15.6
$10,000 to $19,999	8,002	100.0	14.8	21.7	33.9	21.1	8.5
$20,000 to $34,999	5,242	100.0	20.2	25.7	32.5	15.7	5.9
$35,000 and over	3,484	100.0	26.0	26.8	30.3	11.7	5.1

SOURCE: National Center for Health Statistics. "Current Estimates from the National Health Interview Survey, 1989." *Vital and Health Statistics* Series 10, No. 176 (October 1990). Data are based on household interviews of the civilian, noninstitutionalized population.

NOTE: Percentages may not add to 100 percent due to rounding.

[1] Includes unknown health status.
[2] Excludes unknown health status.
[3] The categories related to this concept result from asking the respondent, "Would you say—health is excellent, very good, good, fair, or poor?" As such, it is based on the respondent's opinion and not directly on any clinical evidence.
[4] Includes unknown family income.

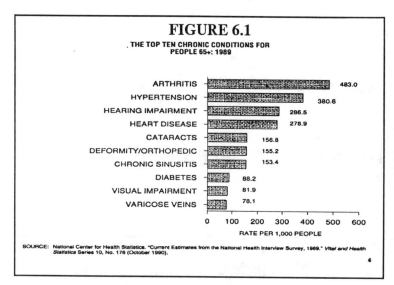

FIGURE 6.1

. THE TOP TEN CHRONIC CONDITIONS FOR
PEOPLE 65+: 1989

Condition	Rate
ARTHRITIS	483.0
HYPERTENSION	380.6
HEARING IMPAIRMENT	286.5
HEART DISEASE	278.9
CATARACTS	156.8
DEFORMITY/ORTHOPEDIC	155.2
CHRONIC SINUSITIS	153.4
DIABETES	88.2
VISUAL IMPAIRMENT	81.9
VARICOSE VEINS	78.1

RATE PER 1,000 PEOPLE

SOURCE: National Center for Health Statistics. "Current Estimates from the National Health Interview Survey, 1989." *Vital and Health Statistics* Series 10, No. 176 (October 1990).

SOCIOECONOMIC DIFFERENCES

Income or socioeconomic status (SES) is directly related to the onset of chronic illness and disability in later years. The more educated and affluent elderly are more likely to be healthy longer. Americans of the lowest SES experience more chronic illness such as cancer, heart attacks, strokes, and lung disease. These illnesses are not as common in upper-SES elderly until after the age of 75.

The number of chronic conditions suffered by an older citizen also varies by SES. Those in the highest SES group reported fewer simultaneous chronic conditions than in the lowest SES.

Possible explanations for the health differences among elderly of different SES include some of the following:

1. a higher incidence of risk behaviors (smoking, high-fat diet, more sedentary lifestyle) among the lower SES;

TABLE 6.2

TOP TEN CHRONIC CONDITIONS FOR PEOPLE 65+, BY AGE AND RACE: 1989
(number per 1,000 people)

Condition	65+	45 to 64	65 to 74	75+	White	Black	Black as % of white
		Age			Race (65+)		
Arthritis	483.0	253.8	437.3	554.5	483.2	522.6	108
Hypertension	380.6	229.1	383.8	375.6	367.4	517.7	141
Hearing impairment	286.5	127.7	239.4	360.3	297.4	174.5	59
Heart disease	278.9	118.9	231.6	353.0	286.5	220.5	77
Cataracts	156.8	16.1	107.4	234.3	160.7	139.8	87
Deformity or orthopedic impairment	155.2	155.5	141.4	177.0	156.2	150.8	97
Chronic sinusitis	153.4	173.5	151.8	155.8	157.1	125.2	80
Diabetes	88.2	58.2	89.7	85.7	80.2	165.9	207
Visual impairment	81.9	45.1	69.3	101.7	81.1	77.0	95
Varicose veins	78.1	57.8	72.6	86.6	80.3	64.0	80

SOURCE: National Center for Health Statistics. "Current Estimates from the National Health Interview Survey, 1989." *Vital and Health Statistics* Series 10, No. 176 (October 1990).

The elderly use professional medical equipment and supplies, dental care, prescription drugs, and vision aids more than people under age 65. Table 6.3 reflects a higher hospitalization rate and average stay among the elderly than any other age group. The average length of hospitalization for an elderly person has declined over the years (Figure 6.2) from 14.2 days per stay in 1968 to 8.5 days in 1986 and up just slightly in 1988 to 8.9 days.

The aging of the American population increases demand for physician care. In 1989, 259 million physician contacts were made by those over 65. Experts predict that in the year 2000, 296 million contacts will be made, an increase of 22 percent (Table 6.4). The year 2030 will reflect a 115 percent increase to 556 million medical visits.

2. greater occupational stresses and hazards in the work environments of the lowest SES;

3. acute and chronic stress among the lower SES;

4. decreased access to medical care among the lower SES.

Figure 6.3 shows how elderly persons in all SES segments rated their health. Their self-reports generally mirror the actual condition of their health.

LIFE EXPECTANCY

Life expectancy for all Americans has increased dramatically since the turn of the century. The

TABLE 6.3

Discharges, days of care, and average length of stay in short-stay hospitals, according to selected characteristics: United States, 1964, 1984, and 1989

[Data are based on household interviews of a sample of the civilian noninstitutionalized population]

Characteristic	Discharges			Days of care			Average length of stay		
	1964	1984	1989	1964	1984	1989	1964	1984	1989
	Number per 1,000 population						Number of days		
Total[1,2]	109.1	114.7	92.6	970.9	871.9	646.6	8.9	7.6	7.0
Age									
Under 15 years	67.6	60.9	44.1	405.7	334.4	256.4	6.0	5.5	5.8
Under 5 years	94.3	96.7	76.6	731.1	595.8	506.2	7.8	6.2	6.6
5–14 years	53.1	41.6	26.7	229.1	193.4	122.8	4.3	4.6	4.6
15–44 years	100.6	81.7	67.0	760.7	530.8	371.8	7.6	6.5	5.5
45–64 years	146.2	160.6	130.5	1,559.3	1,344.5	937.5	10.7	8.4	7.2
65 years and over	190.0	318.0	265.6	2,292.7	2,917.6	2,360.8	12.1	9.2	8.9
65–74 years	181.2	277.7	236.7	2,150.4	2,528.3	2,004.3	11.9	9.1	8.5
75 years and over	206.7	382.6	311.0	2,560.4	3,542.9	2,918.6	12.4	9.3	9.4
Sex[1]									
Male	103.8	114.2	95.0	1,010.2	926.6	690.0	9.7	8.1	7.3
Female	113.7	115.8	91.2	933.4	829.2	615.7	8.2	7.2	6.8
Race[1]									
White	112.4	114.3	92.0	961.4	833.2	635.9	8.6	7.3	6.9
Black[3]	84.0	127.2	105.2	1,062.9	1,247.8	798.9	12.7	9.8	7.6
Family income[1,4]									
Less than $14,000	102.4	150.2	131.3	1,051.2	1,420.3	1,013.0	10.3	9.5	7.7
$14,000–$24,999	116.4	126.6	91.2	1,213.9	991.2	600.5	10.4	7.8	6.6
$25,000–$34,999	110.7	109.4	93.0	939.8	733.1	630.5	8.5	6.7	6.8
$35,000–$49,999	109.2	99.9	75.0	882.6	678.3	476.9	8.1	6.8	6.4
$50,000 or more	110.7	95.9	72.1	918.9	614.8	497.4	8.3	6.4	6.9
Geographic region[1]									
Northeast	98.5	104.5	80.2	993.8	877.5	589.5	10.1	8.4	7.4
Midwest	109.2	125.2	98.4	944.9	965.6	690.2	8.7	7.7	7.0
South	117.8	126.4	106.5	968.0	953.7	721.6	8.2	7.5	6.8
West	110.5	92.9	75.7	985.9	596.7	528.8	8.9	6.4	7.0
Location of residence[1]									
Within MSA	107.5	108.1	89.0	1,015.4	864.6	649.7	9.4	8.0	7.3
Outside MSA	113.3	128.4	105.1	871.9	888.9	639.1	7.7	6.9	6.1

[1]Age adjusted.
[2]Includes all other races not shown separately and unknown family income.
[3]1964 data include all other races.
[4]Family income categories for 1989. Income categories in 1964 are: less than $2,000; $2,000–$3,999; $4,000–$6,999; $7,000–$9,999; and $10,000 or more; and, in 1984 are: less than $10,000; $10,000–$18,999; $19,000–$29,999; $30,000–$39,999; and $40,000 or more.

NOTE: Excludes deliveries.

SOURCE: Division of Health Interview Statistics, National Center for Health Statistics: Data from the National Health Interview Survey.

FIGURE 6.2

TRENDS IN HOSPITAL USAGE BY PEOPLE 65+:
1965-1988

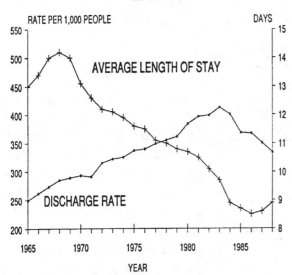

RATE PER 1,000 PEOPLE — DAYS

AVERAGE LENGTH OF STAY

DISCHARGE RATE

YEAR

SOURCES: National Center for Health Statistics. "Trends in Hospital Utilization: United States, 1965-1986." *Vital and Health Statistics* Series 13, No. 101 (September 1989).

TABLE 6.4

PROJECTED PHYSICIAN VISITS AND PERCENT CHANGE IN VISITS
FOR YEARS 2000 AND 2030
(number of people and visits in thousands)

Year	Age		
	65+	65 to 74	75+
2000			
Noninstitutionalized population	34,882	18,243	16,639
Total physician contacts	295,613	147,480	148,133
% change in contacts, 1989-2000	14.2	1.0	31.1
2030			
Noninstitutionalized population	65,604	35,988	29,616
Total physician contacts	555,717	290,932	264,785
% change in contacts, 1989-2030	114.6	99.3	134.4

SOURCE: U.S. Administration on Aging. Unpublished projections based on physician visit rates from the 1989 National Health Interview Survey and population projections from the U.S. Bureau of the Census.

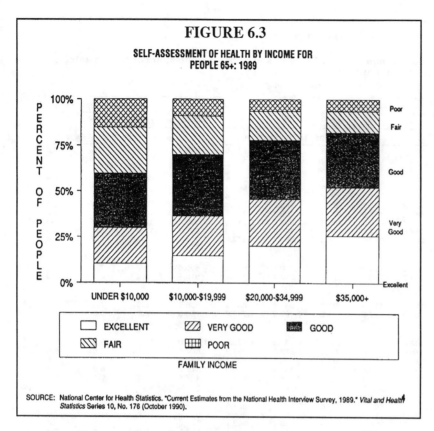

FIGURE 6.3

SELF-ASSESSMENT OF HEALTH BY INCOME FOR PEOPLE 65+: 1989

PERCENT OF PEOPLE

100% ... 75% ... 50% ... 25% ... 0%

UNDER $10,000 $10,000-$19,999 $20,000-$34,999 $35,000+

Poor / Fair / Good / Very Good / Excellent

☐ EXCELLENT   ▨ VERY GOOD   ▩ GOOD
◩ FAIR   ⊞ POOR

FAMILY INCOME

SOURCE: National Center for Health Statistics. "Current Estimates from the National Health Interview Survey, 1989." *Vital and Health Statistics* Series 10, No. 176 (October 1990).

about 1970, when they were passed by black females. Black males have consistently had shorter life spans than any other group.

Reasons for Increased Life Expectancy

During the first half of the century, increased longevity was a result of reducing or eliminating many diseases that killed infants and children and improved methods of delivering babies, so that more people survived to middle age. In recent years, increased life expectancy is attributed to decreasing mortality from chronic diseases among the middle-aged and elderly due to new medical knowledge, practices, and life-sustaining technology. In other words, old people are living to be older.

CAUSES OF DEATH

Seven out of every ten elderly people die from heart disease, cancer, or stroke (Figure 6.4). The leading causes of death and the death rate from each cause in 1988 for age 65 and older are shown in Table 6.6. (Malignant neoplasms refer to cancer, and cerebrovascular diseases include strokes.)

"Still Number One"

The American Heart Association reported that in 1988, 55 percent of all heart attacks occurred in people over 65. Statistically, women have far less coronary heart disease than men until they reach age 65, at which point their numbers approach those of men. Heart disease is the primary cause of death for all Americans, but especially for the elderly. The risk of dying from heart disease increases greatly after age 65, and the death rate

"average" person born in the United States in 1900 could expect to celebrate no more than 40 birthdays. By current estimates, someone born in the year 2000 will live almost twice that long (73.5 years for a man, 80.4 for a woman). Table 6.5 gives projected life expectancy for those born between 1990 and 2050.

Women Live Longer Than Men

As shown in Chapter I, in this century women have lived longer than men and probably will continue to do so. White females have the highest life expectancy of any race-sex group. White males were the second longest-lived group until

TABLE 6.5

PROJECTED LIFE EXPECTANCY AT BIRTH AND AGE 65, BY SEX: 1990-2050
(in years)

Year	At birth			At age 65		
	Men	Women	Difference	Men	Women	Difference
1990	72.1	79.0	6.9	15.0	19.4	4.4
2000	73.5	80.4	6.9	15.7	20.3	4.6
2010	74.4	81.3	6.9	16.2	21.0	4.8
2020	74.9	81.8	6.9	16.6	21.4	4.8
2030	75.4	82.3	6.9	17.0	21.8	4.8
2040	75.9	82.8	6.9	17.3	22.3	5.0
2050	76.4	83.3	6.9	17.7	22.7	5.0

SOURCE: U.S. Bureau of the Census. "Projections of the Population of the United States, by Age, Sex, and Race: 1988 to 2080," by Gregory Spencer. *Current Population Reports* Series P-25, No. 1018 (January 1989).

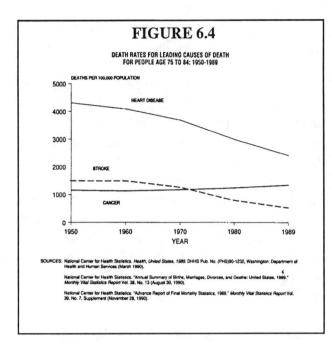

FIGURE 6.4

DEATH RATES FOR LEADING CAUSES OF DEATH
FOR PEOPLE AGE 75 TO 84: 1950-1989

DEATHS PER 100,000 POPULATION

HEART DISEASE

STROKE

CANCER

SOURCES: National Center for Health Statistics. *Health, United States, 1989.* DHHS Pub. No. (PHS)90-1232, Washington: Department of Health and Human Services (March 1990).

National Center for Health Statistics. "Annual Summary of Births, Marriages, Divorces, and Deaths: United States, 1989." *Monthly Vital Statistics Report* Vol. 38, No. 13 (August 30, 1990).

National Center for Health Statistics. "Advance Report of Final Mortality Statistics, 1988." *Monthly Vital Statistics Report* Vol. 39, No. 7, Supplement (November 28, 1990).

TABLE 6.6

DEATH RATES FOR TEN LEADING CAUSES OF DEATH
AMONG OLDER PEOPLE, BY AGE: 1988
(rates per 100,000 population in age group)

Cause of death	65+	65 to 74	75 to 84	85+
ALL CAUSES	5,105	2,730	6,321	15,594
Diseases of the heart	2,066	984	2,543	7,098
Malignant neoplasms	1,068	843	1,313	1,639
Cerebrovascular diseases	431	155	554	1,707
Chronic obstructive pulmonary disease	226	152	313	394
Pneumonia and influenza	225	60	257	1,125
Diabetes	97	62	125	222
Accidents	89	50	107	267
Atherosclerosis	69	15	70	396
Nephritis, nephrotic syndrome, nephrosis	61	26	78	217
Septicemia	56	24	71	199

SOURCE: National Center for Health Statistics. "Advanced Report of Final Mortality Statistics, 1988." *Monthly Vital Statistics Report* Vol. 39, No. 7, Supplement (November 28, 1990).

more than doubles for each age group between 65 and 85. The past three decades have shown a marked decline in death rates for heart disease. Several factors account for the decline. Primary factors are better control of hypertension and changes in exercise and nutrition. Also important is the expanding use of trained mobile emergency personnel(paramedics) in most urban areas. The generalized use of CPR (cardiopulmonary resuscitation) and new emergency medications also increase the likelihood of one's surviving an initial heart attack.

Research on heart disease has historically been done on male subjects, however, recent reports indicate that post-menopausal women not only suffer from the disease as do their male counterparts, but those with the disease are more than twice as likely to die from an initial heart attack than men. The reasons are unknown at this time; however, the suggestion has been made that because of the misconception that women do not experience the disease as frequently, their complaints are not taken as seriously as those of men. Also, physiologic factors as yet unknown may play a role in women's succumbing to heart disease. The need for research on female subjects is clear; demand for such research is being voiced to the medical community.

Cancer

Cancer is the second leading cause of death among the elderly. Success in the cure of certain tumors (Hodgkin's disease, certain forms of leukemia) is equalled by the rise in rates of other cancers, for example, breast and lung cancer. Progress in treating cancer has largely been related to screenings, early diagnosis, and new drug therapies.

Strokes

Strokes are the third leading cause of death and the primary cause of disability among the elderly. The incidence of stroke is strongly related to age; 72 percent of stroke victims are 65 years of age or older.

PHYSICAL PROBLEMS OF THE ELDERLY

Physical ailments can strike anyone at any age, but there are some illnesses and conditions that are more common among the elderly.

Arthritis

Arthritis is an "umbrella term" for a family of more than 100 separate diseases that affect the body's connective tissue. In common usage, it refers to inflammation of the joints. Arthritis is not a disease solely of the elderly, but its prevalence increases with age.

51

The greatest consequence of arthritis is loss of mobility and deformity in the affected tissues or joints. Its impact can be mild or severe, depending on the extent of the disease and the specific type of arthritis. A 1989 study by the National Institute on Aging's Dr. Edward H. Yelin (Arthritis, Rheumatic Diseases, and Related Disorders, NIAMS) found that patients diagnosed with osteoarthritis (a degenerative joint disease) experienced some loss in ability to perform daily functions such as household chores, shopping and running errands, and leisure activities. Patients with rheumatoid arthritis (inflammation of primarily the joint lining) experienced a loss in every activity, and the losses were more severe.

Osteoporosis

Osteoporosis, a decrease in bone mass, has only recently been recognized as a fairly common condition of old age. It is the leading cause of bone fractures in the elderly. Osteoporosis develops slowly over a person's lifetime. After the mid-20s, bone tissue gradually thins out and is not replaced by new bone as quickly as in earlier years.

When osteoporosis advances to the point where 35 to 40 percent of a person's bone density has been destroyed, the vertebrae (bones of the spine) begin to collapse, causing the spine to curve outward in a "dowager's hump." Bone fractures and broken hips become more common, some resulting in permanent damage and even premature death. The disease is difficult to diagnose in its early stages because X-rays can only detect bone loss of more than 30 percent. The recent introduction of photon densitometry, which can measure very small losses in bone density, offers hope of earlier diagnosis.

Osteoporosis affects one out of every four elderly women. Women are far more susceptible to osteoporosis than men, especially those women who are fair-skinned, small boned, of northern European, Chinese or Japanese descent, and who have reduced estrogen levels due to removal of the ovaries or menopause. After menopause women lose bone mass rapidly as loss of estrogen acceler-

ates calcium depletion in the body. At age 65, bone loss rate slows down again.

The disease can be prevented or its effects diminished by measures taken earlier in life. Doctors recommend that women over the age of 40 take between 1,000 and 1,500 milligrams of calcium daily by way of calcium-rich food such as milk, yogurt, cheese, tofu, dark leafy green vegetables, salmon, sardines, and shellfish. It is also important to maintain adequate levels of vitamin D, which helps the body absorb and utilize calcium. Most people get sufficient vitamin D from exposure to sunlight, but the skin loses much of its ability to produce the vitamin as one ages.

Regular exercise, especially walking, jogging, and bicycle riding, also aids in preventing osteoporosis. The risk is increased by smoking, heavy drinking, high caffeine and protein intake, and lack of regular exercise. The newest experimental therapies involve the intake of sodium fluoride, estrogen, calcitonin, and the drug Etidronate.

Diabetes

The elderly are quite susceptible to Type II, or non-insulin dependent, diabetes. (Type I, juvenile or early onset diabetes, usually affects the young.) Frequent complications of diabetes are nerve damage in the legs and feet, sometimes resulting in amputations, and eye problems which can result in blindness. Type II diabetes accounts for over 85 percent of all diabetic cases and can usually be controlled with a diet and weight reduction program. Both forms of the disease require the daily, sometimes even hourly, monitoring of blood sugar and insulin levels. Research is currently being conducted into new methods for administering insulin, such as implants and pumps, and home blood sugar self-test kits are now common for diabetic patients.

Prostate Problems

Prostate problems in men increase significantly after age 50. Often the prostate becomes enlarged and blocks the urethra, the canal through which urine leaves the body, making urination difficult. This condition can be relieved with surgery. Occasionally, cancer can develop in the prostate gland, but, if treated early, it is generally not life-threatening, since prostate cancer progresses very slowly and remains localized for a long time.

Urinary Problems

The National Center for Health Statistics found that 9 percent of noninstitutionalized persons aged 65 and over had problems controlling urination (1986, Advancedata, No. 121, August 27). The problem increases with age, with an estimated 986,000 persons 65 to 74 years old and 1.2 million persons 75 years and older having some urinary difficulty. The problem appears to be more common with women than men.

Urinary problems often have a serious emotional impact. In the above study, people with urinary problems were more likely to report their health as fair to poor and that their health had deteriorated during the previous year. About three-fourths of those with urinary problems suffered some limitation in at least some activity.

Urinary incontinence, the inability to control bladder function, is not a disease, but rather a symptom of other dysfunction. Nor is it a normal function of aging. Specialists report that many people do not report their problems because they are not aware that help is possible. The aggressive marketing of absorbent wear discourages many people from seeking help. Doctors estimate that 85 to 90 percent of sufferers could be successfully treated.

Malnutrition

Even with the emphasis in recent years on good nutrition as a major factor of good health, an estimated one-half of all elderly people maintain eating habits that provide them with less than the recommended daily level of nutrients. If they are inactive, their bodies become less capable of absorbing and using nutrients in the foods they do eat, and certain medications increase the body's needs for particular nutrients.

An individual's eating habits can be affected by many factors-loneliness, depression, lack of money, or lack of transportation. Meals provided by community service organizations, whether they be dinners served at a senior center or home-delivered meals, are one of the most important services offered to the elderly. The older elderly person, those who live alone, and those with limited mobility are more likely to make use of meal services.

Hearing Loss

Hearing loss is a very common problem among the elderly, afflicting 60 to 80 percent of the 65 and older population. Elderly men are much more likely to be hearing-impaired than are elderly women. There are many causes of hearing loss, the most common being age-related changes in the ear's mechanism. People suffering from hearing loss may tend to withdraw from social contact and are sometimes mislabeled as confused or even senile. There is often a reluctance to admit to a hearing problem, and sometimes hearing loss is so gradual that even the afflicted person may not be aware of it for some time. Treatment is available for increasing numbers of patients, if they will seek help. Many physicians are not even aware of the services now available to the hearing impaired, whose options are increasing. Among the solutions now offered are high-tech hearing aids, amplifiers for doorbells and telephones, infrared amplifiers, even companion dogs trained to respond to sounds for the owner.

Vision Changes

Almost no one escapes changes in vision as they grow older. Ninety-five percent of people 65 and older wear glasses. By age 40, a person often notices a change in what may have been perfect vision. It becomes increasingly difficult to read small print or thread a needle at the usual distance. This is often caused by a condition called presbyopia (tired eyes) and is a very common occurrence. People who were previously nearsighted may actually find some improvement in eyesight as they become slightly farsighted.

EYE DISEASES

Much more serious than simple loss of visual clarity are cataracts, glaucoma, and problems affecting the retina, which frequently occur in elderly people.

Cataracts

Cataracts occur when the crystallin structure of the eye lens breaks down. The lens becomes "clouded," limiting the amount of light reaching the optic nerve and distorting images. Most cataracts develop slowly over time, but they can eventually cause almost total blindness. In recent years there has been an increase in lens replacement operations in which the clouded lens is removed and a plastic lens is substituted.

Glaucoma

Glaucoma is caused by pressure building up behind the eyeball. It usually presents no early symptoms, but if undetected in its early stages, it can result in irreversible blindness. Routine glaucoma tests are especially important for older people. Medication (eye drops) can generally manage the condition.

Problems of the Retina

The retina is a thin lining of nerves on the back of the eye. Over time, it can become torn or detached, jeopardizing vision. If treated in time by laser therapy, tears and separations can almost always be repaired.

Senile macular degeneration is a condition in which the macula, a specialized part of the retina responsible for sharp central and reading vision, is damaged. Symptoms include blurred vision, a dark spot in the center of the vision field, and vertical line distortion.

Diabetic retinopathy occurs when the small blood vessels that flourish in the retina do not perform properly. Blood vessels can leak fluid which distorts vision, and sometimes blood is released into the center of the eye causing blindness.

MENTAL DISORDERS OF THE ELDERLY: DEMENTIA

Equally devastating as the decline of a once-healthy body is the deterioration of the mind. As with other disorders, mental impairments can occur in persons of any age, but certain types of illness are much more prevalent in the elderly. In this area more than any other, the differences between individuals can vary dramatically. Some people may show no decline in mental ability until far into old age. Others experience occasional forgetfulness as they enter their "retirement years." A few are completely robbed of all their mental faculties before they reach 60.

Older people with mental problems were once labeled as "senile." Only in recent years have researchers found that physical disorders can cause progressive deterioration of mental and neurological functions. These disorders produce symptoms that are collectively known as "dementia." Symptoms of dementia include "loss of language functions, inability to think abstractly, inability to care for oneself, personality change, emotional instability, and loss of a sense of time or place" (April 1987, Losing a Million Minds, Washington, DC: Office of Technology Assessment).

It is important to note that occasional forgetfulness and disorientation are normal signs of the aging process. True dementia is a disease and is not the inevitable result of growing older. Many disorders may cause or simulate dementia.

Alzheimer's Disease

The most prevalent form of dementia is Alzheimer's disease, named after the German neurologist Alois Alzheimer who, in 1906, discovered the "neurofibrillary tangles" now associated with the disease. Alzheimer's is a degenerative disorder of the brain and nervous system; there is no known cause, cure, or treatment.

Just 10 years ago, Alzheimer's was still a relatively obscure disease that received little study and still less publicity. Symptoms were generally attributed to aging and the victims diagnosed as senile. Even so, Alzheimer's is the fourth leading killer of adults today behind heart disease, cancer, and strokes, claiming more than 100,000 lives each year. Today, Alzheimer's is the subject of intense research and is very much in the public consciousness. Unfortunately, many people have become familiar with the disease because a relative or loved one has been given the diagnosis of Alzheimer's.

Prevalence

As the population ages, Alzheimer's is becoming more of a concern. As many as 10.3 percent of people over the age of 65 with memory problems or other mental impairment probably suffer from Alzheimer's. Up to 3 percent of people between 65 and 74, 19 percent of those between 75 and 84, and 47 percent of those over 85 are likely to have the disease. The National Institute on Aging now estimates that there may be as many as 4 million Alzheimer's victims in the United States today, and by 2050 the number may reach 14 million.

These figures far exceed previous estimates and give an added urgency to finding a cause and a cure.

Accurate assessment of the number of patients is difficult because of the stigma attached to the disease. Scientists report that when they try to trace the inheritance of Alzheimer's in families, they often meet denial and resistance among family members in admitting the presence of the disease in their families.

Symptoms

The diagnosis of Alzheimer's disease can be confirmed only after death. An autopsy of the brain of an Alzheimer's victim reveals abnormal tangles of nerve fibers (neurofibrillary tangles), tips of nerve fibers embedded in plaque, and a significant shortage of the enzymes that produce the neurotransmitter acetylcholine. Research is now taking place to develop a diagnostic test for Alzheimer's in living subjects.

The symptoms of living victims usually begin with mild episodes of forgetfulness and disorientation. Table 6.7 shows the age at onset in one study, reflecting the tendency to develop the disease between the ages of 55 and 80. As the disease progresses, memory loss increases, and mood changes are frequent, accompanied by confusion, irritability, restlessness, and speech impairment. Eventually, the victim may lose all control over his or her mental and bodily functions. Alzheimer's victims survive an average of 10 years after the first onset of symptoms; some live another 25 years.

Suspected Causes

Despite intensified research in recent years, little is known about the cause (or causes) of Alzheimer's. One thing is certain: it is not a normal consequence of aging. It is, rather, a disease that either strikes older people almost exclusively, or, more likely, its symptoms appear and become more pronounced as a person grows older.

TABLE 6.7

Age at symptom onset of 439 patients with a diagnosis of Alzheimer disease only, by sex – California, June 10, 1985–December 31, 1987

Age (yrs) at symptom onset	Men No.	Men (%)	Women No.	Women (%)
Unknown	5	(3.5)	10	(3.4)
45–49	2	(1.4)	3	(1.0)
50–54	6	(4.3)	3	(1.0)
55–59	19	(13.5)	17	(5.7)
60–64	21	(14.9)	35	(11.7)
65–69	22	(15.6)	56	(18.8)
70–74	24	(17.0)	70	(23.5)
75–79	28	(19.9)	58	(19.5)
80–84	12	(8.5)	33	(11.1)
85–92	2	(1.4)	13	(4.4)
Total	141	(100.0)	298	(100.0)

Source: Alzheimer Disease - California, 1985-1987," MMWR, Centers for Disease Control, (Atlanta, GA, February 23, 1990)

There are a several theories on the cause(s) or reasons for the onset of Alzheimer's. Some theories currently being pursued by researchers are:

1. a breakdown in the system that produce acetylcholine;

2. a slow-acting virus that has already left the body before symptoms appear;

3. an environmental toxin such as aluminum;

4. a genetic (hereditary) origin.

Current research is focusing largely on heredity. Several studies have implicated two specific genes on the chromosomes of Alzheimer's patients. Other studies of twins suggest a strong role of heredity in development of the disease.

Caring for the Alzheimer's Patient

There are many victims of Alzheimer's besides the person with the disease. While medications such as tranquilizers may reduce some symptoms and occasionally slow the progression of the disease, eventually most Alzheimer's patients need constant care and supervision. Most nursing homes and health care facilities are not equipped to provide this kind of care, and if they accept Alzheimer's patients at all, they will accept only those in the very earliest stages. Even if long-term care facilities were available, they may be beyond the means of many families, and many children of parents with Alzheimer's desire (or feel a moral obligation) to care for them at home as long as possible.

No matter how willing and devoted the caregiver, the time, patience, and resources required to provide care over a long period of time are immense, and the task can become overwhelming. Recent studies show that the stress of caring for an Alzheimer's patient can affect the caregiver's immune system, making him or her more vulnerable than normal to infectious diseases. Most observers believe that the public services that most of these patients could benefit from are underused. Once again, the stigma of the illness may prevent people from seeking available help.

Alzheimer's and Architecture

The major challenges to caregivers of Alzheimer's patients are often the memory loss, disorientation, and wandering. While such patients may not be experiencing acute medical need, their crises are related to confusion states. Traditional nursing home care is not designed to deal with such disorientation and wandering, but is rather oriented to immediate physical nursing. Nor do Alzheimer's patients, at least in the early stages of the disease, require nursing care in the classical sense.

Experiments with Alzheimer's patients are currently being done with design and architecture. Some authorities suggest that home and institution design can reduce the confusion of these patients and keep them relaxed, safe, and independent as long as possible. The keeping of mementos and familiar objects from one's past, involvement in household chores, and rooms designed with toilets in sight are parts of the experiments being carried out. Alzheimer's is becoming an enormous social problem with great social and financial costs. Such research is vital to understanding the management of this disease.

The Government's Role

The prevalence of dementia (especially Alzheimer's disease), the profound emotional and financial burden of caring for its victims, and the predicted increase in the older population are putting pressure on the federal government to provide more assistance in caring for current victims and to increase funding for research to find the causes and a cure.

In 1989, the National Institutes of Health allocated $123.4 million for Alzheimer's research (up from $5.1 million in 1978). This figure is dwarfed by the estimated billions of dollars the disease costs in terms of care and lost productivity of caregivers as well as patients. As the nation's population ages, federally funded health systems will likely be severely strained.

DRUG USE AMONG THE ELDERLY

The pharmaceutical (drug) industry has revolutionized the treatment of disease in recent decades. New medications are released into the market weekly, many for treatment of conditions common to the elderly. Unfortunately, little is known about the unique physiological response of the older body to chemicals and medication. As a person ages, the body responds differently to chemicals than it would have at a younger age. Medication taken in incorrect dosages, in combination with other drugs, or on complicated schedules easily confuse the elderly person and may result in drug mismanagement. The outcome is often overdose, drug reaction, unsuccessful treatment, or even death.

A second problem for the elderly in drug therapy involves the indiscriminate use of drugs. Patients may be sedated almost routinely when a non-drug therapy may be appropriate. For example, sleep difficulties may be managed not only with medication but by exercise and the elimination of caffeine and naps.

A third medication problem of the elderly is intentional non-compliance. Hospitals report that intentional non-compliance is the second most common factor in drug-related hospitalizations. Elderly persons suffering from depression, resignation, or who have misunderstood their doctor, or who may be attempting suicide, might willfully disregard medication instructions.

Research is now increasing in the study of the elderly. Geriatrics has become an authentic medical specialty. Research in this field will likely help to develop more effective and safer treatment for the elderly.

GETTING AND STAYING HEALTHY

Because of increased educational efforts and general media coverage of health topics, older people, as well as younger, are becoming more aware of personal habits and lifestyles that may contribute to poor health and accelerate the aging process, particularly over a long period of time. Many older people are making a conscious effort to change what may be lifelong bad habits and acquire new ones that can improve their physical and mental conditions.

Among the health practices useful in helping older people to improve and maintain health are: 1) keeping mentally and physically active, 2) proper nutrition, 3) proper use of drugs and alcohol, 4) living in a safe environment, 5) eliminating smoking, and 6) participating in screening programs and tests.

The 1985 National Health Survey showed that the elderly take better care of themselves than the non-elderly. They are less likely to be overweight, smoke, drink, or experience stress than younger people. The elderly have better eating habits than their younger counterparts. They are, however, less likely to exercise (Table 6.8).

Exercise

Exercise provides many benefits for older people. It improves cardiovascular fitness and reduces the risk of heart attack, reduces calcium loss, lowers the risk and impact of high blood pressure, and helps ease the discomfort of arthritis. It also helps maintain proper weight, allows insomniacs to fall asleep more quickly and sleep better, increases energy levels, reduces and/or controls anxiety and mild depression, and improves a person's self-image.

Americans tend to exercise less as they grow older, but a study by the Gallup Organization conducted for *American Health* magazine found that between 1984 and 1986, the percentage of

TABLE 6.8

PERSONAL HEALTH CHARACTERISTICS FOR PEOPLE 18+: 1985

Characteristic (%)	Sleeps 6 hours or less	Never eats breakfast	Smokes every day[1]	Less physically active than contemporaries	Had 5 or more drinks on any one day[2]	Current smoker	30% or more above desirable weight[3]
All people 18+[4]	22.0	24.3	39.0	16.4	37.5	30.1	13.0
AGE							
18 to 29 years old	19.8	30.4	42.2	17.1	54.4	31.9	7.5
30 to 44 years old	24.3	30.1	41.4	18.3	39.0	34.5	13.6
45 to 64 years old	22.7	21.4	37.9	15.3	24.6	31.6	18.1
65+ years	20.4	7.5	30.7	13.5	12.2	16.0	13.2
65 to 74 years old	19.7	9.0	32.4	15.8	NA	19.7	14.9
75+ years	21.5	5.1	27.8	9.8	NA	10.0	10.3

SOURCE: U.S. National Center for Health Statistics, unpublished data. Based on National Health Interview Survey.

[1] Percent of current smokers.
[2] Percent of drinkers who had five or more drinks on any one day in the past year.
[3] Based on 1960 Metropolitan Life Insurance Company standards. Data are self-reported.
[4] Excludes people whose health practices are unknown.

people 50 and older who exercised (46 percent) increased more than the percentage of people in the 18 to 29 age group (20 percent). Most older people engage in low-impact exercises such as walking and swimming.

Social Ties

Contact with other people seems to be a significant factor in lowering mortality rates among persons aged 70 and older, while being married was a major factor for those between 38 and 59 (Seeman, T.E., et al., 1987, Social Network Ties and Mortality Among the Elderly in the Alameda County Study, American Journal of Epidemiology, Vol. 126, No. 4). The importance of social ties may increase with age partly because they compensate for the loss of a spouse. Membership in a church group was associated with decreased mortality in all except the 50 to 59 year age group.

THE ECONOMICS OF HEALTH AND THE ELDERLY

The growing number of elderly is focusing attention on the economic costs of health among the growing older population. The National Institute of Medicine (an advisory panel of the Federal Government) reports that each year the U. S. spends $600 million on research into the ailments of aging. The cost of treating health problems of the old exceeds $162 billion a year. Unless ways are found to prevent or treat certain illnesses, the cost of caring for the disabled elderly will likely double in the next decade. The National Institute of Medicine believes that by delaying the time an elderly person enters a nursing home by only one month, the nation could save three billion dollars a year. Americans 65 years and older make up 13 percent of the population but account for 44 percent of all days in the hospital.

While the demand grows for geriatrics information, and specialists and medical students want training in that area, most medical schools have no qualified staff to train them. Starting in 1994, only doctors who complete fellowships in geriatrics will be eligible for certification. At this time, only about 100 geriatricians are graduated each year from all U.S. medical schools.

CHAPTER VII

MENTAL ILLNESS AND ALCOHOL ABUSE
AMONG OLDER AMERICANS

As the nation ages, older Americans, their lives and their physical and mental well-being, have become topics of increasing interest. Popular magazines evaluate retirement living, while scholarly journals publish the latest research on aging. Mental illness and alcohol abuse are two major areas of concern which are receiving increased attention from the medical profession.

MENTAL HEALTH IS IMPORTANT

Mental health problems can be as debilitating as physical problems. Innumerable studies have been conducted on childhood and adolescence, and most recently, on the challenges of "mid-life." With the large population of baby boomers, the implications of aging take on new significance.

Mental illness in the elderly may be functional, organic, or a combination of the two. Functional causes can include emotional stress, neuroses, or psychoses. Organic factors may include cerebral arteriosclerosis, chemical imbalances, or tumors. Most functional disorders are curable, while an estimated 15 percent of organic disorders are curable. Many more are manageable with therapy or medication.

Geriatric medicine, or the study of the health problems of older people, is a relatively new field, and research is just beginning in this area. More information is needed on the normal mental ranges and capabilities of older people, the relationship between physiological changes and brain functions, as well as between physical illness and mental confusion. As the number of older people in the U. S. continues to increase, the demand for geriatric research and physical and mental health care resources will also grow.

PERSPECTIVES OF A LIFETIME MAY CHANGE AS PEOPLE GROW OLDER

Few personal problems disappear with old age, and many become more acute. Marital problems, which may have been controlled because one or both of the spouses were away at work, may erupt when a couple spends more time together in retirement. A possible "identity crisis" and reduced income due to retirement can aggravate a tense situation and put a strain on both husband and wife, especially if one becomes ill. Old age is often a period of regrets, of "if onlies" and "could have beens," which can lead to mutual recriminations. With the median age of retirement for Americans falling from 65 in 1970 to 62 in 1988 and the life expectancy rising, married couples can now expect to spend many years together in retirement. The transitions required are managed by most elderly couples, although some have problems.

Along with psychological adjustments to aging, the physical effects of aging must also be confronted. If good health habits and necessary medical treatment have not been maintained in early life, a person's health may decline more rapidly, and disease may become more serious. Hearing loss is common, and close correlations have been found between loss of hearing and depression. Vision loss often occurs which limits reading, watching television, driving, and mobility. Loss of sight or hearing can cause perceptual

TABLE 7.1
Suicide Rates, by Sex, Race, and Age Group: 1970 to 1988

AGE	TOTAL [1]			MALE						FEMALE					
				White			Black			White			Black		
	1970	1980	1988	1970	1980	1988	1970	1980	1988	1970	1980	1988	1970	1980	1988
All ages [2]	11.6	11.9	12.4	18.0	19.9	21.7	8.0	10.3	11.5	7.1	5.9	5.5	2.6	2.2	2.4
10-14 years old	0.6	0.8	1.4	1.1	1.4	2.1	0.3	0.5	1.3	0.3	0.3	0.8	0.4	0.1	0.9
15-19 years old	5.9	8.5	11.3	9.4	15.0	19.6	4.7	5.6	9.7	2.9	3.3	4.8	2.9	1.6	2.2
20-24 years old	12.2	16.1	15.0	19.3	27.8	27.0	18.7	20.0	19.8	5.7	5.9	4.4	4.9	3.1	2.9
25-34 years old	14.1	16.0	15.4	19.9	25.6	25.7	19.2	21.8	22.1	9.0	7.5	6.1	5.7	4.1	3.8
35-44 years old	16.9	15.4	14.8	23.3	23.5	24.1	12.6	15.6	16.4	13.0	9.1	7.4	3.7	4.6	3.5
45-54 years old	20.0	15.9	14.6	29.5	24.2	23.2	13.8	12.0	11.7	13.5	10.2	8.6	3.7	2.8	3.8
55-64 years old	21.4	15.9	15.6	35.0	25.8	27.0	10.6	11.7	10.6	12.3	9.1	7.9	2.0	2.3	2.5
65 years and over	20.8	17.8	21.0	41.1	37.5	45.0	8.7	11.4	14.0	8.5	6.5	7.1	2.6	1.4	1.6
65-74 years over	20.8	16.9	18.4	38.7	32.5	35.4	8.7	11.1	12.9	9.6	7.0	7.3	2.9	1.7	2.0
75-84 years over	21.2	19.1	25.9	45.5	45.5	61.5	8.9	10.5	17.6	7.2	5.7	7.4	1.7	1.4	1.3
85 years and over	19.0	19.2	20.5	45.8	52.8	65.8	8.7	18.9	10.0	5.8	5.8	5.3	2.8	.	.

- Represents or rounds to zero. [1] Includes other races, not shown separately. [2] Includes other age groups, not shown separately.

Source; Vital Statistics of the United States, annual, National Center for Health Statistics

disorientation which, in turn, may lead to depression, paranoia, fear, and alienation.

A constant awareness of death can also become a problem during retirement years. Although most of the elderly in good health resolve their concerns with death, some acknowledge denial and fear. How well one accepts the inevitability of death can be a major factor in shaping a person's retirement years.

MOST OLDER AMERICANS CONSIDER THEMSELVES "SURVIVORS"

Because many of today's elderly grew up during the adversity of the Great Depression of 1929 and the early 1930s, most of them do not consider themselves disadvantaged or unable to handle hardship. Instead, many older Americans consider themselves "survivors." This attitude is generally confirmed by studies concerning the mental health of older Americans which show that a small number of the elderly report the need for counseling or consider loneliness to be a very serious problem. The psychological stress of retirement and physical decline may be of concern to some retirees, but not for the majority. In fact, the fifties are more likely to be reported as the years of confrontation with one's mortality and values. Bernice Neugarten, a psychologist at the University of Chicago, reported that the physical and career shifts that occur

in their fifties cause many people to become introspective. By the time they enter their sixties and seventies, they have resolved many of their conflicts.

The loss of work and the decline in social status which often accompanies the loss of employment are two of the major causes of stress during old age. In a work-oriented society, these losses can create feelings of uselessness and lack of self-worth. Such a sense of worthlessness, if not replaced with something meaningful to the individual, can lead to depression, lowered body resistance to disease, and lack of motivation. For those living in poverty, these feelings are compounded by poor housing often in dangerous surroundings, inadequate diets, and worry over paying bills, making the elderly poor more susceptible to mental problems.

TROUBLE WITH COPING - SUICIDE

Loss of a loved one is a major cause of depression and suicide for older people. During the first year after the death of a spouse, the risk of suicide for the remaining partner is 2.5 times greater than the general population; in the second year after a loss, the risk is 1.5 times as great.

The suicide rate among the elderly began to increase in 1981, a reversal of a half-century trend. Table 7.1 shows that, in 1988, the rate of death by suicide for those over 65 was 21 per 100,000 persons, compared to a rate of 12.4 per 100,000 for the general population. White men have, by far, the highest suicide rates, with the oldest old (85+) most likely to kill themselves (Figure 7.1). The incidence among women steadily decreases with age after 55. The increase in suicide among the elderly after 1981 is not an international trend, but peculiar to the U.S.

Suicide figures for the elderly are not always reliable since many suicides are "passive." Persons who are sick, lonely, abandoned, or financially

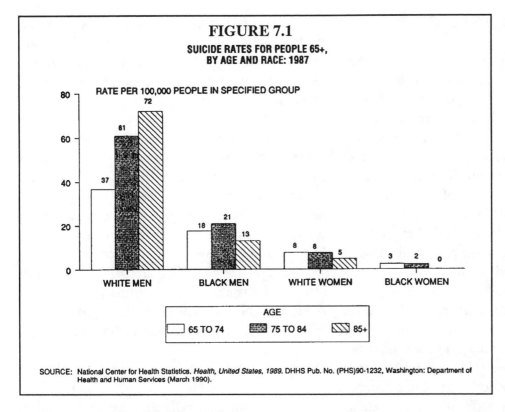

FIGURE 7.1

SUICIDE RATES FOR PEOPLE 65+, BY AGE AND RACE: 1987

RATE PER 100,000 PEOPLE IN SPECIFIED GROUP

AGE
☐ 65 TO 74   ▨ 75 TO 84   ⧄ 85+

SOURCE: National Center for Health Statistics. *Health, United States, 1989*. DHHS Pub. No. (PHS)90-1232, Washington: Department of Health and Human Services (March 1990).

troubled, have been known to starve themselves, not take medication, or mix medications dangerously. Also, the deaths counted as suicides are only those where suicide is named on the official death certificate. Other suicides may be attributed to secondary causes on death certificates. One in six elderly depressives succeeds in committing suicide in contrast to one in 100 in the general population.

The upward trend in suicide among the elderly perplexes health care experts who note that the elderly today are generally more financially secure and healthier than in past generations. The suggestion is made that the technological advances being made to extend life (or postpone death) may have resulted in longer, but less satisfying lives. Experts suggest that older males, who have the highest suicide rates, may become depressed at the loss of job, income, and power status when they retire. Some mental health professionals have noted that the concept of "rational suicide" is gaining popularity. The elderly who are faced with the possibility of extending their lives by medical technologies are weighing the costs, and more of them are

rejecting that option as society's attitude toward suicide changes.

TREATMENT OF MENTAL ILLNESS

While most mental illness among older people can be treated, an estimated 80 percent will never receive treatment. The trend has been to shift the elderly out of the mental health system and into nursing homes, but few nursing homes or intermediate care facilities are equipped to recognize or treat mental illness among the elderly. Older people placed in nursing homes often receive little or no help with mental health problems.

Mental health experts estimate that 20 to 50 percent of all people labeled "senile" have conditions that are either preventable or reversible if detected and treated early. Today, 50 percent of American medical schools have geriatric courses, but since they are elective courses (they are not mandatory), only 2 percent of medical students take them. In 1994, only doctors who complete fellowships will be eligible for certification as specialists in geriatrics. As of 1992, only about 100 geriatricians are graduated each year. In addition, many experienced doctors find older people difficult to treat because their ailments are often more complicated, and their healing process is slower and therefore less satisfying for the doctor when compared to the treatment of younger patients. This unfamiliarity and discomfort in treating the elderly may help explain why mental health services go toward treating the elderly at about half the rate of the general population.

ALCOHOLISM AND ITS EFFECTS

Alcohol is the primary substance of abuse among the older population. Studying the rate of alcoholism among the older population is often more difficult than investigating that of the general population. Because older people are less likely to be employed full-time, job-related problems due to alcohol abuse are not frequent. Since many elderly are widowed, fewer marital conflicts result from alcohol. Older people are less likely to be arrested or brought in to hospitals for alcohol abuse treatment and, once brought in, the proper diagnosis is more likely to be missed.

However, older Americans are also less likely to drink than younger Americans. The percentage of drinkers begins to decline at age 50 and drops very sharply after 60. Several factors may contribute to their overall reduction in alcohol consumption. Older people may suffer negative reactions from alcohol, and the expense may also limit their ability to purchase alcohol. Since elderly women outnumber elderly men, and women are less likely to drink than men, the total number of elderly abstainers is greater. An estimated 10 to 15 percent of older Americans abuse alcohol, although the National Institute of Alcohol and Alcoholism suspects that among those admitted to nursing homes, psychiatric facilities, and hospitals, 20 percent may be alcoholics.

Characteristics of Alcoholism Among Older People

There are three types of older drinkers. They are distinguished by the lengths and the patterns of their drinking histories. The first group are those over 60 who have been drinking most of their lives. This group has been termed "survivors" or "early onset problem drinkers." They have beaten the statistical odds by living to an old age despite heavy drinking. These are the persons likely to show numerous medical problems such as cirrhosis of the liver, brain damage, and psychological problems such as depression.

The second group has histories of "bout" drinking between periods of relative sobriety. These are called "intermittents" because they may revert to heavy alcohol use under the stress and loneliness of aging in our society.

The third group has been characterized as "reactors" or "late onset problem drinkers." The stress of later years, particularly the loss of work or a spouse, may bring about heavy drinking. These people show few of the physical consequences of prolonged drinking and fewer disruptions of their lives. More than two million American men and women over the age of 60 are believed to suffer from alcoholism. About two-thirds have had long-standing alcohol addictions; in the remaining one-third, alcohol abuse develops late in life.

Health-Related Consequences of Alcoholism

Older people generally show a decreased tolerance to alcohol. Consumption of a given amount of alcohol by an elderly person will usually produce a higher blood alcohol level than it would in a younger individual. Chronic medical problems such as cirrhosis may be present, but the need to detoxify (rid the body of poison) and to treat alcohol withdrawal problems is less common. One possible explanation may be that those who have heavily abused alcohol do not survive into old age in great numbers.

Alcohol-induced organic brain syndrome (OBS) is characterized by confusion and disorientation. In elderly alcoholics, it can be confused with, or complicated by, a diagnosis of "senility" (infirmity of body and mind associated with old age). A National Institute on Alcohol and Alcoholism (NIAAA) program diagnosed 61 percent of elderly alcoholics as having OBS. Mortality for alcoholics with OBS is higher than those without OBS.

Since elderly people take more medication than other age groups, they are more susceptible to drug/alcohol interactions. Alcohol can reduce the effectiveness and safety of many medications, sometimes resulting in coma or death. Adverse consequences of alcohol consumption in older people are not restricted to problem drinkers. Older individuals with medical problems including diabetes, heart disease, liver disease, and central nervous system degeneration do not tolerate alcohol well.

Complications In Diagnosis and Treatment

Diagnosis of problem drinking among the aging population is complicated by the fact that many psychological, behavioral, and physical symptoms of problem drinking also occur in people who do not have drinking problems. For example, brain damage, heart disease, and gastrointestinal disorders often develop in older adults but may also occur with drinking. In addition, mood disorders and depression, changes in employment, economics, or marital status often accompany aging as well as alcoholism. The resulting failure to identify drinking in an older person may aggravate health, relationship, and legal problems associated with alcohol abuse.

Older problem drinkers make up a relatively small proportion of the total number of clients seen by most agencies for treatment of alcohol abuse. Chances for recovery among older drinkers is considered good, because older clients tend to complete their therapy more often than younger clients. Problem drinkers with a severe physical disorder or persistent organic brain syndrome (OBS) are often placed in nursing homes, although the staff members have limited experience and training in treating alcoholics.

The elderly may have conceptions of alcoholism that prevent them from realizing their abuse. A 1988 Gallup poll asked if alcoholism was a disease, a mental problem, a lack of will power, or a moral weakness. A smaller proportion of the elderly respondents than the younger considered it a disease, and a proportionately higher number of elderly than younger considered alcoholism a lack of will power or a moral weakness. The theory that alcoholism is a disease originated in recent years, so that an older person may be more likely to attach a stigma or moral judgement to alcoholism.

CHAPTER VIII

CARING FOR THE ELDERLY: THE CAREGIVERS

Societies generally recognize the moral obligation of caring for their needy. In earlier, smaller communities, the care of an elderly person was usually provided by his or her family. The family often included several generations living in close contact with each other and with other members of the community who could share the responsibility and burden. In fact, until recently, family members have been the mainstay of the nation's care system.

In America today, family units are much smaller, and members may live great distances from each other. Communities are often made up of commuters and families with two working parents who may lack the time or desire to meet with their neighbors frequently. Nonetheless, in the absence of satisfactory alternatives, elder care still generally falls to the family, and more specifically, to the wife or daughter.

Table 8.1 shows the numbers of persons needing assistance with activities of daily living (ADLs). After the age of 65, the need for assistance increases sharply as the elderly grow older. Blacks were more likely to need assistance than whites or Hispanics. Table 8.2 indicates that females (68

percent) are more likely to need assistance than males (32 percent). The larger numbers of elderly women in American society result in the situation that most elderly men live in family settings (not with spouses) where they may be more easily assisted, while many elderly women live alone.

Figure 8.1 shows the distribution of ADLs among those requiring help. Forty-seven percent require help with only one activity, 32 percent with two to three activities, and 21 percent need assistance with four or more activities. (See TYPE OF CARE below.)

TABLE 8.1

ESTIMATES OF ADL/IADL DIFFICULTIES OF THE NONINSTITUTIONALIZED U.S. POPULATION AGE 65+, BY SELECTED DEMOGRAPHIC CHARACTERISTICS: 1987

Demographic characteristic	Population age 65+ (in thousands)	At least one ADL or IADL difficulty	At least one ADL difficulty	Number of ADL difficulties		
				1	2 or 3	4 or more
		Percent		Percent distribution		
Total[1]	27,909	19.5	11.4	5.2	3.8	2.4
All						
65 to 69	9,361	9.9	5.9	2.4	2.1	1.3
70 to 74	7,525	13.2	7.9	3.4	3.0	1.5
75 to 79	5,389	19.9	11.5	6.2	3.3	2.0
80 to 84	3,361	34.1	18.6	8.0	7.5	3.2
85+	2,274	56.8	34.5	15.6	9.7	9.2
Men						
65 to 69	4,097	8.0	5.0	1.7	1.8	1.4
70 to 74	3,359	9.2	6.3	2.3	2.3	1.7
75 to 79	2,167	15.5	8.7	4.2	2.7[2]	1.8
80 to 84	1,175	29.5	17.4	7.4	6.6	3.4[2]
85+	743	51.5	26.3	13.0	9.2	4.1[2]
Women						
65 to 69	5,264	11.3	6.5	2.9	2.4	1.3
70 to 74	4,165	16.5	9.2	4.3	3.5	1.3
75 to 79	3,222	22.9	13.3	7.6	3.7	2.0
80 to 84	2,186	36.6	19.3	8.3	7.9	3.1
85+	1,531	59.3	38.4	16.9	9.9	11.7
Ethnic/racial background						
White	24,135	19.1	11.1	5.1	3.6	2.4
Black	2,327	26.3	15.5	6.0	6.4	3.2
Hispanic	863	14.1	7.8	3.7[2]	4.1[2]	0.0[2]
Living arrangements						
Alone	8,985	25.5	13.3	6.5	5.2	1.5
With spouse only	12,744	13.1	7.9	3.5	2.4	1.9
With other relatives	5,631	23.1	15.6	6.7	4.8	4.1

SOURCE: J. Leon and T. Lair. *Functional Status of the Noninstitutionalized Elderly: Estimates of ADL and IADL Difficulties.* DHHS Pub. No. (PHS)90-3462 (June 1990). *National Medical Expenditure Survey Research Findings 4*, Agency for Health Care Policy and Research, Rockville, MD: Public Health Service.

[1] Includes people with other ethnic/racial background, unknown veteran and insurance status, and other living arrangements.
[2] Relative standard error is greater than or equal to 30 percent.

TABLE 8.2
DEMOGRAPHIC CHARACTERISTICS OF IMPAIRED* PEOPLE AGE 65+: 1990

	All people age 65+		Impaired people age 65+	
	Number (thousands)	Percent	Number (thousands)	Percent
Total........................	30,043	100	4,396	100
Men........................	12,469	42	1,408	32
Women	17,574	58	2,989	68

SOURCE: Lewin/ICF, unpublished data, 1990. Estimates based on data from *1984 Survey on Aging (SOA)*, *Current Population Survey (CPS)*, and Brookings/ICF *Long-Term Care Financing Model*.

NOTE: Projections assume constant age, sex, and marital status rates of disability for people living in the community.

Impaired older people are people age 65+ (living in the community) who have limitations in at least 1 of 5 activities of daily living.

CHARACTERISTICS OF AMERICA'S CAREGIVERS

The Majority Are Women

Table 8.3 shows that more than half (55.8 percent) of those caring for an elderly household member were female. More than 18 percent were daughters, 44 percent were spouses, and approximately 25 percent were in a different relationship or nonrelated. Care of the elderly person outside the caregiver's home fell even more to females (67 percent) than to males (33 percent) (Table 8.4),

FIGURE 8.1

ADL LIMITATIONS OF PEOPLE AGE 65+, BY NUMBER OF LIMITATIONS: 1987

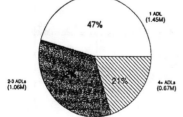

TOTAL = 3.2 MILLION PEOPLE WITH 1+ ADL

SOURCE: J. Leon and T. Lair. *Functional Status of the Noninstitutionalized Elderly: Estimates of ADL and IADL Difficulties.* DHHS Pub. No. (PHS)90-3462 (June 1990). *National Medical Expenditure Survey Research Findings 4,* Agency for Health Care Policy and Research, Rockville, MD: Public Health Service.

even though almost 67 percent of the women caregivers were also employed outside the home. Almost twice as many daughters as sons cared for their elderly parents. Over one-fourth of caregivers in 1986 were elderly themselves.

Competing Demands

As shown above, in 1986, approximately two-thirds of the female caregivers also worked outside the home. With the labor force participation rates of women increasing yearly, it is likely that the percentage is even higher today. Studies report that female caregivers have rearranged their work schedules, taken time off without pay, worked part-time, or quit their jobs to care for aging parents. Although working men report the same conflicts, fewer of them rearrange their work lives to accommodate elderly parents.

Table 8.5 displays the phenomenon of grandparents acting as parents. With drug addiction, alcoholism, divorce, and crime shattering thousands of young American families each year, large numbers of seniors find themselves raising their grandchildren.

In 1990, 29.6 percent of children living in grandparents' homes were cared for by the grandparent with no parent present. This was a decrease from 1980 when the percentage was 42.8. However, the number of children living with grandparents with the mother present increased from 40 percent in 1980 to 49.5 percent in 1990.

TYPE OF CARE

Older people vary greatly in their health and dependency needs. One measure of health status is an elder's ability to perform activities necessary for day-to-day living, such as personal hygiene and moving about. These chores also include meal preparation, housecleaning and laundry, shopping, getting to medical services, using the telephone,

TABLE 8.3

Distribution by Selected Characteristics of Persons Who Provided Assistance to a Household Member, by Type of Assistance Provided: 1986

(Numbers in thousands)

| Characteristic | Assisted with— | | | | | |
	One or more activities	Personal care	Getting around outside	Preparing meals	Doing housework	Keeping track of bills and/ or money
Total..................................	5,791	2,469	2,894	3,734	3,927	1,815
Percent...............................	100.0	100.0	100.0	100.0	100.0	100.0
Age						
Under 18 years	9.6	6.0	4.3	8.0	11.5	0.3
18 to 64 years.........................	64.2	62.9	68.2	63.5	62.5	62.0
65 years and over	26.2	31.1	27.5	28.5	26.0	37.7
Sex						
Male	44.2	32.2	46.1	42.9	47.7	29.4
Female	55.8	67.8	53.9	57.1	52.3	70.6
Race and Hispanic Origin[1]						
White.................................	83.1	80.6	83.8	81.3	82.0	80.7
Black	15.3	17.8	14.1	17.5	16.9	18.3
Hispanic origin[1]	8.1	7.7	7.9	7.9	8.0	6.3
Relationship to Recipient						
Son	11.9	7.4	10.7	10.6	11.6	7.3
Daughter	18.4	18.3	15.2	20.2	22.0	21.6
Spouse	44.0	45.0	49.0	44.6	42.3	38.2
Other relative..........................	19.9	22.9	19.2	18.4	17.9	25.8
Nonrelative	5.8	6.3	5.8	6.3	6.2	7.1
Labor Force Participation Status of Persons 15 to 64 Years						
Male						
In labor force..........................	72.7	67.4	75.4	71.5	69.7	67.7
Not in labor force	27.3	32.6	24.6	28.5	30.3	32.3
Female						
In labor force..........................	55.8	57.6	57.7	55.5	57.2	50.4
Not in labor force	44.2	42.4	42.3	44.5	42.8	49.6

[1]Persons of Hispanic origin may be of any race.

Source: <u>The Need for Personal Assistance with Everyday Activities: Recipients and Caregivers</u>, Bureau of the Census, (WDC, 1990)

TABLE 8.4

Distribution by Selected Characteristics of Persons Who Provided Assistance to Persons Outside Their Household, by Type of Assistance Provided: 1986

(Numbers in thousands)

| Characteristic | Assisted with— | | | | | |
	One or more activities	Personal care	Getting around outside	Preparing meals	Doing housework	Keeping track of bills and/or money
Total..	15,099	3,790	11,656	6,794	7,475	3,456
Percent	100.0	100.0	100.0	100.0	100.0	100.0
Age						
15 to 17 years..........................	2.4	2.8	1.2	2.4	3.9	1.3
18 to 29 years..........................	18.9	18.1	18.0	19.3	21.8	11.7
30 to 44 years..........................	31.9	33.7	32.9	33.6	34.3	31.0
45 to 64 years..........................	32.2	34.0	33.3	31.6	30.5	44.0
65 years and over	14.6	11.4	14.6	13.1	9.5	12.0
Sex						
Male	32.9	26.0	34.0	20.6	25.1	35.2
Female	67.1	74.0	66.0	79.4	74.9	64.8
Race and Hispanic Origin[1]						
White.................................	86.6	81.4	86.7	85.0	85.0	83.8
Black	12.0	17.1	12.1	13.4	13.5	14.7
Hispanic origin[1]	5.6	7.7	5.7	6.1	6.6	6.6
Relationship to Recipient						
Son	12.0	11.8	12.9	8.0	10.1	19.7
Daughter	22.2	26.9	24.2	27.7	29.3	35.2
Other relative	32.6	35.6	31.8	34.5	35.2	31.5
Nonrelative	33.2	25.7	31.1	29.8	25.5	13.6
Labor Force Participation of Persons 15 to 64 Years						
Male						
In labor force..........................	85.1	85.7	86.4	82.9	84.2	84.2
Not in labor force	14.9	14.3	13.6	17.1	15.8	15.8
Female						
In labor force..........................	66.8	65.6	66.6	67.4	67.2	63.2
Not in labor force	33.2	34.4	33.4	32.6	32.8	36.8

[1]Persons of Hispanic origin may be of any race.

Source: <u>The Need for Personal Assistance with Everyday Activities: Recipients and Caregivers</u>, Bureau of the Census, (WDC, 1990)

TABLE 8.5

Living Arrangements of Young Adults, by Sex: 1990, 1980, 1970, and 1960

(Numbers in thousands)

Living arrangement	1990	1980	1970	1960	Percent distribution			
					1990	1980	1970	1960
ADULTS 18 TO 24 YEARS								
Total............................	25,310	29,122	22,357	14,718	100.0	100.0	100.0	100.0
Child of householder[1]...............	13,367	14,091	10,582	6,333	52.8	48.4	47.3	43.0
Family householder or spouse	5,631	8,408	8,470	6,186	22.2	28.9	37.9	42.0
Nonfamily householder..............	2,252	2,776	1,066	354	8.9	9.5	4.8	2.4
Other	4,060	3,848	2,239	1,845	16.0	13.2	10.0	12.5
Male............................	12,450	14,278	10,398	6,842	100.0	100.0	100.0	100.0
Child of householder[1]...............	7,232	7,755	5,641	3,583	58.1	54.3	54.3	52.4
Family householder or spouse	1,838	3,041	3,119	2,160	14.8	21.3	30.0	31.6
Nonfamily householder..............	1,228	1,581	563	182	9.9	11.1	5.4	2.7
Other	2,152	1,902	1,075	917	17.3	13.3	10.3	13.4
Female..........................	12,860	14,844	11,959	7,876	100.0	100.0	100.0	100.0
Child of householder[1]...............	6,135	6,336	4,941	2,750	47.7	42.7	41.3	34.9
Family householder or spouse	3,793	5,367	5,351	4,026	29.5	36.2	44.7	51.1
Nonfamily householder..............	1,024	1,195	503	172	8.0	8.1	4.2	2.2
Other	1,908	1,946	1,164	928	14.8	13.1	9.7	11.8
ADULTS 25 TO 34 YEARS								
Total............................	43,240	36,796	24,556	22,483	100.0	100.0	100.0	100.0
Child of householder..............	4,986	3,194	1,958	2,038	11.5	8.7	8.0	9.1
Family householder or spouse	27,964	26,615	20,332	18,538	64.7	72.3	82.8	82.5
Nonfamily householder..............	5,618	4,411	1,215	642	13.0	12.0	4.9	2.9
Other	4,672	2,577	1,061	1,265	10.8	7.0	4.3	5.6
Male............................	21,462	18,107	11,929	10,896	100.0	100.0	100.0	100.0
Child of householder..............	3,213	1,894	1,129	1,185	15.0	10.5	9.5	10.9
Family householder or spouse	11,998	12,024	9,455	8,557	55.9	66.4	79.3	78.5
Nonfamily householder..............	3,467	2,765	775	398	16.2	15.3	6.5	3.7
Other	2,784	1,424	570	756	13.0	7.9	4.8	6.9
Female..........................	21,779	18,689	12,637	11,587	100.0	100.0	100.0	100.0
Child of householder..............	1,774	1,300	829	853	8.1	7.0	6.6	7.4
Family householder or spouse	15,966	14,591	10,877	9,981	73.3	78.1	86.1	86.1
Nonfamily householder..............	2,151	1,646	440	244	9.9	8.8	3.5	2.1
Other	1,888	1,153	491	509	8.7	6.2	3.9	4.4

[1]Child of householder includes unmarried college students living in dormitories.

Source of 1960, 1970, and 1980 data: U.S. Bureau of the Census, 1980 Census of Population, PC80-2-4B, *Living Arrangements of Children and Adults*, table 4; 1960 and 1970 Census of Population, PC(2)-4B, *Persons by Family Characteristics*, table 2, excluding inmates of institutions and military in barracks.

and financial management. Most caregivers are needed to help with household tasks (meal preparation, housecleaning, and laundry), shopping, and transportation. Assistance in using the toilet and eating is less often needed.

CAREGIVERS NEED CARE, TOO

For many people, the load of caring for an ill or disabled elderly person in addition to immediate responsibilities may, over time, become a burden. Elder caretakers may neglect their own health and needs because no one else is available to care for their elderly spouse or parent. (See also DOMESTIC VIOLENCE AGAINST THE ELDERLY-CHAPTER X.)

Experts agree that even a small break from the responsibilities of elder care can be of enormous benefit to a caregiver, and many believe that it prevents older people from being placed in nursing homes prematurely. Recent attention to the special needs of caretakers has resulted in a variety of formal and informal programs designed to provide some relief for them. While these programs generally provide services to the dependent elderly, their purpose is primarily to assist the caregiver.

Respite Care

Families caring for elderly relatives often do not think of themselves as caregivers. Although they may know they need a break, they may not know the concept of respite care, nor do they know how to arrange it. The dictionary definition of respite is "an interval of temporary relief or rest, as from pain, work, duty, etc." The Foundation of Long Term Care (FLTC) has formulated a working

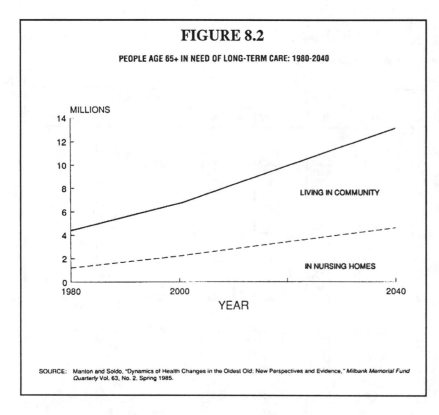

FIGURE 8.2

PEOPLE AGE 65+ IN NEED OF LONG-TERM CARE: 1980-2040

SOURCE: Manton and Soldo, "Dynamics of Health Changes in the Oldest Old: New Perspectives and Evidence," *Milbank Memorial Fund Quarterly* Vol. 63, No. 2. Spring 1985.

The estimated 1,700 adult day care programs around the country provide structured daytime programs where functionally impaired adults can receive the social, health, and supportive services needed to restore or maintain optimal functioning (Von Behren, Ruth, July 1988, Adult Day Care: A Program of Services for the Functionally Impaired, prepared for the National Council on the Aging, Inc.). While not designed specifically to aid caregivers, adult day care programs serve in a similar purpose as formal respite programs by temporarily giving the caregiver physical and psychological relief from the burden of elder care.

definition of geriatric respite care as: "the temporary supportive care of an elder who normally lives in the community with a caregiver, by a substitute caregiver, in order to strengthen and maintain the regular caregiver's well-being and ability to maintain care at home."

In 1987, the FLTC counted formal respite programs in 22 states (Hegeman, Carol R., 1989, Geriatric Respite Care: Expanding and Improving Practice, Albany, NY, The Foundation for Long Term Care). Respite care takes many forms. In some cases, the respite worker comes to the home to take care of the elderly person so that the caregiver can take a few hours for personal needs, relaxation, or rest. Respite care is also available for longer periods so that caregivers can recuperate from their own illnesses or even take a vacation.

FROM INFORMAL TO FORMAL SERVICES

At the same time that the elderly population is increasing, the segment of the general public available to provide unpaid care, generally family members, is decreasing. The once familiar extended family is becoming less common in the U.S. In addition, several other trends will continue to decrease the availability of caregivers, including more women employed outside the home, greater geographical separation of families, high divorce rates, and smaller families. Fewer caregivers will be available to more needy elderly. The result will be a higher proportion of the elderly needing to pay for formal services (See Chapter IX) (Figure 8.2).

PROVIDING HEALTH CARE FOR THE ELDERLY

Providing health care for the elderly is an important issue today, but it will become a concern of gigantic proportions as the elderly population of the United States increases. The elderly are the greatest users of health services, accounting for more than one-third of the nation's total personal health expenditures. Rising costs, demands for additional services, the development of new life-sustaining technologies, and the role of government are, and will continue to be, subjects of intense debate.

In this chapter, health care facilities, costs, and private and government health programs are discussed separately, although in reality, there is considerable overlap between the three areas.

WHERE DO THE ELDERLY GET HEALTH CARE?

Getting proper health care is difficult for many elderly people. Even if they can afford to pay for the best care, and many cannot, they may not be able to find a facility or skilled health care professionals to provide the services they need. As with living arrangements, there is no single answer to health care for the elderly; there are advantages and disadvantages to all the programs.

Home Care

In Their Own Homes

Most Americans prefer to live independently as long as possible. Many elderly people with moderate and even severe health problems manage to remain in their own homes for many years by adjusting their lifestyles, modifying their environments, taking the proper medication, and using outside resources such as relatives, friends, or paid nurses or caregivers to assist them.

At some point, most elderly people with health problems need outside assistance. If family members do not have the time or knowledge to provide the needed care, they must find someone who can. Unfortunately, there is a severe shortage of workers who are trained (and willing) to give at-home medical care. Finding a dependable, skilled caregiver is often very difficult, if not impossible.

In the Homes of Others

When chronic health problems prevent elderly people from living alone or with a spouse, they may move in with their children or other relatives. Families take ill relatives into their homes because they want to care for them as long as possible or because they cannot find suitable or affordable long-term care facilities. Having an elderly, ill parent or relative in the home can place an emotional and/or financial strain on any family, depending on the type and degree of the health problem. In Alzheimer's cases, for example, the burden can be severe and prolonged (see Chapter VI).

Hospitals

Most elderly people receive medical treatment in a doctor's office or health clinic, but the incidence of hospitalization rises with age. In 1988,

TABLE 9.1

TRENDS IN HOSPITAL USAGE BY PEOPLE 65+: 1965-1988

Year	Number of discharges (in thousands)	Discharge rate (discharges per 1,000 people)	Average length of stay per discharge (in days)
1988	10,146	334.1	8.9
1987	10,459	350.5	8.6
1986	10,716	367.3	8.5
1985	10,508	368.2	8.7
1984	11,226	401.3	8.9
1983	11,302	412.1	9.7
1982	10,697	398.8	10.1
1981	10,408	396.7	10.5
1980	9,864	383.8	10.7
1979	9,086	361.5	10.8
1978	8,708	355.4	11.0
1977	8,344	349.2	11.1
1976	7,912	339.9	11.5
1975	7,654	337.3	11.6
1974	7,185	325.7	11.9
1973	6,937	322.3	12.1
1972	6,634	315.6	12.2
1971	5,986	291.1	12.6
1970	5,897	293.3	12.6
1969	5,694	289.3	14.0
1968	5,529	285.5	14.2
1967	5,210	273.2	14.1
1966	4,909	261.7	13.4
1965	4,602	248.2	13.1

SOURCES: National Center for Health Statistics. "Trends in Hospital Utilization: United States, 1965-1986." *Vital and Health Statistics* Series 13, No. 101 (September 1989).

National Center for Health Statistics. "National Hospital Discharge Survey: Annual Summary, 1987." *Vital and Health Statistics* Series 13, No. 99 (April 1989).

National Center for Health Statistics. "1988 Summary: National Hospital Discharge Survey." *Advance Data* No. 185 (June 19, 1990).

TABLE 9.2

SELECTED CHARACTERISTICS OF NURSING HOME AND COMMUNITY RESIDENTS AGE 65+: 1985 AND 1984

Subject	Living in nursing homes 1985	Living in community 1984
Total 65+		
Number (thousands)	1,318	26,343
Percent	100.0	100.0
Age:		
65 to 74	16.1	61.7
75 to 84	38.6	30.7
85+	45.3	7.6
Sex:		
Men	25.4	40.8
Women	74.6	59.2
Race:		
White:	93.1	90.4
Black	6.2	8.3
Other	0.7	1.3
Marital Status[1]		
Widowed	67.8	34.1
Married	12.8	54.7
Never married	13.5	4.4
Divorced or separated	5.9	6.3
With living children	63.1	81.3
Requires assistance in:		
Bathing	91.0	6.0
Dressing	77.6	4.3
Using toilet room	63.2	2.2
Transferring[2]	62.6	2.8
Eating	40.3	1.1
Difficulty with bowel and/or bladder control	54.5	(NA)[3]
Disorientation or memory impairment	62.6	(NA)
Senile dementia or chronic organic brain syndrome	46.9	(NA)

SOURCE: National Center for Health Statistics. Data from the National Health Interview Survey, Supplement on Aging, 1984, and the 1985 National Nursing Home Survey, Advance Data Nos. 115, 121, 133, and 135; Series 13, No. 102; and unpublished data.

1 For nursing home residents, marital status at time of admission.
2 Getting in or out of bed or chair.
3 Although comparable data are not available, the 1984 SOA (see source) found that 6 percent of the community-resident older population had difficulty with urinary control or had urinary catheters.

(NA) Not available.

more than 10 million people age 65 and over were hospitalized. The average length of stay was 8.9 days. Despite the elderly's use of hospitals, their stays have been shortening over time. Table 9.1 shows that from 1965 to 1988, average length of stay dropped from 13.1 days to 8.9 days per hospital stay.

Part of the cost of hospitalization for most elderly patients is covered under Medicare. Since the enactment of the Diagnosis Related Groups (DRG) system (see *How Medicare Pays*, below), Medicare payments to hospitals have fallen below many hospitals' own expenses, forcing some community hospitals to close. Over 50 percent of the closures were in rural communities.

NURSING HOMES

Nursing homes are facilities that provide long-term care for those whose health problems are so severe that they require very specialized, very intensive, or prolonged treatment.

The Nursing Home Population

Approximately 5 percent of the population 65 years and older resides in nursing homes at any one time, but many more will live in nursing homes at some period during their lifetimes. Table 9.2 shows various characteristics of nursing home residents 65 years and older in 1985, the last year for which figures are available. The majority are female, over the age of 75, white, and widowed.

Length of Stay

Contrary to popular belief, most people do not go to nursing homes to die. In fact, in 1985, more than 71 percent were discharged after a median stay of 70 days. However, over 67 percent of those discharged were released to another health facility, usually a hospital or another nursing home.

The Poor May Be Less Welcome

The majority of nursing home residents are there because they suffer from serious health problems, but there are also a number whose problems would not normally require institutionalization. They are usually poor and/or have no one in the community who is able or willing to care for them.

Many, if not most, nursing homes have a limit on the number of Medicaid patients they will accept. A growing number of nursing homes will not accept Medicaid patients at all. Even patients who initially paid their own way but then run out of money may be asked to leave, even though they may still require care.

Conditions Are Slowly Improving

For some people, the prospect of living in a nursing home is terrifying. The unsavory reputation of nursing homes is not entirely undeserved. However, living conditions in these facilities have improved over the past few years. Both physical conditions and workers' attitudes towards residents have improved as a result of media attention, government regulation, demands by families, and the concern of the nursing home industry itself.

The industry recognizes the potential market of an aging population and is anxious to convey a positive image. Nonetheless, reports of abuse and inadequate health care abound. A major problem is retaining good employees. Next to child-care facilities, nursing homes have the highest employee turnover rate of any occupation, especially among unskilled and semi-skilled workers. In many areas of the country, a person can earn a higher hourly wage at a fast-food restaurant than in a nursing home. (See also Chapter X.)

Life-Care Communities

Life-care communities are residential facilities that offer elderly people a place to live (usually apartment-style) and life-time health care. Residents pay an initial entrance fee and an additional monthly fee. Presently, there are few life-care communities in the United States, but their numbers are expected to increase. For a further discussion of life-care communities, see Chapter VIII.

THE HIGH COST OF HEALTH CARE

Americans paid $604.1 billion for health care in 1989. The elderly made up 12 percent of the U.S. population, but accounted for one-third of total personal health care expenditures (i.e., money spent

TABLE 9.3
AVERAGE ANNUAL EXPENDITURES OF CONSUMER UNITS BY TYPE OF EXPENDITURE AND AGE OF REFERENCE PERSON: 1989

Type of expenditure	Amount expended				Percent distribution			
		65+				65+		
	Under 65	Total	65 to 74	75+	Under 65	Total	65 to 74	75+
Total	$30,191	$18,967	$21,152	$15,919	100.0	100.0	100.0	100.0
Housing, exc. utilities	7,394	4,475	4,960	3,795	24.5	23.6	23.4	23.8
Shelter	5,332	2,988	3,283	2,574	17.7	15.8	15.5	16.2
Operations, supplies, and furnishings	2,062	1,487	1,677	1,221	6.8	7.8	7.9	7.7
Transportation	5,751	3,092	3,695	2,248	19.0	16.3	17.5	14.1
Food	4,486	2,912	3,205	2,505	14.9	15.4	15.2	15.7
At home	2,520	1,907	2,048	1,713	8.3	10.1	9.7	10.8
Away from home	1,966	1,004	1,157	792	6.5	5.3	5.5	5.0
Health care	1,211	2,135	1,981	2,351	4.0	11.3	9.4	14.8
Utilities, fuels, public services	1,873	1,694	1,813	1,528	6.2	8.9	8.6	9.6
Cash contributions	849	1,091	1,022	1,187	2.8	5.8	4.8	7.5
Clothing	1,765	902	1,138	576	5.8	4.8	5.4	3.6
Personal insurance and pensions	2,938	740	1,059	295	9.7	3.9	5.0	1.9
Entertainment	1,614	719	843	546	5.3	3.8	4.0	3.4
Other*	2,312	1,207	1,436	888	7.7	6.4	6.8	5.6

SOURCE: U.S. Department of Labor, Bureau of Labor Statistics. "Consumer Expenditures in 1989." Press Release USDL: 90-616 (November 30, 1990).

*Includes tobacco products, alcoholic beverages, personal care products and services, reading, education, and miscellaneous expenditures.

TABLE 9.4

Per capita personal health care expenditures for persons 65 years of age or over, by source of funds, age, and type of service: United States, calendar year 1987

Source of funds and age	Total	Private	Medicare	Medicaid	Other
Personal health care					
65 years or over	$5,360	$2,004	$2,391	$645	$321
65-69 years	3,728	1,430	1,849	245	204
70-74 years	4,424	1,564	2,234	357	268
75-79 years	5,455	1,843	2,685	569	358
80-84 years	6,717	2,333	3,023	908	453
85 years or over	9,178	3,631	3,215	1,742	591
Hospital care					
65 years or over	2,248	333	1,566	110	239
65-69 years	1,682	312	1,144	67	158
70-74 years	2,062	327	1,431	93	212
75-79 years	2,536	341	1,786	127	283
80-84 years	2,935	355	2,070	161	348
85 years or over	3,231	376	2,246	198	411
Physicians' services					
65 years or over	1,107	393	671	17	26
65-69 years	974	380	558	14	22
70-74 years	1,086	389	655	17	25
75-79 years	1,191	398	745	19	29
80-84 years	1,246	407	789	20	31
85 years or over	1,262	420	792	20	31
Nursing home care					
65 years or over	1,085	634	19	395	38
65-69 years	165	94	5	60	6
70-74 years	360	205	11	131	13
75-79 years	802	461	22	292	28
80-84 years	1,603	927	37	584	56
85 years or over	3,738	2,191	56	1,361	131
Other personal health care					
65 years or over	920	644	135	123	18
65-69 years	907	644	142	103	18
70-74 years	916	644	137	117	18
75-79 years	925	644	133	130	18
80-84 years	934	644	128	144	18
85 years or over	947	645	121	164	18

NOTE: Hospital care and physicians' services include both inpatient and outpatient care.

SOURCE: Health Care Financing Administration, Office of the Actuary: Data from the Office of National Cost Estimates.

for the direct consumption of health care goods and services).

An Especially Severe Burden on the Elderly

The cost of health care in the United States is a serious problem for the elderly. Health care is the only budget expense for the elderly which is both a higher percentage of their income and a greater dollar amount than for the nonelderly (Table 9.3).

The House Select Committee on Aging estimated that in 1987 alone, over 600,000 elderly Americans were forced into poverty paying for health care for themselves or for loved ones (April 1987, The Reagan Administration's Fiscal Year 1988 Budget: Undermining the Health of Older Americans, Select Committee on Aging, House of Representatives). Before a family can qualify for some forms of assistance, such as Medicaid, a family must often "spend down," that is, spend their assets to the poverty level. This leaves the surviving spouse and families in financial ruin. Robert M. Ball, chairman of the National Academy of Social Insurance, a non-profit research organization in Washington, DC, stated that, "Sometime in the not-too-distant future, we will get a major national program protecting families against the cost of long term care. . . . I expect it to come, not primarily because of the potential power of the elderly. . . but because of pressure from those middle aged, the sons and daughters of the elderly. They are the ones most at risk."

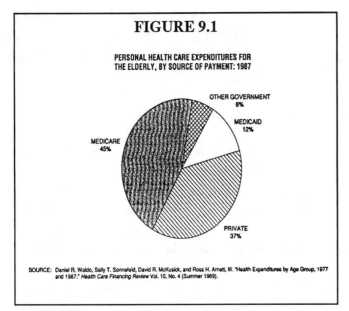

FIGURE 9.1

PERSONAL HEALTH CARE EXPENDITURES FOR
THE ELDERLY, BY SOURCE OF PAYMENT: 1987

OTHER GOVERNMENT
6%

MEDICAID
12%

MEDICARE
45%

PRIVATE
37%

SOURCE: Daniel R. Waldo, Sally T. Sonnefeld, David R. McKusick, and Ross H. Arnett, III. "Health Expenditures by Age Group, 1977 and 1987." *Health Care Financing Review* Vol. 10, No. 4 (Summer 1989).

Where Does the Money Go?

Per capita personal health care expenditures for one year for persons 65 years and older in 1987 are shown in Table 9.4. The average expenditure for the entire age group was $5,360, with hospital costs accounting for 42 percent ($2,248); physicians' services, 21 percent ($1,107); nursing home care, 20 percent ($1,085); and other expenses such as prescription drugs and medical equipment, 17 percent ($920).

Costs increased with age in all four categories of service shown in Table 9.4. People over 85 spend by far the greatest amount per capita on health care, especially nursing home care. Those 85 and over paid more than twice as much for nursing home care as did those 80 to 84, and over

TABLE 9.5

PERCENT DISTRIBUTION OF PERSONAL HEALTH CARE EXPENDITURES,
BY SOURCE OF FUNDS FOR PEOPLE 65+, BY TYPE OF SERVICE: 1987

Source of funds	Total care	Hospital	Physician	Nursing home	Other care
				Type of service	
Total spending...........	100.0	100.0	100.0	100.0	100.0
Private	37.4	14.8	35.5	58.4	70.0
Public.........................	62.6	85.2	64.5	41.6	30.0
Medicare..............	44.6	69.7	60.6	1.7	14.7
Medicaid	12.0	4.9	1.5	36.4	13.3
Other	6.0	10.6	2.4	3.5	2.0

SOURCE: Daniel R. Waldo, Sally T. Sonnefeld, David R. McKusick, and Ross H. Arnett, III. "Health Expenditures by Age Group, 1977 and 1987." *Health Care Financing Review* Vol. 10, No. 4 (Summer 1989).

22 times as much as those 65 to 69. It is often the family of an elderly person who pays for nursing home care. In 1988, an average one-year stay cost $30,000 (Three Year Report, 1986-1987-1988, WDC: the Families U.S.A. Foundation).

Where Does the Money Come From?

Almost all Americans 65 years and older receive help with at least some medical expenses from government programs such as Medicare and Medicaid (see below) and/or are covered by private medical insurance. Many elderly people mistakenly believe that Medicare will pay for all their health costs.

No single government or private program covers all health costs. It is possible, however, to obtain total financial coverage for almost all medical costs with a combination of government programs and private health insurance. The cost of such a package, though, is prohibitive for many elderly people, and qualifications for enrollment in some programs may be difficult or impossible to meet.

GOVERNMENT HEALTH CARE PROGRAMS

The United States is one of the few industrialized nations that does not have a national health care program. In most other developed countries, government programs cover almost all health-related costs, from maternity care to long-term care.

In the United States, the major government health care programs are Medicare and Medicaid. They provide financial assistance for the elderly, the poor, and the disabled. Before the existence of these programs, a large number of older Americans could not afford adequate medical care. Public funds are the major source of health care payments for people over 65 years old (Figure 9.1 and Table 9.5), providing 62.6 percent of the cost. Medicare pays heavily to hospitals and physicians, while Medicaid provided 36 percent of the cost of nursing home care.

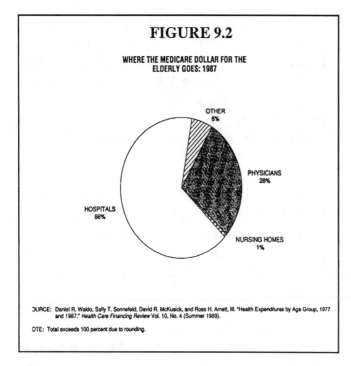

FIGURE 9.2

WHERE THE MEDICARE DOLLAR FOR THE
ELDERLY GOES: 1987

OTHER
6%

PHYSICIANS
28%

HOSPITALS
66%

NURSING HOMES
1%

SOURCE: Daniel R. Waldo, Sally T. Sonnefeld, David R. McKusick, and Ross H. Arnett, III. "Health Expenditures by Age Group, 1977 and 1987." *Health Care Financing Review* Vol. 10, No. 4 (Summer 1989).

NOTE: Total exceeds 100 percent due to rounding.

Medicare

The Medicare program, enacted under Title XVIII ("Health Insurance for the Aged") of the Social Security Act, went into effect on July 1, 1966. The program is composed of two parts:

Part A provides hospital insurance. Coverage includes doctors' fees, nursing services, meals, a semiprivate room, special care units, operating room costs, laboratory tests, and some drugs and supplies. Part A also covers rehabilitation services, limited post-hospital skilled nursing facility care, home health care, and hospice care for the terminally ill.

Part B (Supplemental Medical Insurance or SMI) is elective medical insurance, that is, enrollees must pay premiums to get coverage. It covers private physicians' services, diagnostic tests, outpatient hospital services, outpatient physical therapy, speech pathology services, home health services, and medical equipment and supplies.

In 1987, 29.9 million older persons (and more than 3 million disabled persons) were enrolled in the program, and 768 out of every 1,000 enrollees received some kind of service. The average aged enrollee received $2,945, and disabled enrollees received $3,725 in benefits. Figure 9.2 shows the distribution of Medicare funds for the elderly in 1987.

How Medicare Pays

Doctors are reimbursed on a fee-for-service basis. This system presents a number of problems: because of paperwork, lack of proper compensation, and delays in reimbursements, some doctors will not provide service under the Medicare program; the system includes incentives that may encourage doctors to treat patients in a hospital rather than a less-expensive outpatient setting; and patients may receive treatment that provides only marginal health benefits. The Bush Administration has proposed a new fee schedule to go into effect late in 1992. That schedule would substantially cut payments to doctors. Critics of the proposal claim such reductions could make it harder for elderly people to gain access to health care.

Since 1983, hospitals have received reimbursement under the prospective payment system (PPS), in which a Medicare patient is classified into one of 477 diagnosis-related groups (DRGs). There is a fixed, pre-determined payment for each DRG. Hospitals which can provide care for less than the payment keep the difference; those whose costs run over the payment must absorb the loss. There is, however, a mounting effort within the Medicare program to compensate for different market conditions, for example, between rural and urban hospitals.

Social organizations and members of Congress are concerned that PPS may be affecting the care Medicare patients receive. Since hospitals are paid a fixed reimbursement for a DRG regardless of their expenses, they may find it expedient to provide less service than necessary, to discharge a patient sooner than usual, or not to admit certain patients. Studies report that cost control measures enacted in 1983 did not result in reduced quality of care while an elderly patient was hospitalized, but

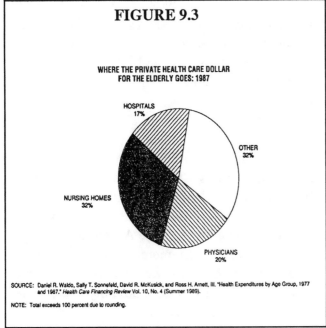

FIGURE 9.3

WHERE THE PRIVATE HEALTH CARE DOLLAR
FOR THE ELDERLY GOES: 1987

HOSPITALS
17%

OTHER
32%

NURSING HOMES
32%

PHYSICIANS
20%

SOURCE: Daniel R. Waldo, Sally T. Sonnefeld, David R. McKusick, and Ross H. Arnett, III. "Health Expenditures by Age Group, 1977 and 1987." *Health Care Financing Review* Vol. 10, No. 4 (Summer 1989).

NOTE: Total exceeds 100 percent due to rounding.

did increase the likelihood that the elderly patient would be discharged in a medically unstable condition.

The Home Health Agency Program

Some people can receive in-home health services from Medicare's Home Health Agency program. Available services include periodic, part-time skilled nursing care; physical, occupational, or speech therapy; part-time home heath aide services; medical social services; and durable medical equipment. To be eligible for services, a person must be enrolled in Medicare, be homebound, and have a plan of treatment developed by an attending physician.

Providing Only Limited Protection

Medicare does not provide complete health care coverage. It does not pay for basic medical expenses such as routine physical examinations, prescription drugs, eyeglasses, prostheses (artificial body parts), and, perhaps most importantly, long-term at-home or nursing-home care. As shown in Figure 9.3, while the elderly pay a relatively small amount of their health-care dollar for hospital expenses, which are largely covered by Medi-

care, they spend 32 cents of each dollar on nursing home care.

Older Americans are, in fact, spending a higher proportion of their incomes on health care now than they were in 1965, before Medicare and Medicaid were enacted (Three Year Study, above). The House Select Committee on Aging reports that Medicare pays less than half (48 percent) of older persons' health care costs (The Reagan Administration's Fiscal Year 1988 Budget, above). Contributing to high health costs are the skyrocketing price of health care in general and the rapid escalation of Medicare premiums, deductibles, and co-insurance.

Older people often find it difficult to locate a doctor who accepts Medicare patients. For the reasons mentioned above, some doctors choose not to participate in the Medicare program, and there is no law that says they must.

The Catastrophic "Catastrophic Coverage Act of 1988"

Concerned about the shortcomings of the Medicare program, Congress enacted PL 100-360, the Medicare Catastrophic Coverage Act of 1988 (MCCA). Among other benefits, the Act limited out-of-pocket expenses for hospital stays by eliminating the limit on the number of covered days and reducing the deductible to once a year instead of for every stay. It also provided increased skilled nursing facility care and home health care, extended hospice care from 210 days to an unlimited stay, set a ceiling on doctor bills, covered up to 80 percent of drug costs (after a $710 deductible), and provided for free mammograms every other year for women over 65.

As with any new government program, the elderly and the general public were confused about the benefits and costs of the MCCA. Debate focused on how the Act would be funded. While most of the Medicare program is financed through a broad range of taxes and government revenues (such as payroll taxes, premiums and deductibles

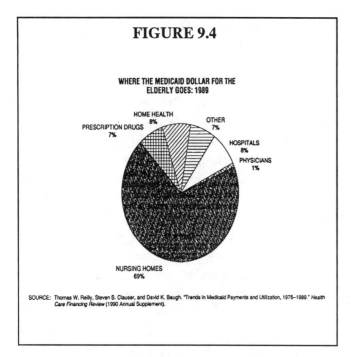

FIGURE 9.4

WHERE THE MEDICAID DOLLAR FOR THE
ELDERLY GOES: 1989

HOME HEALTH
8%

PRESCRIPTION DRUGS
7%

OTHER
7%

HOSPITALS
8%

PHYSICIANS
1%

NURSING HOMES
69%

SOURCE: Thomas W. Reilly, Steven B. Clauser, and David K. Baugh. "Trends in Medicaid Payments and Utilization, 1975–1989." *Health Care Financing Review* (1990 Annual Supplement).

negative publicity (based in part on information disseminated by companies and individuals who sell insurance and health care commodities to the elderly) prevailed, and led Congress to repeal the act in November 1989.

Medicaid

Medicaid ("Grants to States for Medical Assistance Programs," Title XIX of the Social Security Act) is a federal/state program established in 1966 to provide medical assistance to certain categories of low-income Americans: the aged, blind, disabled, or members of families with dependent children. Medicaid covers hospitalization, doctors' fees, laboratory fees, x-rays, and long-term nursing home care.

on Medicare benefits, and general revenues), the MCCA was to be paid for with a surtax imposed on Medicare recipients only. Rarely, if ever, has one segment of the population been required to finance government benefits that they alone received.

The most immediate reaction to the MCAA was an outcry among senior citizens who felt they were being unfairly taxed. Many others were already paying for insurance policies that provided similar coverage. Still others felt that the affluent few should not have to pay for care for the many poor.

The Act also had its advocates. Supporters pointed out that although the amount of the surtax varied with income and marital status, the typical tax would be about $300 per year. Fewer than 6 percent of all Medicare beneficiaries would have been taxed the maximum $800, and 60 percent would have paid no surtax at all. It was estimated that when the program was fully phased in, approximately 22 percent of the Medicare population would receive additional benefits.

Prominent legislators and powerful organizations like the American Association for Retired Persons (AARP) backed the Act, but the flood of

The elderly made up only 14 percent of all Medicaid recipients in 1988 (out of a total of nearly 23 million), but they received 35 percent of Medicaid payments. Medicaid is the principal source of public financing for nursing home care. It is the primary source of prescription drug coverage for a large number of the poor elderly. Although home health services presently account for a small share of Medicaid expenditures for the aged, it is the fastest growing expense (Figure 9.4).

Medicaid is designed to take care of those people who, through poverty or disability, cannot afford medical treatment. However, in 1989, only one-third of elderly poor were protected by Medicaid. In addition, Medicaid recipients are often required to travel long distances and endure prolonged waits before they receive attention, and the care they do receive may be less than adequate.

PRIVATE HEALTH CARE PROGRAMS

Recognizing that Medicare (or Medicaid) will not cover all of their health care costs, many people seek other types of coverage to cover the gap between Medicare benefits and actual expenses. Additional coverage, however, can be costly, and is beyond the reach of some elderly persons.

Employer Health Insurance

Persons over 65 who are actively employed may be covered under a company health care policy. Coverage may not be denied or reduced just because of age or because a person is eligible for benefits under a federal program. Even after retirement, a person may be able to receive continued coverage under a company policy.

Private Health Insurance

An increasing number of private insurance companies are offering policies (also called co-insurance or "medigap" insurance) that pay for services not included in Medicare. These policies can be expensive and, in some cases, do not provide complete coverage. Abuses in the medigap insurance field have included overlapping coverage, selling clients more coverage than they need, and deceptive advertising. Because federal and state laws set a minimum level of benefits for a supplemental policy, one such policy is enough in virtually every case. Yet, in a 1987 study, the Health Insurance Association of America found that 25 percent of such policyholders had more than one policy.

Nearly three-fourths of the elderly have some form of private insurance in addition to Medicare. Older blacks were only half as likely to have supplemental coverage as their white counterparts.

Some of the confusion and abuse surrounding medigap policies has recently been resolved by legislation (PL 101-508) allowing people reaching the age of 65 to buy medigap policies regardless of the condition of their health, provided they do so within six months after enrolling in Medicare. The protections apply to new beneficiaries, approximately 2 million people a year. While critics of the open-enrollment guarantee predict higher costs for the coverage, Representative Ron Wyden (D-Oregon), who sponsored the 1990 law, said that the regulation would standardize policies and put unscrupulous insurance operators out of business.

Health Maintenance Organizations (HMOs)

Health Maintenance Organizations (HMOs) provide health care services for a fixed prepayment. Over the last decade, an increasing number of elderly people have begun participating in HMOs. As one method of controlling growing federal spending for Medicare programs, the Health Care Financing Administration (HCFA) began contracting in 1983 with certain HMOs to provide health care for Medicare recipients. For monthly pre-paid premiums, HMO enrollees receive benefits not available under Medicare alone, such as free prescription drugs, dental care, eyeglasses, hearing aids, and hospitalization. The HMOs, in turn, receive fixed payments from the HCFA.

LONG-TERM HEALTH CARE

Perhaps the most pressing and most difficult health care problem facing America today is long-term care. Long-term care refers to services needed by individuals with chronic illnesses or mental or physical conditions so severe that they cannot care for themselves on a daily basis. Longer life spans and improved life-sustaining technologies are increasing the possibility that an individual may eventually require long-term care.

Options are Limited and Expensive

The options for good, affordable long-term care in the United States are few. One year's stay in a nursing home currently costs an average of $30,000, with actual costs ranging from $20,000 to $50,000 depending on the amount of care required. Even hiring an unskilled caregiver who makes home visits can cost over $25,000 a year; skilled care costs much more. Most elderly people, and young families, cannot afford this expense. Lifetime savings can be consumed before the need for care ends.

A Dilemma for the Entire Family

The inability to care for oneself not only affects the patient, but the entire family. Most people prefer to care for disabled parents or relatives at home as long as they can, but the emotional and financial strain on all family members can be great. As a loved one's condition deteriorates, there may come a time when home care is impossible, and the family has no alternative but to find an outside source of help.

Families who provide long-term care often sacrifice their own needs and wishes to meet the physical and financial obligations inherent in long-term care. They may delay sending a child to college, quit jobs or reduce hours, or they may exhaust their savings or go deeply into debt to pay for a nursing home or specialized care.

Little Relief from Government Programs—

Most government or "social" programs are funded with taxpayer dollars. Yet the elderly, most of whom have regularly paid taxes over a long, productive lifetime are often on their own at a time when they need financial protection the most - when they are old and sick.

The only government program that provides any substantial assistance for long-term health care is Medicaid, the Federal-state health program designed to aid the poor. In order for elderly persons to qualify for nursing home care under Medicaid, they usually must reduce their personal financial status to the poverty level. Often they reach the poverty level by spending most of their hard-earned assets and income on their nursing home care. If the person is married, his or her spouse is now not only alone, but also poor.

—or Private Insurance Policies

A few insurance companies offer policies that claim to cover long-term care. However, they may contain so many loopholes and exclusions that actual coverage is minimal. A joint study by the United Seniors Health Cooperative and the University of North Carolina investigated 77 policies offered by 21 companies in Washington, DC, and found that 61 percent of people now in nursing homes would not have received any benefits from any of the policies.

PROVIDING HEALTH CARE — A NATIONAL CONCERN

As high as they are now, health care costs continue to rise, due mainly to increased prices for services, rising demand for services, and inflation. Americans spent $666.2 billion for health care in 1990. Of that, federal health programs, including Medicare, Medicaid, public health programs, and health research accounted for approximately 29 percent of the cost. Medicare and Medicaid alone represented 10 percent of the total federal budget. By some estimates, health care will account for 15 percent of the gross national product (the total value of a nation's annual output of goods and services) by the year 2000.

How much and what kind of health care protection should be provided by the government for its constituents are on-going questions with no easy answers. The problems have not gone unnoticed by Congress. A wide array of bills have been introduced with proposals ranging from almost total protection under federal programs to almost complete dependence on the private sectors. Even after extensive debate, there is little consensus on a solution. The Catastrophic Coverage Act (see above) is a good example of the complexities of costs and benefits, as well as the effect of public opinion in such emotional issues. Most recently, insurance industry price increases have prompted discussion about national health insurance.

The federal budget, already strained with a huge deficit, cannot provide all things to all people. Priorities must be set and spending decisions made. Faced with an aging population and ever-rising medical costs, the government's and the nation's health dilemma can only worsen.

CHAPTER X

ELDERLY VICTIMS

CRIMES AGAINST THE ELDERLY

In Elderly Victims (Bureau of Justice Statistics, Washington, DC, November 1987), the most recent study of its kind, the U.S. Department of Justice reports that Americans 65 years and older are considerably less likely to be crime victims than younger people (Table 10.1). Similarly, among 1990 murder victims, the elderly were only 5 percent of the total (Table 10.2). However, the consequences of victimization can be much more severe for the elderly.

More than 60 percent of the elderly live in metropolitan areas and many of those live in inner cities where crime rates are highest. Forty-five percent of violent crimes against older people occurred at or near their homes (compared to 22 percent of younger victims), and for victims 75 years and older the rate climbed to 55 percent. For the elderly, homes and neighborhoods, where they generally spend most of their time, do not offer escape from victimization, but in fact, may make them especially vulnerable. As a group, they are more dependent on walking and public transportation which increases their exposure to possible criminal attack.

The number of crimes against the elderly and their rate of victimization (the annual average number of victimizations per 1,000 persons) between 1973 and 1986 is shown in Table 10.3. While the actual number of crimes fluctuated during that period, the victimization rate slowly declined be-

TABLE 10.1

Average annual victimization rates and number of victimizations, by age of victim and type of crime, 1980-85

	Age of victim			
	12-24	25-49	50-64	65 and older
Victimization rate				
Crimes of violence	67.5	34.0	11.3	6.0
Rape	2.0	.8	.1[a]	.1[a]
Robbery	11.4	6.0	3.4	2.7
Assault	54.2	27.1	7.8	3.2
Aggravated	18.4	9.1	2.7	1.0
Simple	35.8	18.0	5.1	2.3
Crimes of theft	126.5	82.4	46.1	22.3
Personal larceny with contact	3.5	2.8	2.8	3.1
Personal larceny without contact	123.0	79.6	43.4	19.2
Household crimes	371.4	242.6	164.4	102.7
Burglary	144.3	86.9	59.4	44.0
Household larceny	196.8	136.5	92.3	53.7
Motor vehicle theft	30.3	19.3	12.7	5.1
Number of victimizations				
Crimes of violence	3,429,700	2,703,500	375,300	154,200
Rape	99,000	65,600	4,600[a]	1,900[a]
Robbery	579,300	480,300	113,800	69,000
Assault	2,751,400	2,157,500	256,900	83,400
Aggravated	934,100	727,200	89,300	24,600
Simple	1,817,300	1,430,400	167,600	58,800
Crimes of theft	6,423,800	6,553,900	1,527,200	576,400
Personal larceny with contact	176,700	225,500	92,500	79,600
Personal larceny without contact	6,247,100	6,328,400	1,434,700	496,900
Household crimes	2,708,700	10,195,400	3,151,300	1,809,500
Burglary	1,052,300	3,651,300	1,138,300	775,100
Household larceny	1,435,600	5,733,900	1,768,800	945,300
Motor vehicle theft	220,700	810,200	244,200	89,100
Number of persons in age group[b]	50,792,400	79,549,900	33,091,500	25,811,700
Number of households in age group[b]	7,293,100	42,018,500	19,178,300	17,614,400

Note: The victimization rate is the annual average of the number of victimizations for 1980-85 per 1,000 persons or households in that age group. Detail may not add to total because of rounding.

[a]Average annual estimate is based on 10 or fewer sample cases; see Methodology.
[b]Annual average for 1980-85.

Source; Crime in the United States - Uniform Crime Reports, 1990, U.S. Department of Justice, (WDC, 1991)

TABLE 10.2

Age, Sex, and Race of Murder Victims, 1990

Age	Total	Sex			Race			
		Male	Female	Unknown	White	Black	Other	Unknown
Total	20,045	15,628	4,399	18	9,724	9,744	345	232
Percent distribution	100.0	78.0	21.9	.1	48.5	48.6	1.7	1.2
Under 18[1]	1,970	1,362	607	1	942	971	38	19
18 and over[1]	17,769	14,038	3,729	2	8,646	8,650	304	169
Infant (under 1)	264	148	116	....	159	98	5	2
1 to 4	317	176	140	1	169	136	10	2
5 to 9	118	51	67	....	61	51	2	4
10 to 14	270	162	108	....	138	125	7	....
15 to 19	2,348	1,994	352	2	918	1,376	28	26
20 to 24	3,472	2,923	549	....	1,485	1,911	52	24
25 to 29	3,405	2,736	669	....	1,519	1,818	40	28
30 to 34	2,773	2,140	633	....	1,307	1,386	53	27
35 to 39	2,051	1,615	436	....	991	994	44	22
40 to 44	1,400	1,108	292	....	774	575	29	22
45 to 49	894	695	199	....	537	322	21	14
50 to 54	586	469	117	....	358	206	17	5
55 to 59	451	332	119	....	271	159	18	3
60 to 64	422	322	100	....	261	152	5	4
65 to 69	284	195	89	....	180	98	5	1
70 to 74	234	129	105	....	167	61	5	1
75 and over	450	205	245	....	293	153	1	3
Unknown	306	228	63	15	136	123	3	44

[1]Does not include unknown ages.

Source; Crime in the United States - Uniform Crime Reports, 1990, U.S. Department of Justice, (WDC, 1991)

tween 1980 and 1986 from 31.4 to 23 per 1000 persons. As shown in Tables 10.4 and 10.5, medical treatment was required for 20 percent of elderly people 75 years or older who were victims of a violent crime such as rape, robbery, or assault, but only 13 percent of persons under 65 needed medical help. At the same time, only 11 percent of victims in the 65-to-74 year age group required medical help.

TABLE 10.3

CRIMES AGAINST THE ELDERLY—NUMBER AND RATE OF VICTIMIZATIONS, BY TYPE: 1973 TO 1986

[Covers persons 65 years old and over. Data based on National Crime Survey; see text, section 5, and Appendix III]

YEAR	PERSONAL SECTOR								HOUSEHOLD SECTOR			
	Total	Violent crimes				Crimes of theft			Total	Bur-glary	Larce-ny	Motor vehi-cle theft
		Total	Rape[1]	Rob-bery	As-sault	Total[2]	Purse snatch-ing	Pocket picking				
NUMBER (1,000)												
1973	625.8	173.0	2.4	101.3	69.3	452.8	29.8	37.1	1,467.2	748.8	644.8	73.6
1975	693.2	166.8	1.2	92.3	73.3	526.4	38.8	31.3	1,707.5	774.1	844.8	88.6
1976	737.5	166.9	1.0	75.1	90.8	570.6	26.3	45.1	1,713.3	742.4	880.5	90.4
1977	698.7	168.3	2.7	75.8	89.8	530.4	24.1	30.0	1,683.4	754.2	871.0	58.2
1978	709.3	180.6	2.4	69.5	108.6	528.7	29.4	37.2	1,618.8	703.9	833.9	81.0
1979	648.1	138.9	.9	58.0	79.9	509.2	38.5	44.6	1,718.2	718.7	917.6	79.9
1980	768.6	165.9	2.8	82.5	80.7	602.7	33.4	56.2	1,826.5	802.1	960.1	64.3
1981	752.6	195.1	2.7	99.3	93.1	557.5	21.1	51.6	2,109.6	921.1	1,077.2	111.3
1982	738.7	146.3	1.5	68.0	76.8	592.4	34.0	45.6	1,744.3	709.4	948.4	88.5
1983	741.6	144.2	1.4	63.9	78.9	597.3	32.8	53.8	1,695.1	754.2	860.2	80.7
1984	660.1	128.7	1.4	57.5	69.8	531.4	21.9	42.9	1,822.1	669.5	851.6	101.0
1985	627.6	122.7	1.5	42.8	78.4	504.9	14.1	57.8	1,455.7	609.5	758.4	87.8
1986	639.2	124.8	-	46.1	78.7	514.4	19.4	49.4	1,477.4	628.4	767.9	81.1
RATE[3]												
1973	30.7	8.5	.1	5.0	3.4	22.2	1.5	1.8	107.9	55.1	47.4	5.4
1975	32.3	7.8	.1	4.3	3.4	24.5	1.8	1.5	118.7	53.8	58.7	6.2
1976	33.8	7.6	.1	3.4	4.1	26.0	1.2	2.1	115.8	50.2	59.5	6.1
1977	31.1	7.5	.1	3.4	4.0	23.6	1.1	1.4	110.9	49.7	57.4	3.8
1978	30.9	7.9	.1	3.0	4.7	23.0	1.3	1.6	104.0	45.2	53.6	5.2
1979	27.5	5.9	(z)	2.5	3.4	21.6	1.6	1.9	107.5	45.0	57.5	5.0
1980	31.4	6.8	.1	3.4	3.3	24.6	1.4	2.3	109.8	48.2	57.7	3.9
1981	30.1	7.8	.1	4.0	3.7	22.3	.8	2.1	124.2	54.2	63.4	6.6
1982	28.9	5.7	.1	2.7	3.0	23.2	1.3	1.8	100.5	40.9	54.5	5.1
1983	28.4	5.5	.1	2.5	3.0	22.9	1.3	2.1	94.8	42.2	48.1	4.5
1984	24.9	4.9	.1	2.2	2.6	20.0	.8	1.6	88.4	36.5	46.4	5.5
1985	23.1	4.5	.1	1.6	2.9	18.6	.5	2.1	78.1	32.7	40.7	4.7
1986	23.0	4.5	-	1.7	2.8	18.5	.7	1.8	79.2	33.3	40.8	4.3

- Represents zero or rounds to zero.   Z Less than .05.   [1] Yearly estimates are based on fewer than 10 sample cases.
[2] Includes personal thefts without contact not shown separately.   [3] Rate per 1,000 persons 65 years old and over; and per 1,000 households headed by persons 65 years old and over.

Source: U.S. Bureau of Justice Statistics, Crime and the Elderly, December 1981 and unpublished data.

Older People Are Considered Easy Prey

Because of their physical limitations, criminals often consider older people easy prey. The elderly usually do not resist a criminal attack. They are aware that they lack the strength to repel a younger aggressor and that they are particularly susceptible to broken bones and fractured hips which could cripple them permanently.

Older people are also a favorite target of fraud and confidence schemes. They often live on fixed incomes and limited savings. "Get rich" schemes that promise economic security for their remaining years can appear very attractive.

The Emotional Impact of Crime

Speaking before the House Select Committee on Aging, Irwin I. Kimmelman, Attorney General for the New Jersey Department of Law and Safety, noted that it is not the number of crimes, but the "terrible and tragic impact that crime has on [the elderly] that is significant. Crime simply causes much more fear among the elderly and has a far more deleterious [harmful] impact on the quality of their lives."

TABLE 10.4		
Attacks, injuries, medical treatment, and hospital care received by violent crime victims, by age of victim, 1973-85		
	Percent of victims	
Crime characteristics	Under 65	65 and older
Victim was:		
Attacked	47%	46%
Injured	30%	29%
Serious	6	7
Minor	24	22
Received any medical care	13%	14%
Hospital care	7	8

Note: Serious injuries are: broken bones, loss of teeth, internal injuries, loss of consciousness, rape or attempted rape injuries, or undetermined injuries requiring 2 or more days of hospitalization. Minor injuries are: bruises, black eyes, cuts, scratches, swelling, or undetermined injuries requiring less than 2 days of hospitalization.

Source: Elderly Victims, Bureau of Justice Statistics, (WDC, 1987)

TABLE 10.5		
Attacks, injuries, medical treatment, and hospital care received by elderly violent crime victims, 1973-85		
	Percent of victims	
Crime characteristics	65-74	75 and older
Victim was:		
Attacked	42%	52%
Injured	26%	35%
Serious	6	8
Minor	20	27
Received any medical care	11%	20%
Hospital care	7	10

Note: Serious injuries are: broken bones, loss of teeth, internal injuries, loss of consciousness, rape or attempted rape injuries, or undetermined injuries requiring 2 or more days of hospitalization. Minor injuries are: bruises, black eyes, cuts, scratches, swelling, or undetermined injuries requiring less than 2 days of hospitalization.

Source: Elderly Victims, Bureau of Justice Statistics, (WDC, 1987)

Crimes against the elderly are particularly cruel because older people are often less resilient than younger people. They may not be able to cope with the trauma and "get on with their lives," especially if their lives are static, with few new pleasant experiences to replace the memory of painful ones. Even so-called non-violent crimes such as purse snatching, vandalism, and burglary can be devastating. Stolen or damaged articles and property are often irreplaceable, either because of the sentimental or monetary value.

Once victimized, older people may become obsessed with the idea that they will be victimized again (a not uncommon reaction in many younger victims, as well). They may develop a negative outlook on life and even alter their lifestyle, as they resort to extreme precautionary measures. Sixty-two percent of violent crimes against the elderly between 1973 and 1985 were committed by a person who was a total stranger to them (Table 10.6). Fear of strangers can make an elderly person reluctant to leave his or her home.

CRIME IS A GREATER REALITY FOR ELDERLY BLACKS

Elderly blacks are far more likely than whites to live in an inner city, where the crime rate is significantly higher. Table 10.7 shows victimization rates for persons aged 65 and older by race and other characteristics. The victimization rate for elderly blacks between 1973 and 1985 was greater than for elderly whites for all crimes of violence, household crimes, and crimes of theft. The only exception was personal larceny without contact, and there the difference was very small. The elderly black victimization rates for robbery and aggravated assault (an attack for the purpose of inflicting severe bodily injury), which are considered crimes of violence, and personal larceny with contact, which is a crime of theft, were more than twice the rate for elderly whites.

TREATMENT BY THE COURTS

Elderly victims are often the most poorly treated clients of the criminal justice system. Because of physical impairments such as poor hearing and vision and slowness of movement and speech, older persons can meet with impatience and insensitivity when they attempt to report a crime against themselves. This kind of treatment only adds to their frustration and sense of helplessness.

Victim compensation for crimes against the elderly is currently provided on the state level, and amounts vary from state to state. Most states

81

TABLE 10.6

Relationship of offenders to victim in crimes of violence, by age of victim and type of crime, 1973-85

Type of crime and age of victim	Total	Percent of victimizations involving offenders who were:					
		Relatives	Well known, not relatives	Casual acquaintances	Known by sight only	Not known at all	Relationship not ascertained[a]
Crimes of violence[b]							
Under 65	100%	7%	17%	15%	10%	47%	4%
65 and older	100	5	11	6	6	62	9
Robbery							
Under 65	100	4	10	8	6	68	4
65 and older	100	1[c]	4	2	2	82	9
Assault							
Under 65	100	8	19	16	11	42	4
65 and older	100	9	17	10	10	46	8

Note: Percentages may not total to 100% because of rounding. The closest relationship to any offender was used to classify multiple-offender victimizations.
[a]Includes responses of "don't know."
[b]Includes data on rape, not shown as a separate category.
[c]Estimate is based on 10 or fewer sample cases; see Methodology.

Source: Elderly Victims, Bureau of Justice Statistics, (WDC, 1987)

compensate for medical, counseling, and physical therapy expenses associated with the crime and reimburse for lost wages, loss of support to dependents, and for funeral expenses.

DOMESTIC VIOLENCE AGAINST THE ELDERLY*

Domestic violence against the elderly is a phenomenon that has only recently gained public attention. It is impossible to determine exactly how many elderly people are the victims of domestic violence. As with child abuse, the number of actual cases is larger than the number of reported cases. Even when it is reported, definitions of abuse and reporting methods vary greatly both between states and among different government agencies. Several authorities have concluded that more than one million elderly persons suffer from some form of domestic abuse every year.

Types of Mistreatment

Research on domestic elder abuse is still in its infancy, but studies conducted over the past 10 years have revealed several recurring forms of abuse. Dr. Richard L. Douglass, in Domestic Mistreatment of the Elderly - Toward Prevention (1988, prepared for the American Association of Retired Persons, Washington, DC), identifies the following categories of mistreatment:

Passive Neglect - unintentional failure to provide basic necessities such as food and medical care due to caregiver indifference, inability, or ignorance.

Psychological Abuse - inflicting mental anguish by, for example, name calling, humiliation, making threats, or isolation.

Material (Financial) Abuse - exploiting or misusing an olderperson's money or assets.

Active Neglect - intentional failure to provide needed care which includes food deprivation, deliberate abandonment, not providing glasses or dentures, denying access to health-related services.

Physical Abuse - inflicting physical pain or injury.

Stress

Most experts agree that stress is a major contributing factor in abuse of the elderly. Meeting the daily needs of a frail and dependent elderly relative may be overwhelming for some family members. When the elderly person lives in the same household as the caregiver, crowding, differences of opinion, and constant demands often add to the strain of providing physical care. If the elderly person lives in a different house, the added pressure of having to commute between two households, doing extra housekeeping chores, and being on call at a moment's notice may be too much for the caretaker to cope with.

---

* For a complete discussion of domestic violence against the elderly, see Domestic Violence — No Longer Behind the Curtains, Information Plus, Inc., 1991, Wylie, TX.

TABLE 10.7

Victimization rates of persons age 65 and older, by sex, race, and marital status of victim and by type of crime, 1973-85

| | Sex | | Race | | Marital status | | | | |
Type of crime	Male	Female	White	Black	Married	Widowed	Never married	Divorced	Separated
Crimes of violence[a]	9.3	5.5	6.4	12.8	5.5	7.0	9.4	20.1	31.6
Robbery	4.1	2.5	2.7	7.3	2.1	3.5	5.7	9.4	14.8
Aggravated assault	1.7	.9	1.1	2.3	1.1	1.2	1.4	2.4	5.1
Simple assault	3.4	1.9	2.5	2.9	2.3	2.3	2.2	7.7	11.7
Crimes of theft	27.4	19.9	22.7	25.3	22.3	20.9	28.5	42.2	44.0
Personal larceny with contact	2.4	3.6	2.7	6.8	2.0	3.8	6.7	6.0	10.5
Personal larceny without contact	25.0	16.3	20.0	18.6	20.3	17.2	21.8	36.1	33.5
Household crimes	117.0	100.3	105.2	151.5	111.8	104.8	85.5	163.3	136.2
Burglary	48.4	48.0	46.0	70.7	43.6	50.4	45.4	75.1	76.1
Household larceny	62.0	48.7	54.3	73.0	61.6	50.4	36.6	80.4	58.1
Motor vehicle theft	6.6	3.6	5.0	7.7	6.6	4.0	3.5	7.7	2.0[b]

Note: Detail may not add to total because of rounding. Characteristics of victim are used for crimes of violence and theft; characteristics of head of household are used for household crimes. Victimization rates are average annual rates per 1,000 persons (households).

[a] Includes data on rape, not shown as a separate category.
[b] Estimate is based on 10 or fewer sample cases; see Methodology.

Source: Elderly Victims, Bureau of Justice Statistics, (WDC, 1987)

The Financial Burden

In many cases, caring for an elderly person places a financial strain on a family. Elderly parents may need financial assistance at the same time that their children are raising their own families. Instead of an occasional night out, a long-awaited vacation, or a badly needed new car, young families may find themselves paying for ever-increasing medical care, prescription drugs, physical aids, special dietary supplements, extra food and clothing, or therapy. Saving for their children's college education, for a daughter's wedding, or for retirement becomes difficult. Resentment can build quickly, and it can lead to emotional if not outright physical abuse.

The Cycle of Abuse

Some experts believe that persons who abuse an elderly parent or relative were themselves abused as children. Dr. Suzanne K. Steinmets, Director for Resources for Older Americans at the University of Delaware and a recognized expert on domestic violence, found such a pattern in her studies of elderly abusers. She found that only one out of 400 children treated non-violently when they were raised attacked their elderly parents; one out of two children who were violently mistreated as they grew up abused their elderly parents (Elder Abuse: The Hidden Problem, Washington, DC, 1980). Chicago psychiatrist Mitchell Messer, who treats adults who care for elderly parents, notes, "We find parent beatings when the parents set the example of solving problems through brutality when the children were growing up. . . . The response is simply following the example his parents set." As adults, formerly abused children often have financial, marital, or drug problems which they blame on their parents and which make them even more abusive.

Invasion of Privacy

Most Americans believe that home is a place a person should be able to call his or her own. When that home must be shared, there is an inevitable loss of a certain amount of control and privacy. Movement may be restricted, habits may need to be changed, rivalry frequently develops between generations over decision-making, and young children may play the adults against each other to get what they want. Frustration and anxiety result as both parent and supporting child try to suppress angry feelings, sometimes unsuccessfully.

83

Loss of Freedom

An adult child may be obligated to care for an adult parent just at the time when his or her own children are leaving home. The resentment of being once again tied to the home, this time to care for a frail, perhaps bedridden parent, pushes many caregivers to the breaking point. To make matters worse, they may feel guilty and ashamed of their negative feelings. The dependent parent, in turn, often senses this resentment and may respond by withdrawing or becoming even more demanding. According to Dr. Richard Douglass (see study above), the average length of home care for a severely dependent person who is over 70 is between five and six years. In many cases it is much longer.

Additionally, an adult child (usually a daughter) with children still in the home may find herself in the position of caring also for an elderly parent. The term "sandwich generation" has been coined to describe these caregivers who may have anticipated enjoyment of their own interests at exactly the same time they are required to assume care for an aged parent. At the same time, it should be emphasized that the overwhelming majority of caregivers who suffer these many types of stress do not abuse the elderly people they are caring for.

Reverse Dependency

A study of 42 physically abused elderly persons and 42 non-abused elderly (the control group) by Dr. Karl Pillemer indicates that people who abuse an elderly person may actually be quite dependent on that person (December 1985, "The Dangers of Dependency: New Findings on Domestic Violence Against the Elderly," Social Problems, Vol. 33, No. 2). Dr. Pillemer found that the abused elderly in the study were no more likely to have had a recent decline in health or be seriously ill or hospitalized in the previous year than the non-abused elderly - in fact, as a group, the abused elderly were more self-sufficient in preparing meals, doing ordinary housework, and climbing stairs than were the non-abused elderly.

On the other hand, the abusing caregivers were found to be more dependent on their victim for housing, financial assistance, and transportation than were the caregivers in the control group. They appeared to have "few resources [and] were frequently unable to meet their own basic needs. . . . Rather than having power in the relationship, they are relatively powerless." From these findings, Dr. Pillemer concluded that abusing caregivers may not always be driven to violence by the physical and emotional burden of caring for a seriously disabled elderly person but may have emotional problems of their own that can lead to violent behavior.

The Abusive Spouse

Dr. David Finkelhor of the Family Violence Research Program of the University of New Hampshire, along with Dr. Karl Pillemer, have concluded that most elderly people are abused not by adult children but by spouses (November 1986, "The Prevalence of Elder Abuse: A Random Sample Survey," Durham, NH). Spousal abuse is possibly the result of the fact that more elderly people live with a spouse than with an adult child, so the opportunity for spousal violence is greater. Violence against an elderly spouse may be the continuation of an abusive relationship that began years earlier - abuse does not end simply because a couple gets older. Sometimes, however, the abuse (almost always by the husband toward the wife) may not begin until later years, in which case it is often associated with alcohol abuse, unemployment, post-retirement depression, and/or loss of self-esteem.

Intervention and Prevention

Most states (and the District of Columbia) now have laws dealing specifically with adult abuse, but as with laws concerning child abuse and spousal abuse among younger couples, they are sometimes ineffective. The laws and the enforcing agencies vary from state to state and even from county to county within a given state. No standard definition of abuse exists among enforcement agencies. In many cases, authorities cannot legally intervene and terminate an abusive condition unless a report is filed, the abuse is verified, and the victim files a formal complaint. An elderly person could understandably be reluctant, physically unable, or too fearful to accuse or prosecute an abuser.

The best way to stop elder abuse is to prevent its occurrence. As noted above, researchers have identified specific situations where abuse is likely to occur and the type of person that is likely to be an abuser. Older people who know that they will eventually need outside help should carefully analyze the potential difficulties of living with a child and, if necessary and possible, make alternate arrangements. In any event, they should take care to protect their money and assets to ensure that they cannot be easily taken over by someone else.

Young families or persons who must care for an older person, voluntarily or otherwise, must realize that their frustration and despair do not have to result in abuse. Social agencies can often work with families to help relieve anger and stress. Sometimes there are ways to offset the financial burden of elder care, for example, through tax deductions or subsidies for respite care (see Chapter IX).

INSTITUTIONAL ABUSE

Abuse of the elderly also occurs outside the private home in nursing homes charged with the care of the aged and ill patient. An April 1990 report of the Office of Inspector General, "Resident Abuse in Nursing Homes," found that:

1. Abuse is a problem in nursing homes;

2. Physical neglect, verbal and emotional abuse are the most frequent types of abuse;

TABLE 10.8

PRIMARY ABUSER OF NURSING HOME RESIDENTS ACCORDING TO RESPONDENTS

ABUSER → / PROBLEM	NURSING HOME STAFF	MEDICAL PERSONNEL	OTHER PATIENTS	FAMILY OR VISITORS
PHYSICAL ABUSE	89 %	3 %	17 %	3 %
MISUSE OF RESTRAINTS	56 %	48 %	1 %	2 %
VERBAL/EMOTIONAL ABUSE	89 %	7 %	13 %	10 %
PHYSICAL NEGLECT	88 %	15 %	0 %	3 %
MEDICAL NEGLECT	25 %	80 %	1 %	3 %
VERBAL/EMOTIONAL NEGLECT	84 %	6 %	2 %	21 %
PERSONAL PROPERTY ABUSE	79 %	1 %	18 %	15 %

NURSING HOME STAFF — ALL STAFF EXCLUDING RNS, LVNS AND DOCTORS

MEDICAL PERSONNEL — LICENSED NURSES AND PHYSICIANS

RESPONDENTS = 206 ◯ PRIMARY ABUSER OF NURSING HOME RESIDENTS

TOTAL PERCENT MAY EXCEED 100 PERCENT AS SOME RESPONDENTS GAVE MORE THAN ONE PRIMARY ABUSER IN A CATEGORY.

Source: Resident Abuse in Nursing Homes - Understanding and Preventing Abuse, U.S. Department of Health and Human Services, (WDC, 1990)

3. Nursing home staff, medical personnel, other patients and family or visitors also may be abusive; however, aids and orderlies are the main abusers in all categories except medical neglect, where medical personnel are deemed responsible (See Table 10.8);

4. Nursing home staff often lack training to handle stressful situations;

5. Staff training and certification will help to deter abuse.

The recommendations made by that report include additional training for personnel, reporting of abusive personnel and incidents of abuse, and education of residents in dealing with such problems.

In an effort to improve the quality of care and eliminate abuse in nursing homes, government regulations and laws are requiring greater supervision of nursing homes. In 1987, President Ronald Reagan signed into effect a landmark law, the Omnibus Budget Reconciliation Act (P.L. 100-203), to protect patient rights and treatment. The law went into effect October, 1990. Compliance with the law varies from state to state and from one nursing facility to another. Families are increasingly filing (and winning) court suits against irresponsible nursing facilities.

CHAPTER XI

TRENDS AND PROJECTIONS

As indicated in preceding chapters, aging in America has become the aging of America. Since by the year 2030 one-third of the population will be over 55, the aging of the nation means definite shifts in its economic, political, and demographic makeup.

"GRAY POWER" — A POLITICAL BLOC?

People in the 55 to 74 age group vote more than any other group. The growing number of Americans in this age group will make a sizeable political impact. Organizations such as the American Association of Retired Persons (AARP) already exercise considerable influence in lobbying and in educating political leaders on certain issues. That influence will undoubtedly grow as lawmakers respond to the voting power of the elderly, who are among the most active voters.

Issues such as age discrimination, quality of care in nursing facilities, medigap coverages, and reform in pension plans and Social Security are vital topics for older Americans. Other areas that must be addressed are expansion in senior citizen benefits and discounts, changes in traffic and architectural design, and implications posed by medical technology.

A SHIFTING ECONOMY

Increasing numbers of aged Americans will alter the work force as industry seeks both to accomodate the elderly and to profit from their resources. The first baby boomer turns 60 in 2006, so most of the changes in the work force will not occur until late in the first decade of the next century. At the same time, the already growing retirement-related industries are expected to increase. Businesses will seek to fill the needs of the older population. Health and fitness concerns will demand additional geriatricians, physical therapists, cataract and hearing specialists, and nutritionists. Already a market has emerged for "beepers," remote control and monitoring devices for those living alone. Comfort and security become more important as people age; they are more likely to purchase products based on comfort, value, and ease of use. Older adults are more likely to be attracted to products and appliances that they believe to be "user friendly," that is, easily understandable and useable. Many recreation centers and community programs have expanded their post-55 services. The hotel and travel industries offer discounts and accomodations tailored to the needs of the increasingly mobile mature market and its considerable discretionary income. Restaurants have responded by preparing smaller portions and lowering prices on senior citizen menus.

Certain communities are luring older people in an effort to combat economic decline. Many rural towns have found it profitable to attract retirees, with their pensions and savings, who make fewer demands on expensive local public services such as schools.

As the nation's population grows older, more older persons are on the streets both as drivers and as pedestrians. Insurance companies are now offering reduced premiums to the elderly who enroll in driver's safety classs. Highway safety engineers are studying the design of intersections and signs in an effort to keep older citizens driving safely as long as possible.

Universities report an increase in the age of students. This "graying" of the campus reflects the influx of older students, some of whom are elderly Americans, in response to a changing job market as well as greater mobility and vitality among older people. This new population has prompted changes in college life, including more flexible class schedules and greater accountability from faculty since the older student is known to be more demanding.

Another institution affected by the age of our society is the penal system. Prisons report changing needs as its inmate population grows older. These prisoners are expected to require additional medical and psychological services that will further stretch the already exorbitant cost of inmate care.

The increasing complexity of American society and the growing needs of the aged who have no one else to assist them have led to the emergence of two new types of service professions-private care managers and claims companies-that provide, for a fee, what family members may once have provided. Private care (or case) managers are social workers who provide one-to-one assistance in arranging care or housing or in referral to government agencies that serve the elderly. Medical claims companies assist the aged in filling out the complicated insurance forms - for a charge or a percentage of the benefits received.

According to Aging in America -Trends and Projections-1991 (1991,WDC), prepared by the U.S. Senate Special Committee on Aging, in conjunction with the AARP, the Federal Council on the Aging, and the United States Administration on Aging, in 1980, twenty-eight percent of all American men over 65 were veterans. By the year 2000, sixty percent of all elderly men will be veterans who are eligible for veteran's benefits. Due to the growth in the number and proportion of older veterans, a strain on the Veterans Administration medical system will result, and put further pressure on community resources (Figure 11.1).

ALTERNATIVE LIFESTYLES

The increasing diversity of the aging population and the shortage of caregivers of long term care for them will demand new ways of living. The disabled will still need nursing facilities. Hospices are increasingly emerging as humane solutions to terminal illness, especially in light of recent medical technology and in the ethical issues of death and dying.

Less physically impaired elderly may need new kinds of home care or adult day care. Acces-

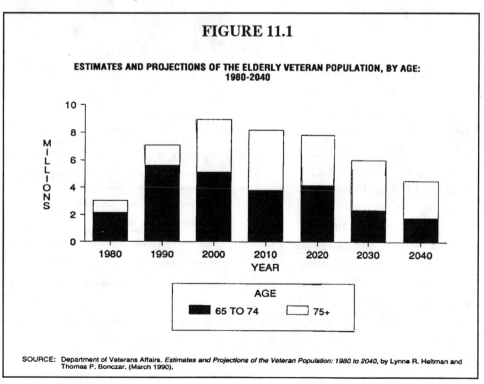

FIGURE 11.1

ESTIMATES AND PROJECTIONS OF THE ELDERLY VETERAN POPULATION, BY AGE: 1980-2040

SOURCE: Department of Veterans Affairs. *Estimates and Projections of the Veteran Population: 1980 to 2040*, by Lynne R. Heltman and Thomas P. Bonczar. (March 1990).

87

sory apartments, shared housing and housing designed for the elderly will become more available. Home equity conversion and reverse mortgages, in which an aged person "sells back" his mortgage in a gradual liquidation (as opposed to selling the house and living on the proceeds or leaving an estate for payment of debts upon one's death) may ease the housing problem for some elderly.

For the economically disadvantaged elderly, the possibility of homelessness may be all too real. American society is increasingly challenged by an economy that forces growing numbers of aged, infirm, mentally impaired, and unemployed residents to live in its streets.

"QUITTING TIME" - RETIREMENT BECOMES AN INSTITUTION

A longer lifespan gives people the opportunity to spend more time in all the major activities of life-work, education, and retirement. <u>Aging in America - Trends and Projections-1991</u> reports that as more and more people leave the work force before 65, retirement has become as much an institution in American life as the other two major stages of life - education and work (Figures 11.2 and 11.3). For those who choose to retire, the retirement years assume increasing importance. For older persons who need or want to continue working, unemployment and age discrimination pose serious hardships.

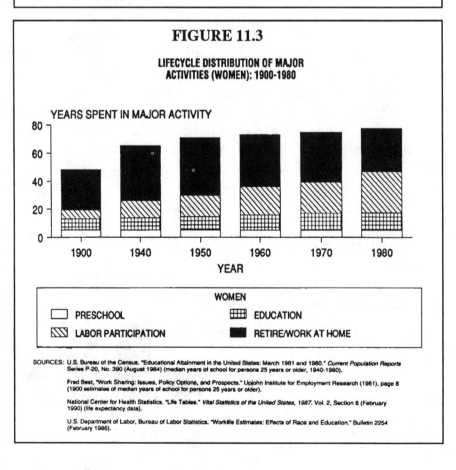

FIGURE 11.2

LIFECYCLE DISTRIBUTION OF MAJOR ACTIVITIES (MEN): 1900-1980

YEARS SPENT IN MAJOR ACTIVITY

MEN
- □ PRESCHOOL
- ▨ LABOR PARTICIPATION
- ▦ EDUCATION
- ■ RETIRE/WORK AT HOME

SOURCES: U.S. Bureau of the Census. "Educational Attainment in the United States: March 1981 and 1980." *Current Population Reports* Series P-20, No. 390 (August 1984) (median years of school for persons 25 years or older, 1940-1980).

Fred Best, "Work Sharing: Issues, Policy Options, and Prospects." Upjohn Institute for Employment Research (1981), page 8 (1900 estimates of median years of school for persons 25 years or older).

National Center for Health Statistics. "Life Tables." *Vital Statistics of the United States, 1987.* Vol. 2, Section 6 (February 1990) (life expectancy data).

U.S. Department of Labor, Bureau of Labor Statistics. "Worklife Estimates: Effects of Race and Education." Bulletin 2254 (February 1986).

FIGURE 11.3

LIFECYCLE DISTRIBUTION OF MAJOR ACTIVITIES (WOMEN): 1900-1980

YEARS SPENT IN MAJOR ACTIVITY

WOMEN
- □ PRESCHOOL
- ▨ LABOR PARTICIPATION
- ▦ EDUCATION
- ■ RETIRE/WORK AT HOME

SOURCES: U.S. Bureau of the Census. "Educational Attainment in the United States: March 1981 and 1980." *Current Population Reports* Series P-20, No. 390 (August 1984) (median years of school for persons 25 years or older, 1940-1980).

Fred Best, "Work Sharing: Issues, Policy Options, and Prospects." Upjohn Institute for Employment Research (1981), page 8 (1900 estimates of median years of school for persons 25 years or older).

National Center for Health Statistics. "Life Tables." *Vital Statistics of the United States, 1987.* Vol. 2, Section 6 (February 1990) (life expectancy data).

U.S. Department of Labor, Bureau of Labor Statistics. "Worklife Estimates: Effects of Race and Education." Bulletin 2254 (February 1986).

What do the elderly do with their time? Men are likely to increase the amount of time spent on traditional female tasks, such as cooking and housework. In addition to travel, study, and socializing, the media claim the largest share of the elderly person's day, with television consuming more than half the newly-freed time. (See Table 11.1). The differences in time use between the elderly and the general population result from less time spent working, not solely from the physical effects of aging. Loss of employment income may also limit the pastime activities possible for some older Americans.

DEATH AND DYING

The elderly are, by far, the most frequent beneficiaries of the advances in medical technology are . Technology that may enhance life is now recognized as capable of, in certain instances, prolonging life (as well as dying) at the expense of quality of life and without regard for individual wishes. The legal, ethical, religious, and economic questions raised by such technology have yet to be resolved and will certainly touch the lives of an increasing number of older Americans.

Among those technologies at issue are cardiopulmonary resusitation, respiratory ventilation, organ transplants, dialysis, nutritional support and hydration, antibiotics, and recently, euthanasia and suicide-enabling paraphernalia and procedures.

Controversy involving medical technology will generally center around terminology such as "quality v. quantity" of life, the "high cost of dying," "living wills," and "the right to die." Court cases increasingly challenge accepted procedure. Under the newly passed Patient Self-Determination Act (HR 5835) effective December 1, 1991, all individuals receiving medical care in hospitals, nursing homes and certain other facilities receiving Medicare and Medicaid funds must be advised of two rights, (1) the right to make decisions about their care - including the right to refuse that care, and (2) the right to prepare binding documents stating their desire or not for life-sustaining intervention in the event of their incapacitation-a "living will."

The lengthening of a person's life span can present a serious problem for some people. Some observers believe that extending a patient's life by technology is not necessarily a benefit for the person. Despite the fact that the elderly are healthier and more affluent than previous generations, the suicide rate among the elderly has risen steadily since 1981. According to records of the National Center for Health Statistics, the suicide rate among persons 65 and older is 21.6 per 100,000 people, compared to an overall national rate of 12.8 (See Chapter VII).

Dynamics in Aging

As the elderly population swells in the decades ahead, it will also become increasingly diverse. Tomorrow's elderly will likely be more educated and wealthier than today's elderly, just as today's older Americans are better educated and more well-to-do than their grandparents. And with the variety of living arrangements needed and the differences between individuals in health and personality, the older generation will reflect more variation than ever before.

CHAPTER XII

PROGRAMS ESPECIALLY FOR THE ELDERLY

The image of the elderly person sitting at home in a rocking chair gazing forlornly out the window, in poor physical and mental health, helpless and defenseless, is, sometimes, an unfortunate reality. But older people do not necessarily have to face their problems or live their lives alone - many organizations provide support to older Americans.

While some of these organizations are government programs, a large number are private, run not only for, but by, older people. They receive financing from various sources, including government grants, membership fees, private contributions, and product sales. Most are non-profit. Services range from home-delivered meals to discount cruise tickets. Older persons can find groups that lobby Congress on elderly-rights legislation or clubs made up solely of sports enthusiasts over age 55. They can obtain legal advice and gardening tips for a minimal fee or free-of-charge.

Unfortunately, many poor elderly people, and especially those who live alone, do not know these organizations exist. Often the person who most needs their services is least able to obtain them. Many organizations, especially those with greater financial resources, advertise extensively and enjoy national recognition, but others have limited budgets with which to publicize their services.

GOVERNMENT-SPONSORED PROGRAMS - THE OLDER AMERICANS ACT

When President Lyndon Johnson signed the Older Americans Act (OAA) (PL 89-73) on July 14, 1965, he saw it as a clear affirmation of "our nation's high sense of responsibility toward the well-being of older citizens." The OAA established a network of federal, state, and local government agencies to provide services for the elderly through programs and grants for social services, research and demonstration projects, and personnel training. From a modest $6.5 million in 1966, OAA appropriations rose to $683.8 million in 1981, and President Bush requested $1.2 billion for the programs in his 1991 budget proposal.

The OAA network offers a broad range of services which are available to all elderly people but are aimed primarily at those with the greatest economic or social need. These services include health screening, congregate meals, in-home services such as home repairs, shopping assistance, counseling, advice on long-term care options, legal advice, volunteer opportunities, senior centers, and telephone reassurance. Every state government has a department or unit devoted to the elderly that can provide information about local OAA programs.

PRIVATE AND COMMUNITY ORGANIZATIONS

Over the last 40 years, as people have lived longer, interest in older persons in our society has increased dramatically. The number of organizations dedicated to improving the overall quality of life for senior citizens has grown from a few to many dozens. The following list provides an overview of some of these groups.

The American Association of Retired Persons(AARP)

Probably the largest and best known organization is the American Association of Retired Persons (AARP). Founded in 1958 by Dr. Ethel Percy Andrus (who also founded the National Retired Teachers Association), there are over 33 million members in 3,700 local chapters.

AARP was created to serve four basic purposes:

1. to enhance the quality of life for older persons,

2. to promote independence, dignity and purpose for older persons,

3. to lead in determining the role and place of older persons in society, and,

4. to improve the image of aging.

AARP is active in almost every area of concern to older persons, from politics to health issues. It publishes brochures, booklets, and a magazine featuring articles on subjects of special interest to the elderly as well as broad social issues. AARP provides its members with such diverse services as programs on crime prevention, divorce counseling, and retirement planning. Members are entitled to group health insurance, a group travel program, an investment program, discounts on pharmacy services, and more. Membership is limited to people 50 or older and costs $5 per year (including spouse). AARP's headquarters are located at 601 E Street, N.W., Washington, DC 20049, (202) 434-2277.

Gray Panthers

The Gray Panthers is a coalition of old and young people working together to combat ageism. It was founded in 1970 by Margaret Kuhn. Its "media watch" program monitors the media for demeaning and prejudicial characterizations of the elderly and the aging process. Its headquarters are at 311 S. Juniper Street, Philadelphia, PA 19107, (215) 545-6555.

National Council of Senior Citizens

The National Council of Senior Citizens (NCSC) is primarily an advocacy group dedicated to protecting the rights of senior citizens. It was formed in 1961 during the struggle to enact Medicare. Since then it has helped increase Social Security benefits, created senior centers and nutrition sites, initiated community employment and low-income senior housing projects, and provided social services under the Older Americans Act.

Its 4.5 million members can obtain health care insurance, travel discounts, prescription drug discounts, and help in dealing with government agencies. NCSC encourages its members to participate in social and political activities. The NCSC newsletter, *Senior Citizens News*, keeps members informed on political issues and other relevant matters. Its office is located at 925 15th Street, N.W., Washington, DC 20005, (202)347-8800.

National Council on the Aging

The National Council on the Aging (NCOA) is made up of individuals and organizations who have an active interest in making society more equitable for older persons, in protecting their rights, and in making sure their needs are met in a humane, effective, and efficient manner. Its members include, among others, health care professionals, adult day care providers, educators, volunteers, gerontologists, and senior citizens.

NCOA conducts research and demonstration projects, identifies improved service techniques, develops standards, conducts conferences and training, produces a variety of publications, and advocates on behalf of the elderly. It is a leading resource for professionals serving the aged. Its main office is at 600 Maryland Avenue, S.W., Washington, DC 20024, (202)479-1200.

Older Women's League

The Older Women's League (OWL) refers to itself as "the first national grassroots membership organization to focus exclusively on women as they age." Its goals are to provide mutual support for its members, achieve economic and social equity for women, and improve the image and status of older women.

Recognizing that women generally suffer more severely, and in greater numbers, from the problems of old age, OWL is active in pension reform, support for caregivers, combating age and sex discrimination in the work place, ensuring affordable, quality health care, protecting Social Security benefits and lobbying for increased benefits, and helping women control their lives during their later years. It currently has chapters in 36 states, with a main office at 730 11th Street, N.W., Washington, DC 20001, (202)783-6686.

American Association of Homes for the Aging

Founded in 1961, the Association of Homes for the Aging (AAHA) is a national organization of not-for-profit nursing homes, senior housing, continuing care retirement communities, and community services for the elderly. Taking its mandate from religious and historical attitudes of respect and reverence for the elderly, AAHA is dedicated to providing older people with the care and support they need to live out their lives with dignity.

AAHA's 37 affiliated associations supply the elderly and their families with information about housing options, caregiving, nursing home reform, and most issues that directly affect their lives. They take a leadership role in representing and promoting the interests of their constituents through advocacy, education, professional development, research and services. AAHA is headquartered at 1129 20th Street, N.W., Suite 400, Washington, DC 20036-3489, (202)223-5920.

National Citizens' Coalition for Nursing Home Reform

Twelve citizen advocacy groups formed the National Citizens' Coalition for Nursing Home Reform (NCCNHR) in 1975 to improve care and life for nursing home residents and provide information and leadership in legislation and government policy. Today, its 250+ member groups promote community involvement in nursing homes, assist in resolving complaints and problems, monitor regulatory activities, and support resident and family councils and other forms of consumer empowerment. The NCCNHR Clearinghouse serves consumers, researchers, educators, policymakers, etc., with information, ideas, and referrals. Its main office is at 1424 16th Street, N.W., Washington, DC 20036, (202)797-0657.

National Association for Home Care

The National Association for Home Care (NAHC) is a trade association representing home health agencies, homemaker-home health aide organizations, and hospices. Its mission is to promote and protect the well-being of the nation's sick, disabled, and elderly. NAHC advocates home care, whenever possible, as the most humane, cost effective method of delivering care to those in need. It provides information on the role of Medicare, home health expenditures, the need for home care services, and the benefits of home care. NAHC headquarters are located at 579 C Street, N.E., Washington, DC 20002, (202)547-7424.

National Hospice Organization

A hospice is usually thought of as a place where the terminally ill receive care during their final days. The National Hospice Organization (NHO) regards hospice as a concept of care consisting of an interdisciplinary program of supportive services for terminally-ill people and their families. The purpose of hospice is not to prolong life, but to make the remaining weeks or months of life as pain-free, dignified, and meaningful as possible.

As the only non-profit membership organization in the United States devoted exclusively to hospice, NHO actively addresses areas of concern to established and newly forming hospices, including standards criteria, ethics, research and evaluation, legislation, and education. Its main office is at 1901 N. Moore Street, Suite 901, Arlington, VA 22209, (703)243-5900.

Mobility International USA

Many older people dream of traveling when they retire, only to find that they are confronted with problems that make travel difficult or impossible, such as access to medical care, getting around in a wheelchair, and dietary restrictions. Mobility International promotes travel among the elderly and disabled by offering information on how to make traveling easier and less expensive. The mailing address is P.O. Box 3551, Eugene, Oregon, (503)343-1289.

The Salvation Army

The Salvation Army has a special program that addresses the physical, emotional, and spiritual needs of senior citizens. It operates centers that provide hot lunches, classes in crafts, foreign languages and other interests, pre-retirement seminars, and referral services. Other services include low-cost residential facilities, transportation to hospitals and doctors' offices, telephone reassurance, and visits to the elderly who are isolated. Salvation Army camps, some of which offer year-round programs, give the elderly a chance to enjoy natural surroundings and the opportunity to make new friends. Its headquarters are at 120 West 14th Street, New York, NY 10011, (212)337-7200.

National Hispanic Council on Aging

The National Hispanic Council on Aging (NHCoA) is a membership group dedicated to promoting the well-being of the Hispanic elderly and eliminating the "social, civic and economic inequalities experienced by elders of Hispanic descent." NHCoA seeks to accomplish its goals through empowerment and self-help. It maintains an active relationship with other public and private agencies to ensure that the Hispanic elderly receive the benefits and services available to them.

NCHoA activities include publishing educational material, conducting seminars and workshops, administering internship programs in gerontology (the study of aging), developing programs that are culturally and linguistically appropriate for elderly Hispanics, and preparing funding proposals. Its seven chapters are located in the Southwest, New Jersey, and New York, with headquarters at 2713 Ontario Rd., N.W., Washington, DC 20009, (202)265-1288.

National Senior Citizens Law Center

The National Senior Citizens Law Center (NSCLC) was established in 1972 to help older Americans live with dignity and free from poverty by providing legal services on behalf of elderly poor clients and client groups. NSCLC offers litigation assistance, research and consulting support, national policy representation, and on-site training and training manuals on legal matters. NSCLC's office is located at 2025 M Street, N.W., Washington, DC 20036, (202)887-5280.

Pension Rights Center

The Pension Rights Center was organized in 1976 to educate the public about pension issues and protect and promote the pension interests of workers and retirees. It seeks solutions to the many problems of current private and government pension systems, and its ultimate goal is to bring about a retirement income system that is economically feasible while meeting individual needs. Its offices are at 918 16th Street, N.W., Washington, DC 20006, (202)296-3776.